Laylah

Laylah: The Life of Leila Waddell
Copyright © 2025 Darren Francis
All Rights Reserved.

ISBN 978-1-915933-54-6 (Hardcover)

A CIP catalogue for this title is available from the British Library.
10 9 8 7 6 5 4 3 2 1

Printed by TJ Books, Cornwall

Published in 2025
Hadean Press
West Yorkshire
England
hadean.press

Laylah

THE LIFE OF LEILA WADDELL

DARREN FRANCIS

ACKNOWLEDGMENTS

Many thanks to Michele Lyle for all her support, Una Maria Blyth, Philip Young of the Warburg Institute for granting me access to their Crowley archive, and the staff of the York Collection itself for their assistance during my visit.

CONTENTS

L.A.Y.L.A.H., *The Book of Lies*, Wieland and Co., 1913, p. 98.

OUR LADY BABALON
(An Introduction)

I think it was her eyes that drew me in at first, focussed yet wistful, and fixed on the observer. Her hair parted at the forehead, so dark it could almost be black, and hanging down to and covering her breasts. Topless, hands linked across her chest and with both thumbs elevated. It's an image familiar to anybody with at least a passing knowledge of Aleister Crowley, and arguably one of the most famous in twentieth century occultism.

The next photograph of her I saw was just as intriguing if not so immediately striking. In this one she is seated upright, again looking directly at the viewer, a sly yet inscrutable expression on her face. She wears an ankle-length robe with a cross at the chest, a violin in her left hand and a violin-bow in the right.

Leila Waddell, the subject of those two images, has long fascinated me, since I first saw them and before I had any idea who she was or even knew much about Crowley or the occult. I was somewhat smitten, truth be told.

My interest in matters esoteric is long-standing since my teens, though is chiefly an academic one, and I can't say that Crowley has held any great allure for me despite my recognising his impact and historical significance. It was the people on the periphery of his story that fascinated me rather than Crowley himself, the women in particular, and above them all in my mind was Leila Waddell. I'd wanted to write about her for a long time though it wasn't until April 2023 that I began to do so, with a book-length biography in mind. I was surprised that nobody had done so already. After my first weeks of research, I realised why, stumped by how little I had managed to discover. Few past authors had taken the time to look at her life in much depth, and all I could find, beyond mentions in books about Crowley, were half a dozen or so short biographical articles which largely paraphrased the same points. For a while I doubted whether I'd be able to gather enough material to write anything longer than article-length, and it was only by looking beyond the obvious sources and into newspaper archives that I began to fill in the numerous gaps in the narrative. As it transpired there was much that I had to leave out when writing, regarding Crowley specifically rather than Waddell. In order to tell her story, it was necessary to also tell his, the difficulty being that there was a tremendous amount of material to draw upon regarding him and considerably less for her. I wanted enough

Crowley in the book to convey the nature of the man and their relationship, but not too much as to let him overbalance things.

To address the comment from one advance reader that I present Crowley in an unflattering light, I would respond that I don't think I give an opinion of him at all; rather, I sought to capture something of his essence as a man, his life and ideas, and particularly his relationship with Leila Waddell, using his own words where I could. Also, please don't ask 'why didn't you include x or y?' in Crowley's story. I'm aware that I left a great deal out. I had to be selective in including only what seemed most relevant or was pertinent to Waddell and their relationship. Besides, this book is about her and not him, and if you want more Crowley there are plenty of other books that already have you covered. I even recommend a few in mine.

There are two things that still surprise me about Leila Waddell. The first is the repeated mention of her considerable musical talent. There have been several articles and even some Crowley authors I've read that describe her as a violinist of middling or substandard ability. Every contemporary media report demonstrates this to be untrue. Even at age eighteen it was said of her that

> the mastery that this young lady has acquired over the difficult instrument is something wonderful in one so young. She plays with delightful grace and ease – all the technical difficulties vanishing before her touch. Nor is this superior proficiency in technique her only merit. She is besides a real musician, and plays with real sympathy and power.[1]

A decade later she would be claimed as 'Australia's finest violiniste.'[2] The notion that Leila Waddell was a sub-par musician likely derives from Crowley's 'autohagiography' *The Confessions of Aleister Crowley*, wherein amongst other insults he refers to her as a 'fifth rate fiddler', though I'd rather trust the myriad newspaper articles that speak of the high calibre of her playing than I would her ex-fiancé's memoir.

The second surprise is that she has remained unsung for so long. Her life and talents tell a remarkable tale, and I found that the more I researched and wrote about her, the more I liked her. Sadly, she has been overshadowed in the years since by her association with Crowley; hopefully this book will go some way towards rectifying her relative obscurity.

---

1 *The Sydney Morning Herald*, 7 December 1898.
2 *The Bournemouth Graphic*, 27 May 1909.

One final point of note: early in the conception of this biography I located my paperback copy of *The Confessions of Aleister Crowley* on a far shelf, intent on re-reading it by way of research. The book was old and in poor shape, having been inherited some years prior from the collection of my deceased father. Returning to my seat with book in hand, I dropped it and it split along the spine, falling open at the exact page that features that photo of Leila Waddell with which this introduction begins. I took it as a sign, whether from Waddell or my father I couldn't decide, and began writing in earnest.

IÁ LAYLAH!

Love, I love you! Night, night, cover us! Thou art night, O my love;
and there are no stars but thine eyes.
Dark night, sweet night, so warm and yet so fresh, so scented yet so
holy, cover me, cover me!
Let me be no more! Let me be Thine; let me be Thou; let me be
neither Thou nor I; let there be love in night and night in love.
N.O.X. the night of Pan; and Laylah, the night before His threshold!

'The Southern Cross', Aleister Crowley
Liber CCCXXXIII: The Book of Lies, Wieland and Co.,
London, 1913, p. 39.

THAT EASE AND GRACE WHICH SHOWS
A TRUE ARTIST
(1880-1909)

Leila Waddell, or more fully Leila Ida Nerissa Bathurst Waddell, was born on 10 August 1880, a home birth at her parents' residence on Durham Street, Bathurst, in the Central Tablelands of New South Wales, Australia. Now a city, in the eighteen-fifties Bathurst – approximately forty miles west of Sydney – was a rural gold-rush town, being the site of the first discovery of gold in Australia in 1851 and with the town acting as central hub and point of export for the numerous surrounding deposits.[3] A railroad to Sydney was constructed in 1876 and Bathurst boomed, and by 1885 the town had a population of 8,000 with up to 20,000 in the wider vicinity.

Leila was the third of eleven children of David Waddell, born 1849 or 1850 in Randwick, and Mary Gertrude Waddell *née* Crane, born 1858 of Bellevue Hill. They were wedded some time before 1876; the precise date is not known, nor is when they settled in Bathurst. David worked for the family firm Waddell Brothers of Bathurst and Sydney, wool-scourers, with his brothers Thomas, John, Robert, and James. Unlike them he was an employee of the company rather than a partner, until his retirement on 6 February 1893 with his brothers carrying on the business without him. David Waddell was something of a figure in the Bathurst community and a Freemason, and on 1 June 1888 was elected or 'installed' as a Master Elect at the Phoenix Lodge, Bentinck Street, Bathurst, as well as being appointed as a local Alderman on 29 October 1889.

David and Mary had two daughters before Leila: Emmeline Eva Waddell born 30 September 1876, and Minerva MacRie Waddell, born 11 September 1878. Leila arrived on 10 August 1880, and was christened at St Barnabus Church on 3 October. Additional children of the family included Ivy Minerva Laurie Victoria Waddell, born 26 December 1882, Muriel Ruby Laura Myrtle Adelle Waddell born 24 July 1885, Selwyn Osmond Edgar Reginald David Redfern Waddell born 4 July 1887, Wallace Montgomery Allaway Abernethy Clive Steven James Waddell, born 18 April 1890, Wellesley Mervyn Stuart Waddell born 26 September 1892,

---

3 One of which, Hill End, was the site of the largest single piece of gold ever found anywhere, a 630 lb mass of quartz and gold discovered on 20 October 1871 containing roughly 205 lb of gold.

Beaufort Errington Havelock Waddell, born 1 May 1895, Marie Enid Thelma Waddell born 19 August 1897, and Beaupre Una Doris Waddell, born 17 August 1901.

Until recently little was known of Leila Waddell's parents or siblings or wider family, which led to speculation – in particular by the Australian writer Toby Creswell[4] and occult author Francis King[5] in his books *Magic: The Western Tradition* and *The Magical World of Aleister Crowley* – that she may in fact have been a New Zealander, and part-Maori. Though this notion seems to have reframed the popular conception of her, and the part-Maori myth still gets repeated in some Crowley biographies,[6] there is no evidence for it. Quite the contrary; New South Wales records also give details of her grandparents, John Crane (who hailed from Coventry, England) and Jane McKenzie (from Fort William, Inverness-shire, Scotland) on her mother's side and John Waddell and Elizabeth McAnally (both from County Monaghan, Ireland) on her father's. She was an Australian of UK descent through and through. It is said that Waddell's grandparents fled Ireland Australia-bound to escape the great Irish famine which killed around a million of the country's population, and though this is certainly possible – the famine lasted 1845 to 1852 – we don't know with any surety.

Leila Waddell began violin tuition in 1887 at the age of six or seven. As to what led her to the instrument, an article in *What's On* of London dated 15 October 1910 sheds light;

> Miss Waddell tells an interesting story of the way she learned to play, and how she had to start afresh when she had acquired quite a repertoire. She was born in an up-country town, where music was at a discount. One day the local barber disclosed himself to her father as a violin player who desired to give lessons. Mr Waddell said he would allow one of his daughters to learn. She learnt easily, and soon had at her fingers' ends pieces and exercises simple and difficult. After two years the barber died. In his stead a stranger

---

4 See *Notorious Australians: the Mad, the Bad and the Dangerous* by Toby Creswell, p 57-60.

5 George Francis King (1934-1994) was an editor and author of more than thirty books on esoteric and occult subjects. *Magic: The Western Tradition* and *The Magical World of Aleister Crowley* are among his better-known. He later angered the Ordo Templi Orientis with his 1973 volume *The Secret Rituals of the OTO*, which gave details of their rites.

6 For example *Do What Thou Wilt: A Life of Aleister Crowley* by Lawrence Sutin, p 206, or *Perdurabo: The Life of Aleister Crowley* by Richard Kaczynski, p 212.

came to town, and she was transferred to the new virtuoso. For a time all went well; then suddenly during one lesson he said: 'You should play C sharp not C natural.' The promising pupil could not comply. It was then discovered that she knew not a note of music. She had learnt 'like a parrot,' so to speak. She had observed the barber closely and copied him, watching his fingers and imitating the sounds by ear. The new virtuoso took her right back to the beginning, and with good results.[7]

Aside from violin, Waddell's education was unremarkable. She attended the Convent of Mercy High School, Bathurst, receiving an upper second class for reading and recitations on 13 December 1889 and a prize awarded in the arts (possibly for music) from the Mayor. The first media note of Waddell playing in public comes from *The Bathurst Free Press and Mining Journal* on 28 October 1891, which mentions a conversazione for St Stephens' Presbyterian Church held in Bathurst Masonic Hall where she performed a violin solo aged eleven. At a benefit concert for All Saints' School organ fund on 7 December that year 'Little Miss Waddell played a violin solo, which did her infinite credit.'[8] She was also one of several musicians playing for the patients of Bathurst Hospital on 31 December 1891; her solo was described as 'the gem of the evening.'[9]

What else we know of Waddell's early life was unexceptional. She spent some seven or eight years studying violin under a Mr Henri Staell[10] – likely the aforementioned 'new virtuoso' – and she swiftly became an accomplished player. Her favourite composers were the Belgian Henri Vieuxtemps[11] and the Polish Henryk Wieniawski,[12] both nineteenth century violinists of

---

7 *What's On*, London, 15 October 1910.

8 *The National Advocate*, 8 December 1891.

9 Ibid., 1 January 1892.

10 Sometimes also spelled 'Stael'.

11 Henri François Vieuxtemps was a Belgian violinist and composer of substantial ability. Born 1820, he played in public for the first time aged six, and was soon giving performances in Liege and Brussels and beyond despite his young age. By fifteen he was also composing, and played his first self-written concerto c. 1835. He performed and wrote prolifically over the next forty years, composing more than eighty separate pieces of music. His career as a violinist ended following the second of two strokes in 1879, and he died in an Algerian sanatorium in 1881, aged sixty-one.

12 Henryk Wieniawski, born 1835, was a Polish violinist and composer widely considered one of the greatest ever violinists. He played from an early age and studied at the Paris Conservatoire from 1843 (despite only being aged eight at the

formidable repute. She joined the Amateur Orchestral Society and Sydney
Philharmonic Orchestra young, performing a violin solo at the latter's sixth
grand concert at Bathurst Masonic Hall on 26 January 1892. She appeared
again to give a solo at Bathurst Church fair on 1 December 1892, and at a
moonlit concert at Vale Church, Bathurst on 13 February 1894.[13]

Waddell's then-youngest sister Ivy Waddell was killed in a horse-riding
accident on 4 December 1894, when Leila was fourteen. Ivy had been out
riding with her father, journeying home from Victoria Park, Bathurst, when
her horse threw her off before falling on top of her. She died at home hours
later. Events were set out in detail in local media:

> A sad accident occurred this morning in Durham Street, resulting
> in the death of a young girl, in her thirteenth year,[14] named Ivy
> Waddell, youngest daughter of Mr David Waddell. On Sunday
> last the family were down at Broadwater, when a halter was left
> by mistake, and this morning Mr Waddell, accompanied by his

time; special provision had to be made to admit him). He began composing in 1847,
the first of many works throughout his short life. His concertos in particular are
renowned for the difficulty of performing them. He died in 1880 from a heart attack,
aged forty-four.

13 There are numerous other mentions of Waddell's public playing in the media
archives of this period, but this author doesn't feel the need to itemise them all
in the main body of the text; they included at All Saint's College on 20 December
1892, at St Stephen's Church on 28 September 1893, at Bathurst Masonic Hall on 15
November 1893, at Bathurst School Of Arts on 19 March 1894, at Wesleyan Church
on 9 April 1894 for Harvest Thanksgiving, at Oddfellow's Hall on 17 May 1894, at All
Saints Organ Recital on 30 May 1894, at Bathurst Presbyterian Church on 29 August
1984, at Wesleyan Church on 26 January 1895, at All Saints Church on 29 May 1895,
at a concert at Convent High School on 30 October 1895, at St Stephen's Church
in Bathurst on 25 December 1895, at Bathurst School Of Arts on 25 July 1895, at
Bathurst Masonic Hall on 13 August 1895, at Trinity Church, Kelso, on 3 December
1895 at Bathurst Masonic Hall on 16 December 1895, at St Stephen's Church on 25
December 1895, at Wesleyan Church on 23 February 1896, at Bathurst School of Arts
on 18 May 1896, at William Street Wesleyan Church on 23 February 1886 and again
on 22 March 1896, at Bathurst Picnic Race Club Ball on 20 April 1896, at Bathurst
Masonic Hall on 14 May 1896, at Bathurst School of Arts on 18 May 1896, at St
Barnabas Church, Bathurst, 25 June 1896, at Bathurst Masonic Hall on 7 July 1896,
at Kelso Reading Room on 29 July 1896, at Bathurst Masonic Hall on 9 September
1896, for Bathurst Choral Society on 1 December 1896, at St Stanislaus College on 8
December 1896, at Convent of Mercy High School on 17 December 1896, and at St
Stephen's Church on 27 December 1896.

14 She was actually eleven if the date of birth of 26 December 1882 we have for her
is correct.

daughter Ivy, started out for a ride at about 4 o'clock, returning to town soon after 10. Ivy was riding a creamy pony, exceedingly quiet and easily controlled. As they passed the hospital they started into a canter, but had not gone more than a few hundred yards when the pony Ivy was riding tripped on a stone, and before its rider could pull up she was thrown, the pony falling upon her. The accident happened near Mr Sinnott's residence, and Mr Sinnott was standing in the verandah as the riders passed. He saw the pony trip, and says he noticed it turn a complete somersault and fall with its full weight on to the girl. Mr Waddell was riding slightly in front of his daughter, his horse having gained somewhat and he was therefore powerless to assist. As soon as possible assistance was at hand and the injured girl was taken into Mr Sinnott's residence. She was still conscious, but it was plainly seen that she was seriously injured. Mr Sinnott, junior, rode with all haste to Dr Kirkland's residence, and that gentleman was speedily on the spot. He saw that the injuries were fatal, and had her at once removed to her father's home, within a quarter of a mile from the scene of the accident. With all possible care the sufferer was removed and placed in bed. Temporary relief was afforded her, but within two hours life had passed away. The unfortunate girl retained consciousness to the last, and within a few moments of her death responded in an audible tone to the prayer offered by Rev Dean Marriot. Noticing the grief of her parents she implored them not to grieve for her, and in reply to a question from the Dean she said she was indeed badly injured. The parents, hoping that the injuries were not so serious as were at first anticipated, urged for a consultation with medical men, and this was arranged; but within a short time after Dr Kirkland left the house death ensued – the injuries received being internal. The pony deceased was riding is injured and has a cut in the forehead showing with what force it struck the ground. At this spot there are a number of loose stones, and it was no doubt on one of these that the pony slipped. Ivy was a bright, intelligent girl, the life of her home and a general favourite. Her 13th birthday is on Boxing Day and arrangements were being made for celebrating the event. Mr Waddell has had a great deal of trouble during this year, and this crushing blow is severely felt by the family.[15]

15 *Bathurst Free Press and Mining Journal*, 4 December 1894.

Leila Waddell was listed as 'leader'[16] of the orchestra for St Stephen's Church Annual Conversazione held at Bathurst Masonic Hall on 26 September 1895, remarkable perhaps given that she was fifteen at the time. Her eldest sister Emmeline, then aged seventeen, appeared on first violin. At a Convent High School concert on 30 October 1895 'the success of each song was considerably enhanced by violin obbligatos contributed by Miss Leila Waddell'.[17] She passed intermediate level violin examinations with honours at Trinity College on 19 December 1895, for which she was awarded

> a gold medal of chaste design... for the highest pass for practical work (violin)... It is in the shape of a maltese cross, and is nicely engraved, having on one side the recipient's name and on the other the words: 'Trinity College, London. For the highest pass – 85 – gained with honors.'[18]

Her tutor was then listed as Mr W G Smith. At St Joseph's Church on 5 January 1896, she 'made a great impression by her really clever manipulation of the violin; while the dancing of her two sisters [actually cousins], Miss Elsie and Esther Waddell, also evoked much praise from all quarters.'[19] On 14 September 1896 she passed Musical Knowledge with 98 marks (with sisters Emmeline and Edith scoring 93 and 86 respectively). At a further Convent of Mercy student performance on 21 October 1896 Waddell

> has succeeded in reducing that rebellious instrument into perfect subjection, and it emits, at her magnetic touch, sounds of most pleasing harmony and delight. Her style is faultless, and with a little more energy and power she will have completely escaped from the thraldom of that enemy of art in music – amateurdom.[20]

Mention is made of Waddell passing Senior Violin with honours at Trinity College on 22 December 1896 with 84 marks. Her appearance at Ashfield School in Bathurst was given special mention in *The National Advocate* on 24 August 1897 under the heading *A Talented Violinist*:

---

16 Ibid., 27 September 1895.

17 *National Advocate*, 31 October 1895.

18 *Bathurst Free Press and Mining Journal*, 18 December 1895.

19 *National Advocate*, 6 January 1896.

20 *The Catholic Press (Sydney)*, 24 October 1896.

Miss Leila Waddell whose appearance before a Bathurst audience is always so much appreciated has been giving an Ashfield audience a taste of the quality of her manipulation of the King of Instruments... The audience warmly applauded the effort and the young amateur's performance reflects credit both on Mr W G Smith, her teacher, and on the city of her birth... The violin solos, viz, *Legende* and *2nd Mazurka* (Wieniawski), played by Miss Leila Waddell, were so well executed that this young amateur should continue to pursue her musical studies. The young violinist was presented with a beautiful bouquet of flowers.[21]

It is notable that Waddell was, even at this young age, performing a Wieniawski piece, compositions renowned amongst violinists for their difficulty. It is eloquent testament to her then-capability as a player.

Waddell and her violin were a regular fixture around Bathurst and beyond by the late eighteen-nineties, with her making frequent public performances,[22] often solo but sometimes in a duet or ensemble. She was becoming something of a minor local celebrity, with the Bathurst newspapers frequently remarking on her talents. At the annual prize-giving at St Mary's Rosebank College on 8 December 1898, *The Sydney Morning Herald* deemed her

a marked feature of the performance... The mastery that this young lady has acquired over the difficult instrument is something wonderful in one so young. She plays with delightful grace and ease – all technical difficulties vanishing before her touch. Nor is this superior proficiency in technique her only merit. She is besides a real musician, and plays with rare sympathy and power. Readers of the Catholic Press will remember that we referred in high terms of praise to the young lady's performance on the violin at an entertainment given in the Convent School, Bathurst, in honour

21 *The National Advocate*, 24 August 1897.

22 At Wesleyan Church on 29 March 1897, at St Michael and St John's Cathedral on 9 May 1897, at Bathurst Masonic Hall on 20 July 1897, at Ashfield School of Arts, 18 August 1897, at Wesleyan Church on 24 October 1897, at Bathurst Masonic Hall on 3 November 1897, at St Mary's Convent of Mercy on 18 November 1897, at St Stanislaus College on 8 December 1897, at Bathurst Hospital on 28 December 1898, and at Bathurst School of Arts on 25 January 1899 at Bathurst School of Arts on 26 January 1899 and again on 5 July 1899, at Bathurst Cathedral on 9 January 1900, and at Bathurst Patriotic Concert (venue unknown) on 26 January 1900.

of the Hierarchy of Australasia, on the occasion of their visit to that city, to assist at the solemn re-opening and dedication of the Cathedral. Since then, however, she has made marked progress, and there can be no doubt now but that she will largely add to the fame that Australia is acquiring as being a land whose children are pre-eminently gifted with high musical ability.[23]

Waddell's eldest sister Emmeline was wedded on 30 January 1899 to Edward J Curran, at which ceremony Leila acted as one of three bridesmaids. Emmeline and Edward – who went on to train as a doctor – later emigrated to London and then to Kansas City, where she died in 1953. Leila Waddell also relocated, from Bathurst to Sydney to continue her musical studies. She likely arrived some time in early September 1900 as mention is made in the *Bathurst Free Press and Mining Journal* on 11 September of

> Miss Leila Waddell, who is a native of Bathurst, and before removing to Sydney for the purpose of completing her musical education, frequently charmed her audiences by the excellency of her performances, receives the following flattering notice in a recent issue of the Catholic Press: 'Those who attended Mrs Theodor Boesen's usual fortnightly "At Home" last Wednesday had the pleasure of listening to one who bids fair to surpass all her compatriots as a violinist. Young Miss Waddell is the happy possessor of rare talents, and has been fortunate enough to have been trained by one who is recognised as the violinist of Sydney, Mr Henri Staell. Certainly, the pupil has profited to a marvellous degree by the tuition given her, if one may judge by her sympathetic, as also by her intellectual, rendering of the various solos she played. Miss Waddell is also a graceful player and has full control of her instrument, as could be seen by the way the rich deep and broad tones were given. The Sydney public will soon have an opportunity of appreciating the worth of such genius, as it is expected that she will appear on a public platform in a few months.[24]

Waddell's Sydney debut was quick in coming, at an 'at home' for a Mr and Mrs Cairos Rego at Nicholson's Music Salon on 22 September 1900, where

23 *The Sydney Morning Herald*, 7 December 1898.
24 *Bathurst Free Press and Mining Journal*, 11 September 1900.

there was a large attendance of visitors... Miss Leila Waddell, a talented young violinist, with the promise of a firm, true style, who will shortly be introduced to the public, rendered the Mendelssohn Violin Concerto to a pianoforte accompaniment finely played by Mrs Theodor Boesen.[25]

Waddell likely studied at the Sydney School of Arts, as we find mention of her playing at an event there in January 1901 which compliments 'a violin solo by Miss Leila Waddell. The piece selected was Sarasate's *Spanish Dance*, and to say the least it was very ably and pleasingly rendered, and the audience were thoroughly satisfied, as was instanced by the applause.'[26] It is also possible that she was working in a bank for a brief time around this period, as *The Evening News of Sydney* makes note of her performing at a staff event for the Bank of New South Wales in May 1901.[27]

Barely in her twenties, Waddell taught violin between 1901 and 1906, initially at Presbyterian Ladies' College, a girls-only boarding school located in Croydon, a western Sydney suburb, before moving on to tutor at Ascham School, eastern Sydney, also girls-only though non-denominational, and thence to Kambala Church of England Girls' School in Rose Bay. The first of these positions – as 'junior professor of the violin' – was secured for her by her former tutor Henri Staell, who held the chief musical professorship at Presbyterian Ladies' College.

Waddell made her public debut as a paid and professional musician at a farewell concert given by a Miss Fanny Bauer at Sydney Town Hall on 7 May 1902. She was twenty-one. *The Daily Telegraph* noted that

Miss Leila Waddell, a promising young violinist, created a good impression in Vieuxtemps' *Adagio Religioso*, but more particularly in Saint-Saëns' *Le Cygne*... which was bracketed by Wieiawski's *Sielenka*. In the Saint-Saëns selection, Miss Waddell showed to advantage her good tone, firm bowing, and admirable style.[28]

Waddell maintained public performance throughout the early nineteen-hundreds, all the while tutoring. Amongst other appearances,[29]

25 *The Sydney Morning Herald,* 24 September 1900.

26 *Bathurst Free Press and Mining Journal,* 11 January 1901.

27 *The Evening News (Sydney),* 20 May 1901.

28 *The Daily Telegraph* (Sydney), 7 May 1902.

29 Including at Bathurst School of Arts, 21 May 1902, at Sydney Town Hall on

at Miss Donnelly's song recital on 1 January 1903 she 'simply charmed the audience, and the young artist was greeted with storms of applause at the finish of each item. Miss Waddell played with that ease and grace which shows a true artist, and the splendid reception accorded her was full of well-deserved merit.'[30]

By February 1903 Waddell was also giving lessons in violin at Pleyel's, 35 George Street, Bathurst. At Heylen's Hall, Sydney, she 'received a well-merited encore for each of her numbers'[31] on 2 March. At Sydney Town Hall on 18 April she

> exhibited a round, sweet tone in her rather too careful interpretation of Bach's *Air for G String*. Later the young violinist played brilliantly Wieniawski's difficult *Valse Caprice*, in which her bright and taking executive power [sic.] led to a hearty encore.'[32]

At St Stephen's Church, Bathurst, on 8 June

> Miss Leila Waddell, who is well-known to Bathurst audiences as a talented violinist, was specially engaged, and treated her hearers to some excellent music. She has perfect control over the instrument, and is fast becoming – if she has not already attained the position – a finished musician. Never before in Bathurst has she been heard to better advantage.[33]

At Paling's Showrooms on 19 December she 'played smoothly in the difficult chromatic passages and always with sympathy of tone, Vieuxtemps'

---

20 December 1902, Bathurst Masonic Hall on 31 December 1902, at St Stephen's Church, Bathurst, 4 January 1903, at Kelso Cathedral, 25 January 1903, at an 'at home' for Mrs Theodor Boesen on 11 March 1903, at Sydney Town Hall on 2 June 1903, at Sydney Town Hall on 13 June 1903, at Centenary Hall, Sydney, 2 July 1903, at Sydney Town Hall on 17 July 1903, at St John's Parish Hall, Sydney, 21 September 1903, at North Sydney School of Arts on 23 September 1903, at St Stephen's Presbyterian Church, Sydney, 7 October 1903, at Sydney Town Hall on 11 December 1903, at Palings Showrooms, Sydney, 19 December 1903, and at Sydney Hospital on 23 December 1903.

30 *The National Advocate*, 2 January 1903.

31 *Lithgow Mercury* (New South Wales), 6 March 1903.

32 *The Sydney Morning Herald*, 20 April 1903.

33 *Bathurst Free Press and Mining Journal*, 9 June 1903.

Andante, a violin composition chiefly distinguished by its melancholy grace.'[34]

Waddell undertook a trip to Tasmania for an engagement at Hobart Masonic Hall on 21 January 1904 where

> the concert was opened with Grieg's well-known *Sonata in C Minor* for pianoforte and violin by Miss Fast (piano) and Miss Waddell. Many prefer this sonata to almost any of Grieg's instrumental works, being so full of beautiful themes. It was very creditably and sympathetically performed on the part of both instrumentalists, eliciting hearty applause from an appreciative audience. Miss Leila Waddell played Wieniawski's captivating *Capriccio Valse* with great delicacy and brilliancy, exciting prolonged applause.[35]

She returned to mainland Australia later that month, resuming teaching duties on 1 February. A regular staple of the Sydney concert circuit, she appeared every few weeks at one or another event around the city.[36] At Leeholme it was noted that

> this charming violinist held the company almost spellbound with her exquisite playing. To make a violin solo acceptable something more than mere technical dexterity is needed, and that something which for want of a better name I call feeling or soul is a quality fully possessed by Miss Waddell.[37]

---

34 *The Sydney Morning Herald*, 21 December 1903.

35 *The Mercury (Hobart, Tasmania)*, 22 January 1904.

36 Including in 1904 at Sydney Town Hall, 5 and 14 March; at Centenary Hall, Sydney, 2 April; at Prince Alfred Park Grand Horticultural Fete, 21 April; at Centenary Hall, Sydney, 28 May; at Bathurst School of Arts, 6 July; at All Saints' Cathedral, Bathurst, 19 July; at Sydney Town Hall, 25 July, 20 August, 8 September and 11 October; at St James' Hall, Sydney, 22 October; at Sydney Town Hall, 10 December; in 1905 at All Saints' Cathedral, Bathurst, 18 January; at Sydney YMCA, 1 February; at Palings Concert Hall, Sydney, 21 February; at Sydney Town Hall, 25 March and 1 April; at St Stephen's Church, Bathurst, 5 July; at Sydney Town Hall, 15 July, 26 July, 12 August and 26 August; at Sydney YMCA, 12 September and 18 December; at Sydney Town Hall, 10 March; in 1906 at Rockdale Town Hall, 4 April; at Sydney YMCA, 1 May; with Dulwich Hill Choral Society, 14 June; at The Australia Winter Garden, 24 July; at Sydney Town Hall, 28 July and 2 August; at Rockdale Town Hall, 15 and 18 August; at St James' Hall, Sydney, 1 September; at Sydney Town Hall, 3 October; and at Palings Hall, Sydney, 3 November.

37 *The National Advocate*, 26 July 1904.

At the Liguria Band Hospital Concert 'Miss Leila Waddell's strong yet sympathetic tone was well employed in Schumann's *Abendlied*, and the violinist then rendered with spirit Wieniawski's captivating *Sielenka*.'[38]

A concert was held in tribute to Waddell on 21 November 1906, an event agreed upon following a meeting at Paling's Concert Saloon in Sydney presided over by a Mr H N Southwell 'at which he explained that the many friends and admirers of Miss Leila Waddell wished to organise a concert in her honour, in recognition of her brilliant talents as a violinist, her high personal character and her frequent services in the cause of charity.'[39] Those assembled – who included a judge, the city organist, and Waddell's former tutor Henri Staell – were in agreement, and the event soon arranged. 'Much enthusiasm was shown in Miss Waddell's interests, and there can be no doubt that the esteemed artist will be heartily supported by the great body of concert goers.'[40] That this event was mooted, let alone that it took place, is apt demonstration of the esteem in which Waddell was held in the city at the time. The concert, at Sydney YMCA Hall, 'drew a large audience most deservedly, for the programme presented was excellent, and was carried through with finish and charm by a strong combination of some of Sydney's best-known musicians.'[41] Waddell also performed that night and

> played remarkably well, her best contribution being the *Ballade and Polonaise* of Vieuxtemps. In suavely mellow tones the violinist expressed the plaintive beauty of this eminently melodious piece, whilst her rendering of the fascinating but difficult polonaise was characterised by a welcome measure of animation and decision. The enthusiasm was prolonged, an abundance of fresh flowers graced the scene, and the player then responded by adding as encore Bach's *Air for G String*.[42]

Following the commemorative concert Waddell set sail for Wellington on the Wimmera on 1 December 1906, arriving on 5 December to join the Brescians, a European concert party under Henry Hayward,[43] undertaking

---

38 *The Sydney Morning Herald*, 9 September 1904.

39 Ibid., 20 October 1906.

40 Ibid., 20 October 1906.

41 *The Sydney Mail and New South Wales Advertiser*, 28 November 1906.

42 *The Sydney Morning Herald*, 22 November 1906.

43 Henry Hayward (1865-1945), founder of the Brescians, looks to have been an interesting character. Further to his musical career he went on to write books

tours of Australia and New Zealand between December 1906 and August 1908.[44] The Brescians, consisting chiefly of members of Hayward's own family and the Martinego family who hailed from Brescia in Italy – Flavell Hayward, Rudall Hayward, Domenica Martinego, Antonia Martinego, Adelina Martinego, together with Maurice Chenoweth and Fred Mills – performed in traditional Italian festival costume and also played as accompaniment to early cinematograph shows by J T West's Modern Marvel Company. West's shows consisted of exhibits of scientific curiosities of the time including Urban-Bioscope system films and X-rays and the like. West told *The Feilding Star* on 14 December 1906 that

There seems to be no lack of interest in the cinematograph, and day by day the demand increases for the right kind of material, as much at home as in the colonies. How is it accounted for? Well, I

---

promoting rationalism, including *Here's to Life: The Impressions, Confessions, and Garnered Thoughts of a Free-Minded Showman*, published in 1944.

44 Known tour dates for Waddell with the Brescians included Hawera Opera House, New Zealand, 10 and 11 December 1906, Wanganui Opera House, New Zealand, 12 and 15 December 1906, Feilding Drill Hall, New Zealand, 19 and 20 December 1906, Wellington Town Hall, New Zealand, 24 and 29 December 1906 to 5 January 1907, Christchurch Cathedral, New Zealand, for two weeks in February 1907, Sydney Lyceum 29 March to 4 May 1907, Lithgow from 11 May 1907, Mudgee 16 and 17 May 1907, the Masonic Hall, Dubbo, from 23 May 1907, Oddfellows Hall, Goulburn, 29 May to 1 June 1907, Nixon's, Cootamundra, 5 to 8 June 1907, Oddfellows Hall, Wagga Wagga, 15 to 18 June 1907, Mechanics' Institute, Albury, 19 June 1907, Shire Hall, Benalla, 25 and 26 June 1907, the Athenaeum Hall, Melbourne, 1 July to 29 August 1907, Adelaide Town Hall, 31 August 1907 to at least 7 September 1907, His Majesty's Theatre, Perth, 21 September to 23 October 1907, Her Majesty Theatre, Kalgorlie, 27 October to 2 November 1907 (with West's show without The Brescians on 25 and 26 October), King's Theatre, Freemantle, 4 to 11 November 1907, His Majesty's Theatre, Perth, 1 to 15 November 1907, the Town Hall, Hobart, Tasmania, 27 November to 13 December 1907, the Academy of Music, Launceston, Tasmania, 19 December 1907 to 8 January 1908, Westbury, Tasmania, 9 January 1908, Deloraine, Tasmania, 10 and 11 January 1908, the Town Hall, Davenport, Tasmania, 13 and 14 January 1908, Oddfellows' Hall, Latrobe, Tasmania, 16 January 1908, Penguin, Tasmania, 17 January 1908, Burnie, Tasmania, 18 to 20 January 1908, Gaiety Theatre, Zeehan, Tasmania, 21 to 24 January 1908, Queenstown, Tasmania, at least 27 January 1908, the Town Hall, Hobart, Tasmania, 3 to 13 February 1908, Theatre Royal, Nelson, New Zealand, from 11 March 1908, Town Hall, Blenheim, New Zealand, from 14 March 1908, His Majesty's Theatre, Gibsone, New Zealand, April 1908, Masonic Hall, Wellington, New Zealand, at least 27 and 28 May 1908, the Theatre Royal, Rockhampton, 15 to 20 June 1908, and the Centennial Hall, Brisbane, 4 July to approximately 30 August 1908.

think indeed I am sure that many of the scientific methods I have been able to introduce, and incorporate with the cinematograph, such as the silhouette system, the adaptation of the stereoscope, and harnessing of the microscope to the camera whereby it is poscope, and the harnessing of the microscope to produce such striking and educative results, account in a great measure for the marvellous success I have obtained at home and abroad.[45]

West's show was praised in the 24 December 1906 *Wellington Evening Post*:

Though living pictures in fair abundance have flitted through Wellington in recent months, the public cannot be said to be surfeited, especially when the films are shown by the West Company. It was this organisation that really introduced enjoyable kinematographic sketches. In the old days – they are not so very old – the living picture was a puny, blinding thing, interesting, wonderful and all that, but very painful to the eyes. The pictures were living, but they had measles or some other disease which broke out in spots and patches. The West management brought out a healthy family of views, and the people mustered in thousands throughout New Zealand to relish the novelty. Added to this attraction came the Brescians, bright-robed melodists, whose voices and various instruments made a delicate dessert after the main feast of sightseeing.'[46] [47]

---

45 *The Feilding Star*, Feilding, New Zealand, 14 December 1906.

46 *The Wellington Evening Post*, 24 December 1906.

47 One incident that occurred on the tour, in the town of Seymour some forty miles north of Melbourne around 27 or 28 June 1907, even made the local papers under the header 'Robbing an Actress': 'Miss Leila Waddell, a member of the West Brescians Company, has complained to the Seymour police of the loss of 20 sovereigns and a lady's patent leather shoe either on the 27th or 28th ult. Miss Waddell states that she had the money in a steel purse, which she carried on a steel chain satchel on her arm, in which she also had 18/6 in silver and two cheques. She placed the satchel under the mattress of a spare bed in the room she slept in, and at 11.20pm. on the 27th ult. she left the room for ten minutes. Next morning she took the satchel, but did not miss the money. At 1pm. on the 28th she placed the satchel under the mattress again, and went to lunch, and an hour afterwards she went for a walk. On returning she opened the satchel, and the money was gone, the purse having been taken, but the 18/6 and cheques were left in the satchel.' (Benalla Standard, 2 July 1907).

A review of the Brescians' performance at the Lyceum from *The Sydney Morning Herald* gives us an idea of the nature of their shows:

At the Lyceum, the Brescians presented programmes, both afternoon and evening, of chiefly sacred or classic music in harmony with the spirit of the fast day, and instead of wearing the gala costumes of the Italian peasants of Brescia, the ladies were attired in white or cream-coloured crepe de chine. The orchestra, which has now been joined by that experienced artist Miss Leila Waddell, as second violin, opened with a smooth and animated rendering of the charming *Andante* from Haydn's Surprise Symphony, and the audience was even more pleased with the many familiar melodies included in the company's rendering of *Memories of Wallace*, arranged by Signor Lardelli. Mr Fred Mills, who in the regular programme gives a broadly humorous monologue, won applause with the recitation *Amen Corner*. Miss Adelina Martinego played brilliantly the graceful *Rondo* for violin from De Beriot's *8th Concerto*. In addition to an effective rendering of *Comfort Ye* by Mr Maurice Chenoweth, the lyric tenor of the party, soprano and contralto excerpts from the *Messiah* were welcomed from Miss Antonia Martinego and Miss Domenica Martinego. Mr Rudall Hayward sang with power and fluency *Why Do The Nations*, and one of the best items on the sacred programme was the beautiful quartet, *God is a Spirit*, an excerpt from Sterndale Bennett's cantata *The Woman of Samaria*, which is often chosen as the anthem over the graves of the great at Westminster Abbey. Mr J T West, both before and after the concert, exhibited a choice series of moving pictures. The programmes this afternoon and evening will be entirely of a popular holiday character.[48]

By October 1908 Waddell had left the Brescians for her next gig, as a member of the Viennese Ladies' Orchestra, performing Oscar Strauss' 1907 operetta *A Waltz Dream*.[49] On 3 October the ensemble set sail on the Orontes bound for Plymouth in England, then still possessor of a world-spanning empire of which Australia had until recently been a part, having only been granted nation status as the Commonwealth of Australia on 1 January 1901

---

48 *The Sydney Morning Herald*, 30 March 1907.

49 *Ein Walzertraum* in the original German. A German silent film adaption – with the operetta performed as soundtrack – appeared in 1925.

after years of political struggle for independence. The trip was facilitated through Waddell's association with J T West and managed by him.

It is not recorded precisely how long Waddell's ocean passage from Sydney to Plymouth took. It was a journey that could then be up to a hundred days or – at the very best – around half that. The ship arrived at its destination some time in November. An article to this effect in *The Sydney Mail* dated 13 January 1909 headed 'Miss Leila Waddell Arrives in London' informs us that 'Miss Leila Waddell, the talented young New South Wales violinist, who has toured Australasia with the Brescians for two and a half years, has arrived in London. Miss Waddell leaves shortly under engagement for a month's tour of the provinces.'[50] It well-demonstrates the acclaim in which Waddell was then held in her homeland that such a minor news item regarding her activities on the other side of the world could make it into a local newspaper. She spent some time in London with her sister Emmeline and Emmeline's husband Dr Edward J Curran before beginning her concert commitments. It is not noted precisely when Emmeline and Edward had emigrated from Australia to England, but this would likely have been the first time the three had seen each other for some years.

The first UK concert by Waddell with the Viennese Ladies' Orchestra was on 20 December 1908 at Kings Theatre, Glasgow 'staged with great brilliance',[51] followed by performances on at least 26 December and 1, 2, 4, 5, 6, 9, and 16 January 1909. We also know of dates at the Royal Lyceum Theatre, Edinburgh, between 18 and 30 January and at Prince's Theatre, Manchester from 1 February for three weeks (described in *The Manchester Courier* as 'one of the the brightest operettas of the day'),[52] the New Theatre, Cardiff from 22 February, and the Theatre Royal, Bradford for six nights from 2 March. The Gaiety Theatre, Dublin was next, from 8 March, thence to Shaftesbury Hall, Bournemouth for twice-daily performances from 26 April to 1 May. Strangely the adverts and posters for the Bournemouth shows proclaimed them 'First Appearance in the Country of Miss Leila Waddell, the Famous Australian violinist', which was not the case at all, her first English show having taken place in Bradford six weeks previously.

The full extent of Waddell's UK excursion with the Viennese Ladies' Orchestra was indicated in a 24 April piece written by Waddell herself for *The National Advocate*, dated 17 March and sent from Newcastle-upon-Tyne, headed 'A Bathurst Native on Tour in Great Britain':

---

50 *The Sydney Mail*, 13 January 1909.

51 *The Glasgow Herald*, 21 December 1908.

52 *The Manchester Courier*, 2 February 1909.

Dear Editor – It has just occurred to me that Bathurstians may be interested in hearing of my doings this side of the world, hence the following:- I was very fortunate since I secured a 20 weeks excellent engagement to tour Scotland and the provinces a fortnight after my arrival – and have met with great success. Six weeks in beautiful Scotland, Manchester, Cardiff, Bradford, Leeds, Dublin, Newcastle, Nottingham, Hull, Liverpool, Birmingham, Blackpool, Bournemouth, so am having an excellent opportunity of seeing the Midlands and great manufacturing towns. In Glasgow I met some relatives. My uncle, R D Waddell, is a very wealthy man and collector of famous violins. He owns the celebrated Betts Strad, the fancy price or value of which is £5000, and the best Guadagnini in the world which he has presented to me – a noble instrument with a tone like a cello for which Hart of London has a ready buyer for £3000 – so that I consider myself extremely lucky in owning such a celebrated instrument. My uncle's collection also embraces two fine Amatis, two Joseph Guarnerius – two Jacob Stainers, a Carlo Brgonzi. Vuillaume, Laudolphi, a maggini Viole, and some splendid cellos – The Betts Strad is the envy of all dealers – it has the most silvery tone, luscious quality – a very beautiful instrument – 25 violins, and historical bows – The whole collection is valued at £50,000.[53] I played all the violins whilst staying at my Uncle's house, and was in my element. I thought Edinburgh a lovely city with its interesting, old castles and world famous Princess Street. Such a winter, ever so much snow, but I have enjoyed it thoroughly. The Country clad in white is a veritable fairyland to me, especially the leafless trees which add a note of weirdness. English people consider it a phenomenal winter heavy snow in March being almost unknown for a generation. I am sorry to have missed the Opera at Covent Garden, but am looking forward to the Wagner festival at Bayreuth in July, a whole week of Wagner – including the Ring. I am well booked ahead engagements, so cannot agree with the theory that it is foolish for Australians to come to London.

'Yours faithfully
Leila Waddell On Tour.[54]

---

53 And would today be worth approximately £1,225,000.
54 *The National Advocate*, 24 April 1909.

Waddell attracted much press attention on her first UK outing, with her Bournemouth performances at Shaftesbury Hall in particular singled out for praise. *The Bournemouth Daily Echo* on 27 April made mention that 'Miss Leila Waddell, the Australian violiniste, who is making her first appearance in this country, proves herself a performer of exceptional ability alike in her powers of technique and expression, with a particularly good tone.'[55] The same paper wrote again on 5 May that 'the charming Colonial artiste, Miss Leila Waddell, is still with West's [Pictures] and her performance of such items as the *Perpetuum Mobile* of Rice, entitles her to a very high place in the ranks of violin soloists in this country.'[56] On 6 May *The Bournemouth Graphic* noted that 'during the week Miss Leila Waddell, the charming young Australian violiniste, has increased her circle of admirers, and she has gained here an artistic reputation which should serve her in good stead in her after career.'[57]

The Viennese Ladies' Orchestra returned to Bournemouth later that month, giving two performances daily at 3pm and 8pm from 24 May to 5 June. Adverts for these shows billed Waddell as 'the Queen of Australian Violinists.' On 26 May *The Bournemouth Daily Echo* wrote that 'the return engagement of Miss Leila Waddell was a triumph for the charming Australian violinist, and she was accorded a well-deserved ovation. She was presented by musical admirers with some choice flowers.'[58] *The Bournemouth Graphic* felt that 'a remarkable reception was given to the charming Leila Waddell upon her second appearance here this season. This lady is claimed as Australia's finest violiniste, and her renderings are worthy of any concert hall in this country.'[59]

While in London Waddell took the opportunity to study under the acclaimed French violinist and tutor Émile Sauret,[60] who was at that time Professor of Violin at Trinity College in the city, a position he was appointed to in 1908. Sauret himself had been a pupil of both Henri Vieuxtemps and Henryk Wieniawski, Waddell's favourite composers, and she no doubt

55 *The Bournemouth Daily Echo*, 27 April 1909.

56 Ibid., 5 May 1909.

57 *The Bournemouth Graphic*, 6 May 1909.

58 *The Bournemouth Daily Echo*, 26 May 1909.

59 *The Bournemouth Graphic*, 27 May 1909.

60 Émile Sauret, born 1852, studied violin from age six and began performing publicly two years later. His extensive career saw him perform throughout Europe and America. He is less remembered for his compositions, in part due to their difficulty. He taught violin in Berlin and Chicago, before settling in London where he died in 1920.

found the opportunity to learn under him enlightening. Sauret was initially dismissive of her for having played in vaudeville, to which she countered that she had to in order to be able to afford his fees. Sauret gifted her an Amati violin which she carried with her and played for the rest of her life (indeed it is very possibly this instrument she is playing in the photographs we have of her), so impressed was he with the fact that she had committed to memory a book of etudes he had written. Later said to be worth in the region of £1,000, she never had any inclination to sell it.

Alongside her hectic performance and study schedule Waddell also attended as many shows as she could as a spectator. While at a concert in London – a Chopin recital by Vladimir de Pachmann – she was introduced to Katherine Mansfield,[61] an up-and-coming New Zealand writer and journalist who had also not long been in London, having arrived in 1907. The two rapidly became good friends, travelling together to see the Bayreuth Festival in July 1909, a musical event held in Bayreuth, Germany and featuring performances of Wagner operas. The festival had been set up by Wagner himself in the eighteen-seventies to present his own work, in particular *Der Ring des Nibelungen* and *Parsifal*. Wagner had fixed ideas as to how his works should be staged and also supervised the design and construction of the theatre, with modifications needed to fit the sizeable orchestras for which he wrote. With the first performances taking place in 1876, the festival is still held to this day and is a biannual or sometimes annual event. Due to the many Wagner fans worldwide wishing to attend, the wait for tickets can be five or ten years or longer.

A further lengthy letter from Waddell appeared in the pages of *The National Advocate* on 25 September 1909, headed 'A Bathurstian in England'. Dated 14 August, and with return address given as Upper Addison Gardens, Kensington, W London, England, presumably where she was staying at the time, it reads:

---

61 Born Kathleen Mansfield in 1888, Katherine Mansfield was a New Zealand journalist and writer of more than sixty short stories, and is now regarded as one of the most significant modernist authors. She began writing from an early age, having her first stories published in her high school journal in 1898, and achieved wider publication soon after. She resettled in England from New Zealand aged 19, having previously studied in the UK, and befriended Virginia Woolf, D H Lawrence, and others of the famed Bloomsbury group. Extensively published throughout her life, she was diagnosed with pulmonary tuberculosis in 1917 and died five years later, aged 34.

Dear Mr Editor, After leaving Birmingham upon the completion of a highly successful and thoroughly enjoyable tour, I went to Bournemouth, where I played at two performances a day for one month, under Mr J T West's management, and, being in my best solo form, quite crept into the hearts of those enthusiastic people who form absolutely some of the most musical and critical audiences in England. They have been splendidly educated by the excellent opportunities offered at the Winter Gardens by Mr Dan Geoffrey and his fine orchestra, so that they insist upon listening only to the best music.

Then I returned to London, and all its manifold wonders struck me afresh after my 20 weeks absence. The streets seemed so busy after the provincial towns, and I felt that it was good to again watch that rushing tide of humanity, also the veritable monarch on the streets – the London omnibus – which seems to me the most popular vehicle in the wide world, in spite of the fact that it possesses less inherent romance than any other known means of transit. And although the method of the omnibus is essentially one of leisured dignity, the colossal traffic on the streets forbids anything else. It is the attempt of the motor buses to override existing conditions that has resulted in their co-operative failure, for rushing along at a restless pace they not infrequently find that ignominious resting-place in the gutter – what time that unrivalled master of repartee, the driver of a passing omnibus, makes amusing remarks, such as 'Any dead 'uns this time, Bill?' I think that the chief glory of the omnibus is the splendid opportunity it affords for easy and restful views of the city, when time is of no particular importance, and close inspection not convenient; and there is so much going on simultaneously that one is sure to be entertained, amused, and interested all the time. The taxi-cab has become tremendously popular, and is indeed a delightfully comfortable way of getting about, and seems very cheap for the first eight pence, but after that the two-pences seem to register with amazing rapidity. Although there are many hundreds of taximeters in London, it is very difficult to secure one after the theatre, especially in Piccadilly Circus or Leicester Square where the theatres are so congested. But what struck me most of all upon my return to this marvellous city was the unparalleled beauty of the parks. Hitherto, I had only seen the leafless trees in November, looking very quaint but decidedly bleak, so that my first glimpse of them clad in their summer glory simply delighted me. What a wonderful place Hyde Park is? In the heart of it one could almost imagine oneself in the country, with hundreds of sheep grazing, quite unconcerned at the increasing procession of carriages, motors and horsemen. Then the Serpentine is so beautiful, and most popular for boating. And the fairy-like trees, with their dainty foliage and varied greens are so much more beautiful than anything we get in Australia or New Zealand. There are two delightfully pretty spots in Hyde Park (one near Queen's Gate and the other near to Kensington Gardens), which always reminds me of scenes in *The Midsummer Night's Dream* and *As You Like It*. Well, there are so many diversions in London, and I seem to have wandered far from my subject, for I meant to talk of matters musical. During the musical season in May and June, when for two weeks in May there were on an average 50 concerts a week (Thing of it as compared with all the concerts in Australia in a year). I heard Ysaye and Pugno in three Sonata recitals, each of which proved memorable performances, for both violinist and pianist were artists of absolutely equal calibre, and I shall never forget their wonderful rendering of the celebrated Kreutzer Sonata; then that truly delightful violinist, Fritz Kreisher, who plays old-world music, collected in many instances from the old monasteries, and arranged by himself; also the technically perfect Jaques Thiband, whose beautiful tone and dainty style of playing sounded to perfection at his recital in the Bechstein Hall. An interesting feature was the presence of every celebrated violinist – in London for the season. They were scattered all over the hall, and formed a most critical, but enthusiastic, audience. During his performance of the Bach *Chaconne*, Thiband's E string broke, and Kubelik (who was present) had the very same experience in the same solo show a week later at the Queen's Hall, a truly strange coincidence! Kubelik returned from Australia with a warmth of tone and abundance of expression, which he lacked when I heard him in Brisbane, and was much commented upon in London. His playing simply forms the embodiment of executive genius, and at his two recitals he was in magnificent form. I also heard from Busoni, Godowsky, Montz Rosenthal, and many lesser lights in the pianofore world. I cannot say which of these four really great artists I preferred, each was wonderful in his own way. There were delightful vocal recitals by Elena Gerhardt, Marie Breme and Norodca, endless delightful concerts conducted by

Arthur Nikisch, Weingartner, Richter, Dr Cowen, Henry Woods, also Thomas Beecham, who conducts the new Symphony Orchestra, and who, by the way, is a son of the celebrated Beecham's pill man. I must not forget to tell you of Vea-dimer de Pachmann, the greatest Chopin player in existence, who gave a wonderfully enjoyable Chopin recital at the Queen's Hall. It was indescribably beautiful – his conceptions of that great master are unrivalled. He is very eccentric, and at times almost pantomimic in his gestures; for instance, whilst playing a most delightful passage he turned to the audience saying 'Isn't that lovely? Last time I played it differently, but I think I prefer this reading. Ah, you are so good to listen to me. I am sorry, I have forgotten the A flat ballade (touching his forehead); it is gone, but I shall play you the Fantasie Impromptu instead.' Most of his remarks were addressed to Marie Corelli who sat in the front row of the sofa stalls, facing the great Pachmann. I saw *The Merry Widow* four times, to which Londoners proved so faithful for two years, and enjoyed very much the delightful acting of Lily Elsie and Joseph Coyne. Huntley Wright was inimitable in *The King of Cadonia*, and Ellaline Terris proved most dainty in the name part of *The Dashing Little Duke*. Gertie Miller and George Grossmith carry off the honours in Our Miss Gibbs. Rost Stahle was excellent in *The Chorus Lady*, and in that very clever comedy *What Every Woman Knows*. Gerald Du Maurier, Hilda Tevelyan and Edmund Gwenn acted most beautifully. Julia Neilson and Fred Terry made a huge success with *Henry of Navarrai*, as did Guitz in his powerful French play at the Adelphi. Weedon Grossmith had made a big hit in Mr Preedy and the Countess, and Irene Vanburgh is drawing London to se her as *The Woman in the Case*, also Marie Tempest in *Penelope*, and *The Best People* at Wyndham's is a big success. The bollies always provide a delightful evening's amusement in their imitations and burlesques, and Adelaide Genee is fascinating crowding audiences nightly at the Empire with her wonderful dancing, in whose particular dainty and fairy-like style she stands alone. I have seen all these productions, so you see I am making good use of my time. Then at last, but not least, the Covent Garden grand opera season. What a quaint old building, and what an extraordinary position next to the markets! I thought the design, with so many tiers of boxes most fascinating, especially when one saw those boxes occupied by beautifully dressed women, with their dazzling displays of diamonds. Such marvellous wealth is almost appalling, especially after the opera, when one sees unfortunate beggars crouched against the market stalls looking absolutely hungry. I saw Tetrazina in the *Rigolette, Traviata, Lucia di Lammermoor,* and *La Sonnambula,* and thought her extremely overrated, for although a better actress, as a singer and artiste she does not compare with Melba. Her upper register is marvellous in its strength and beauty of tone, especially from C to F, but she gets the effects in a most inartistic way, and her lower register is very ordinary indeed. Rumour hath it that she will not sing at Covent Garden next year. And everywhere one could hear complaints of Melba being so much missed. Kirby Lunn (the only great English lady vocalist) possesses a most beautiful voice, and she used it to perfection in *Aide and Sason,* and *Delila,* and her rendering of the famous excerpt (so often heard on the concert platform) in the second act, was truly magnificent. Mdlle Destinn, the famous young dramatic soprano, made a delightful *Madam Butterfly.* I also heard the great Scotti and Sammarco, Zenatello and Anselmi during the season. Fortunately, some friends of mine had a box, and so I saw the operas under most luxurious conditions, and shall always remember the season with great pleasure. I have played at many At Homes, including one at the house of Mr Alfred Beit, the South African millionaire, for which I received a magnificent fee of 30 guineas. I also played at the Ritz Hotel, Savoy and Waldorf. On August 30, I began a 15 weeks' tour as conductor and leader of the ladies' band in George Edwards and Charles Frohman's production of Strauss' *Waltz Dream.* I am to be paid an excellent salary, and only 20 minutes playing at each performance, in the band stand on the stage, second act, which is supposed to be Viennese Garden. In my next, I shall tell you of my visit to Bayreuth. With regards to all in dear old Bathurst.

Leila Waddell.[62]

Waddell remained in the UK for the rest of 1909 and into 1910, touring with The Viennese Ladies' Orchestra performing *A Waltz Dream.* Among known dates were Belfast Grand Opera House from 17 September until at least 24 September, the Royal Lyceum Theatre, Edinburgh from 11 to 16 October, and the Lyceum, Sheffield on at least 15 November, but there were

---

62 *The National Advocate,* 25 September 1909.

others, and shows in Europe are also indicated. She made the pages of *The Sydney Morning Herald* again on 11 December under the heading 'Music and Drama Miss Leila Waddell':

> Miss Leila Waddell, a violinist with a refined and artistic style well-known in Sydney concert-rooms, who has been in England nearly a year, is completing a six months' tour in *The Waltz Dream* [*sic.*] as leader of the ladies' orchestra on the stage, and as soloist behind the scenes, and is getting an excellent salary. This artist may revisit Australia, and also has tempting theatrical offers for further tours.[63]

When in London in between concert commitments Waddell would often spend time with her new friend Katherine Mansfield. The two began to visit the famed Café Royal at 68 Regent Street,[64] close to Piccadilly Circus, thus ensuring Waddell's introduction to the musicians, artists, authors, and poets of London Bohemia. The Café Royal was established in 1865 by a French wine merchant named Daniel Thomas Thévenon who had fled bankruptcy in his homeland and changed his name to Daniel Nicols, intending to start afresh in London. It rapidly became the go-to place for Londoners who wanted to see and be seen and was reputed to have one of the finest wine cellars in the world. Oscar Wilde, W B Yeats, Aubrey Beardsley, Walter Sickert, Augustus John, Frank Harris, James McNeill Whistler, Ernest Dowson, Paul Verlaine, and George Bernard Shaw were among its patrons, and it was very possibly here that Leila Waddell first met Aleister Crowley.

---

63 *The Sydney Morning Herald*, 11 December 1909.

64 Presently 15-17 Glasshouse Street. Now a Grade II-listed building, between 2008 and 2012 the Café Royal was converted into a five-star hotel while retaining many of its original fixtures and fittings.

LEILA AS 'THE INTERPRETER'. *THE EQUINOX* VOL. I NO. IV, SEPTEMBER 1910, P. 198. CARL HENTSCHEL PH. LC.

Behold! I have lived many years, and I have travelled in every land
that is under the dominion of the Sun, and I have sailed the seas
from pole to pole.
Now do I lift up my voice and testify that all is vanity on earth,
except the love of a good woman, and that good woman LAYLAH.
And I testify that in heaven all is vanity (for I have journeyed oft,
and sojourned oft, in every heaven), except the love of OUR LADY
BABALON. And I testify that beyond heaven and earth is the love
of OUR LADY NUIT.
And seeing that I am old and well stricken in years, and that my
natural forces fail, therefore do I rise up in my throne and call upon
THE END.
For I am youth eternal and force infinite.
And at THE END is SHE that was LAYLAH, and BABALON, and
NUIT, being............

'Starlight', Aleister Crowley
Liber CCCXXXIII: The Book of Lies, Wieland and Co.,
London, 1913, p. 108.

AGATHA AND PERDURABO
(1910)

Aleister Crowley was born Edward Alexander Crowley on 12 October 1875 in Royal Leamington Spa, Warwickshire, England. A tremendous amount of sensationalism and nonsense has been written about him in the years since and this author hopes not to add to it, endeavouring to keep matters succinct and factual.[65] Crowley's parents were wealthy due to his father's share in Crowley's Alton Ales, a family brewing business. He was their first and only surviving child. Both parents were devout Plymouth Brethren[66] and raised him in the faith. Though they were not close he admired his father Edward Crowley, 'his hero and his friend',[67] who died of tongue cancer in March 1887 when Crowley was eleven. His mother Emily found him a difficult child, referring to him as 'the Beast', a name he embraced. He remembered her as 'a brainless bigot of the most narrow, logical and inhuman type.'[68]

One of the first things Crowley did upon entering Trinity College, Cambridge in October 1895 was change his first name to Aleister, having been told – wrongly – that it was the correct spelling of the Gaelic form of his

---

65 A full and extensive Crowley biography is beyond this author's remit, and readers seeking more information will find that there have been many books about him over the years, ranging from the excellent to the serviceable to the poor. Among the better ones, *Do What Thou Wilt: A Life of Aleister Crowley* by Lawrence Sutin, *Perdurabo: The Life of Aleister Crowley* by Richard Kaczynski, and *A Magick Life: A Biography* of Aleister Crowley by Martin Booth are good places to start.

66 The Plymouth Brethren are a Christian movement that originated in Dublin c.1825. Their central belief is that The Bible – the King James version specifically – is the sole authority in all matters, and should be taken as literal truth. Priests and intermediaries are seen as unnecessary, with all worshipers deemed equal. They are somewhat apocalyptic in outlook, anticipating the world's imminent end and preparing accordingly. Books other than the Bible are mostly forbidden, and Christmas considered a pagan tradition and not celebrated. Crowley's father in particular was dedicated to his beliefs, spending time as a traveling preacher, and family Bible readings after breakfast were a daily occurrence in the Crowley household.

67 Aleister Crowley, *The Confessions of Aleister Crowley*, p 22. Crowley wrote the first three chapters of *Confessions* – covering the period prior to his father's death – in third person, as if he considered it the defining event that set his life in motion.

68 Aleister Crowley, *The Confessions of Aleister Crowley*, p 8.

middle name Alexander.[69] Admitted to university to study moral sciences, he swiftly switched to classics. He read extensively but seldom attended lectures, favouring chess, climbing, poetry and sex with local Cambridge women. The inconvenience of time expended seeking out partners vexed him, 'the stupidity of having had to waste uncounted priceless hours in chasing what ought to have been brought to the back door every evening with the milk!'[70] He had his first homosexual union in Stockholm on New Year's Eve 1896, and though always free with his sexuality, his relations with men were destined to mostly be more casual than those with women. It was also in Stockholm that he had his first mystical experience, being

> awakened to the knowledge that I possessed a magical means of becoming conscious of and satisfying a part of my nature which had up to that moment concealed itself from me. It was an experience of horror and pain, combined with a certain ghostly terror, yet at the same time it was the key to the purest and holiest spiritual ecstasy that exists. At the time, I was not aware of the supreme importance of the matter. It seemed to me little more than a development of certain magical processes with which I was already familiar.[71]

That the two – the sexual and the mystical – were entwined should not be surprising considering what we know of Crowley's later life. He left Cambridge in 1898 without finishing his degree, feeling little inclination or necessity to do so. Though he'd received a not inconsiderable inheritance from his deceased father in the region of £40,000[72] (equating to more than £1,000,000 today), he mulled over career options, briefly deliberating becoming a poet or a professional chess player – his ability at the game was formidable – and even entertaining the idea of international diplomacy[73] before choosing a life dedicated to the occult and esoteric:

---

69 Which should actually have been Alaisdair. Crowley had no desire to be known as Edward, since he disliked all abbreviated forms of it and since it had also been his father's name. Neither was he keen on his childhood nickname Alick.

70 Aleister Crowley, *The Confessions of Aleister Crowley*, p 97.

71 Ibid., p 109.

72 Other sources indicate that Crowley's inheritance could have been as little as £16,000 or even as much as £100,000, though most agree on a sum in the region of £40,000. Regardless of how much it was Crowley easily managed to spend his way through it, finding himself destitute in later years.

73 Some writers contend that Crowley did in fact act as an agent for British

In October, 1897, he... experienced a trance, in which he perceived the utter folly of all human ambition. The fame of an ambassador rarely outlives a century. That of a poet is almost as ephemeral. The earth must one day perish. He must build in some material more lasting. This conception drove him to the study of Alchemy and Magick.[74]

Throughout his life Crowley consistently wrote a great deal of poetry, and had a very high regard for his own work;[75] 'it has been remarked a strange coincidence that one small county [Warwickshire] should have given England her two greatest poets – for one must not forget Shakespeare.'[76] He self-published his first poetry books before he'd even left university; *Aceldama: A Place to Bury Strangers In*, and *White Stains*, the latter having to be typeset and printed in Amsterdam due to its sexually explicit content.[77] He deemed *Aceldama* 'my first published poem of any importance, I attained, at a bound, the summit of my Parnassus. In a sense, I have never written anything better. It is absolutely characteristic. Its technical excellence is remarkable and it is the pure expression of my unconscious self.'[78] Though

intelligence for much of his life, alongside his magical career. This author has never been convinced, though that doesn't necessarily mean there's no truth to any of it. The argument is beyond the remit of this book; for more information, see *Secret Agent 666: Aleister Crowley, British Intelligence and the Occult* by Richard D Spence, and *Aleister Crowley: The Biography* by Tobias Churton.

74 Aleister Crowley, *The Equinox of the Gods*, online edition; Crowley writes about himself in the third person again here. <https://ia804602.us.archive.org/28/items/Equinoxs/Eq-gods.pdf>

75 Which frequently went in hand with a dismissal of the literary abilities of others, with anybody who didn't see in Crowley's poetry a genius at work clearly being jealous of the magnitude of his talent. When Crowley first encountered the Irish poet W B Yeats at an 1899 London Golden Dawn meeting for example, and shared some of his verse with him, Yeats 'glanced through them. He forced himself to utter a few polite conventionalities, but I could see what the truth of the matter was.... black, bilious rage.. shook him to the soul... What hurt him was the knowledge of his own incomparable inferiority. ' (Aleister Crowley, *The Confessions of Aleister Crowley*, p 157).

76 Aleister Crowley, *The Confessions of Aleister Crowley*, p 7.

77 Crowley self-published a total of five poetry books in 1898, including *The Tale of Archais, Songs of the Spirit*, and *Jephthah*. These latter three sold about as well as *Aceldama* and *White Stains* did, that is poorly. *Jephthah* for example sold a total of ten copies in five years. All of course are now highly sought after and expensive to procure in their original editions,.

78 Aleister Crowley, *The Confessions of Aleister Crowley*, p 126.

Crowley's poetry does have merit he exhibited little in the way of creative or editorial control, deeming every word and phrase that flowed from his pen to be genius. His excessive use of exclamation marks and alliteration might also grate to modern tastes.

It may surprise the reader to learn that Crowley's approach towards magick – he later chose to spell it thus to differentiate it from stage magic,[79] 'to distinguish the Science of the Magi from all its counterfeits'[80] – was chiefly a pragmatic one. In the book *Liber 0* he wrote of

> Sephiroth and the Paths; of Spirits and Conjurations; of Gods, Spheres, Planes, and many other things which may or may not exist. It is immaterial whether these exist or not. By doing certain things certain results will follow; students are most earnestly warned against attributing objective reality or philosophic validity to any of them.[81]

Towards the end of his life he stated that 'magic is something we do to ourselves. It is *more convenient* to assume the objective existence of an Angel who gives us new knowledge than to allege that our invocation has awakened a supernatural power in ourselves.'[82]

On 18 November 1898 Crowley was initiated into the Hermetic Order of the Golden Dawn, a western magical organisation founded in London a mere decade earlier[83] by three Freemasons, William Wynn Westcott (1848-1925), Samuel Liddell MacGregor Mathers (1854-1918), and William

---

79 Resurrecting an archaic Early Modern English spelling.

80 Aleister Crowley, *Magick*, p 45.

81 Aleister Crowley, *Liber 0*, online edition. <https://hermetic.com/crowley/libers/lib6>

82 Aleister Crowley, quoted in *Museum Piece: The Education of an Iconographer* by James Laver, p 228. Italics in original.

83 There is some controversy as to the origins of the Hermetic Order of the Golden Dawn. Westcott alleged that the source was a sixty-page manuscript in cipher and of Renaissance origin found in a second-hand bookstore, featuring rituals and occult teachings. An enclosed document led Westcott to Anna Sprengel, a Stuttgart-based Rosicrucian who claimed to be head of a German magical order named Die Goldene Dämmerung, the Golden Dawn. The two corresponded, leading to the establishment of the Isis-Urania Temple of the Hermetic Order of the Golden Dawn in London as the English branch of an existing organisation. The provenance of the manuscript however has long been disputed, as indeed has Sprengel's existence; more likely is that Westcott, Mathers, and Woodman invented the whole story, and wrote the rituals and teachings themselves.

Robert Woodman (1828-1891). Prominent members have included Arthur
Machen, W B Yeats, Arthur Conan Doyle, A E Waite, Algernon Blackwood,
Sax Rohmer, and Florence Farr. Upon initiation Crowley assumed the
magical name Frater Perdurabo, translated as 'I will endure to the end', an
apt moniker considering his lengthy occult career and one that he would
continue to use long after he had tired of the Golden Dawn itself. The other
members did not impress him,

> for the most part muddled middle class mediocrities... an abject
> assemblage of nonentities... as vulgar and commonplace as any
> other set of average people... [They] possessed no individuality;
> they were utterly undistinguished either for energy or capacity.
> There is not one of them today who has made any mark in the
> world.[84]

He was taught Goetia[85] and Kabbalah[86] and ceremonial magick by
Golden Dawn member Allan Bennett,[87] the two living together in London
as pupil and tutor in a 67-69 Chancery Lane flat rented by Crowley. Bennett
used a number of drugs prescribed to help with his asthma including opium,

---

84 Aleister Crowley, *The Confessions of Aleister Crowley,* p159-160.

85 Evocations of demonic entities from *The Lesser Key of Solomon,* a seventeenth
century grimoire of anonymous authorship which may have been derived from earlier
sources. When Crowley met Allan Bennett for the first time, Bennett exclaimed
'Little brother, you have been meddling with the Goetia!' Upon Crowley stating that
he hadn't, Bennett replied 'In that case, the Goetia has been meddling with you.'

86 A system of Jewish mysticism which has numerous spellings – including Qabalah
and Cabala – and central to which is the cosmological model of the Tree of Life,
comprising ten emanations or sepiroth and their connected pathways. Each sepiroth
has its own properties and correspondences, ascending from the base or mundane
to the divine. Crowley saw knowledge of the Kabbalah as an essential component
of magical training. 'The Tree of Life has got to be learnt by heart; you must know
it backwards, forwards, sideways, and upside down; it must become the automatic
background of all your thinking. You must keep on hanging everything that comes
your way upon its proper bough.' (Aleister Crowley, *Magick Without Tears,* p 49).

87 Born Charles Henry Allan Bennett (1872-1923), an early Hermetic Order of the
Golden Dawn member (Order name Frater Iehi Aour) and a friend and teacher to
Crowley. He also studied as a Buddhist and was influential in introducing Buddhism
to England. Crowley reports that Bennett's physicality disgusted him; 'he revolted
against being an animal; he regarded the pleasures of living (and above all, those of
physical love) as diabolical illusions devised by the enemy of mankind in order to
trick souls into accepting the curse of existence.' Aleister Crowley, *The Confessions of
Aleister Crowley,* p 173.

cocaine, chloroform, and morphine, and served as Crowley's introduction to drugs not merely for recreation but also as an aid to mystical experience.

> [Bennett] suffered acutely from spasmodic asthma. His cycle of life was to take opium for about a month, when the effect wore off, so that he had to inject morphine. After a month of this he had to switch to cocaine, which he took till he began to 'see things' and was then reduced to chloroform. I have seen him in bed for a week, only recovering consciousness sufficiently to reach for the bottle and sponge. Asthma being a sthenic disease, he was then too weak to have it any more, so he would gradually convalesce until, after a few weeks of freedom, the spasms would begin once more and he would be forced to renew the cycle.[88]

Crowley took to drugs with great gusto, and continued to use many and varied substances to one degree or another throughout the rest of his life. Cocaine, morphine, opium, heroin, and others now prohibited as class A drugs were then still legal and readily available,[89] being prescribed for a variety of ailments, and their addictive properties were only just beginning to be understood.

In November 1899, Bennett having moved to Ceylon to further his own Buddhist studies and where the climate better-suited his perilous health,[90] Crowley purchased Boleskine House overlooking Loch Ness[91] in

---

88 Aleister Crowley, *The Confessions of Aleister Crowley*, p 173.

89 At least until the passing of the 18 August 1920 Dangerous Drugs Act, which while not strictly outlawing drugs began to exert legal control over them. Addiction was deemed a criminal offence and not an affliction, and heroin, cocaine, morphine, and opium among other substances were made available for export, import, and sale only by licence.

90 A relocation paid for with £100 which Crowley requested with no intent to pay it back from a married woman with whom he was having an affair, the delightfully named Lilian Horniblow (also known as Laura Grahame).

91 Regarding the monster purported to lurk therein, one curious theory has it that this is not a flesh-and-blood beast at all but something non-corporeal (hence the difficulty in finding or even photographing it), and was the result of one or another Crowley ritual, something summoned and never properly banished. Crowley wondered along the same lines himself, writing in later life 'Maybe the Lake of Loch Ness is suffering from the same Magical phenomena as the Manor of Boleskine. I do not know, but I am extremely interested in the ultimate end of the investigations into the existence of the monster which has created such excitement.' (quoted in *Aleister Crowley: The Biography* by Tobias Churton, p 110).

Scotland, styling himself as the Laird of Boleskine and dressing the part in traditional Scots garb despite having no Scottish ancestry. His chief purpose in relocating was to find somewhere remote and secluded where he could carry out the ritual workings of the Sacred Magic of Abramelin[92] the Mage,[93] the ultimate goal of which was 'attainment of the Knowledge and Conversation of the Holy Guardian Angel.'[94] He soon found that 'the demons connected with Abramelin do not wait to be evoked; they come unsought.'[95] The house

> became peopled with shadowy shapes, sufficiently substantial, as a rule, to be almost opaque. I say shapes, and yet the truth is that they were not shapes properly speaking. The phenomenon is hard to describe. It was as if the faculty of vision suffered some interference; as if the objects of vision were not properly objects at all. It was as if they belonged to an order of matter which affected the sight without informing it.[96]

Though projected to take six months the Abramelin working was cut short in Crowley's case, ultimately not being completed until 1906.

Crowley had achieved much in occult knowledge and capability since his Golden Dawn initiation and felt ready for further advancement within the Order to the grade of Adeptus Minor 5°=6°[97] but this was declined.

---

92 Often also rendered Abra-Melin.

93 There is some debate as to precisely how old the text from which Crowley was working, *The Book of the Sacred Magic of Abramelin the Mage*, actually is. Though often claimed to have originally been translated from Hebrew into French in 1458, an original manuscript of this translation has never been found and it is now thought more likely to have originated some time in the eighteenth century. The translation Crowley used was a recent one, by Hermetic Order of the Golden Dawn co-founder Samuel Liddell MacGregor Mathers.

94 More than a mere watchful and protective spirit, the Holy Guardian Angel of western occultism is conceived of as a divine intelligence – which may be an independent discarnate entity or one's subconscious 'higher self' depending on how one chooses to look at it – connection with which is essential in facilitating spiritual and magical development and ascendancy. Numerous methods of contact have been indicated, including the Abramelin procedure and the later Crowley-written Liber Samekh ritual, which was intended as a more straightforward means.

95 Aleister Crowley, *The Confessions of Aleister Crowley*, p 176.

96 Ibid., p 182.

97 The grade system of the Hermetic Order of the Golden Dawn was not straightforward, and the naming of its degrees can be confusing. Its structure was

Many of the group's London members disapproved of his reputation and libertine lifestyle, his numerous affairs, bisexuality and drug use. Crowley went directly to Order head Samuel Liddell MacGregor Mathers, resident in Paris, who elevated him to the next degree on 13 January 1900, creating a schism between Mathers and Crowley on one side, and much of the rest of the London lodge on the other. Disillusioned, Crowley travelled to America and to Mexico and thence to Hawaii, Japan, China, and on to India. Despite his magical accomplishments, doubt wracked him; 'I exist not; there is no God; no place; no time: wherefore I exactly particularise these things.'[98] In Ceylon he met up again with his former instructor Allan Bennett, now living as a Buddhist monk. He spent six weeks learning yoga and meditation, practices that would later form a key part of his own magical curriculum. By November 1902 he was once more in Europe, where he stayed a while in Paris before returning to Boleskine House the following April. Inevitably, wherever he went and whatever he did an interminable amount of poetry ensued, especially when he had a woman around – which was usually the case – to act as muse. He self-published his poetry volumes as quickly as he wrote them, accumulating an extensive body of work. Back at Boleskine he felt dispirited with his magical endeavours; 'It is strange to look back on myself at twenty-seven,' he later wrote, 'completely persuaded of the truth of the most extravagant claims of mysticism and magick, yet completely disillusioned with regard to the universe.'[99] He even found himself suddenly unable to write; 'The condition of my soul is clearly indicated by my output. The fount of lyric poetry had run completely dry.'[100]

On 12 August 1903 Crowley wedded Rose Kelly[101] in a union of

---

based on the Kabbalah and had three 'layers', an Outer Order, a Second Order, and an Inner Order, with degrees to be attained within each. By this point Crowley had ascended through the four ranks of the Outer Order and sought entry into the Second Order.

98 Aleister Crowley, diary, 1 August 1900.

99 Aleister Crowley, *The Confessions of Aleister Crowley*, p 377.

100 Ibid., p 378.

101 Rose Kelly, born 1874, is best-remembered for her marriage to Crowley and her involvement in the Cairo Working that led to the reception of *The Book of the Law*. Crowley regarded her as one of the most significant of his Scarlet Women (see the chapter *Mother of Heaven, Sister Cybele, Laylah (1911)* elsewhere in this book for more information on Scarlet Women) and always acknowledged her role in the birthing of Thelema. Following their divorce the two remained in contact. Though Kelly is commonly reported to have been committed to an asylum by Crowley in September 1911 for dementia brought on by her alcoholism, this may not have been the case; see *Aleister Crowley in Paris* by Tobias Churton, p 228. Kelly was remarried

convenience, she being pressured by her family into marriage and seeking a way out. Kelly had already accepted proposals from two men and was having an affair with a third. Her family, tired of her ways, demanded that she marry one of the men – which was her choice – to resolve the matter. Crowley suggested she marry him instead, and she accepted. Though intended as a purely practical arrangement to get her out of the mess she was in, the two soon fell in love once they got to know one another, he deeming her 'one of the most beautiful and fascinating women in the world'.[102]

> Physically and morally, Rose exercised on every man she met a fascination which I have never seen anywhere else, not a fraction of it. She was like a character in a romantic novel, a Helen of Troy or a Cleopatra; yet, more passionate, unhurtful. She was essentially a good woman. Her love sounded every abyss of lust, soared to every splendour of the empyrean.[103]

They entered an extended honeymoon period, 'an uninterrupted sexual debauch'[104] during which they travelled widely and Crowley wrote love poetry to his new bride.[105] He found her easy enough to control;

> Once, in the first three weeks or so, Rose took some trifling liberty; I recognised the symptoms, and turned her up and spanked her. She henceforth added the qualities of perfect wife to perfect mistress. Women, like all moral inferiors, behave well only when treated with firmness, kindness, and justice... When trouble is not suppressed permanently by a little friendly punishment, it is a sign that the virtue has gone out of the master.[106]

In April 1904 while the pair were in Cairo, Crowley – with Kelly's assistance in her role as Ourada[107] the seer – was contacted by an entity

---

in 1912 to Dr Joseph Gormley (a doctor who had treated her), and died in 1932 of liver failure caused by her excessive drinking.

102 Aleister Crowley, *The Confessions of Aleister Crowley*, p 387.

103 Ibid., p 393.

104 Aleister Crowley, quoted in *A Magick Life: A Biography of Aleister Crowley* by Martin Booth, p 182 (and elsewhere).

105 Published as *Rosa Mundi* in 1905.

106 Aleister Crowley, *The Confessions of Aleister Crowley*, p 388.

107 A name bestowed on her by Crowley, being the Arabic for rose.

calling itself Aiwass,[108] a messenger of Hoor Paar Kraat or Harpocrates, which took the form of a disembodied voice;

> The Voice of Aiwass came apparently from over my left shoulder, from the furthest corner of the room. It seemed to echo itself in my physical heart in a very strange manner, hard to describe... The voice was passionately poured, as if Aiwass were alert about the time-limit... Of deep timbre, musical and expressive, its tones solemn, voluptuous, tender, fierce or aught else as suited the moods of the message. Not bass – perhaps a rich tenor or baritone.[109]

Crowley transcribed over three days between 8 and 10 April in three one-hour sessions the text that would come to be known as *Liber AL vel Legis*, more commonly called *The Book of the Law.*

The Book of the Law and its teachings would form the core of the magical philosophy and practice known as Thelema, and – after some scepticism and rejection – Crowley devoted much of the rest of his life to understanding and promoting its contents. The word 'Thelema' is an English transliteration of the Greek θέλημα, or 'will.' Thelema's central tenets include the famed 'Every man and every woman is a star', 'Do what thou wilt shall be the whole of the law,'[110] and 'Love is the law, love under will.' 'Do what thou wilt shall be the whole of the law' in particular has been much misunderstood. It does not simply mean 'do whatever you want', rather 'find your True Will and live in accordance with it.' 'It is the apotheosis of Freedom; but it is also the strictest possible bond.'[111] Central to Thelema is the idea that every

---

108 Sometimes spelled Aiwaz or Airwas. Crowley would later come to regard Aiwass as his own Holy Guardian Angel.

109 Aleister Crowley, *The Equinox of the Gods*, online edition. <https://ia804602. us.archive.org/28/items/Equinoxs/Eq-gods.pdf>

110 As noted by other writers, 'do what thou wilt' isn't a phrase unique to Crowley. Rabelais' novels Gargantua and Pantagruel feature an 'Abbaye de Thélème' with the words 'Do what you will' inscribed above its door. In a fifth century sermon, St Augustine of Hippo stated 'Love and do what you will.' William Blake's *The Everlasting Gospel* includes the lines 'Do what you will, this life's a fiction / And is made up of contradiction.' Elizabethan occultist John Dee wrote 'Do that which most pleaseth you... Wherefore do even as you list.' Sir Francis Dashwood, at his Hellfire Club at the abbey of Medmenham, had the slogan 'do what thou wilt' painted above the door, styled after Rabelais. The notion of an Abbey of Thelema would be revisited by Crowley in 1920; see the chapter *Love Alway Yieldeth: Love Alway Hardeneth (1914-1923)* later in this book.

111 Aleister Crowley, *The Message of the Master Therion*, published in *The Equinox*

individual has their own unique True Will, or purpose, which they should uncover and pursue by magical means (though there are and always have been theoretical Thelemites who don't practice magick). 'So with thy all; thou hast no right but to do thy will. Do that and no other shall say nay. For pure will, unassuaged of purpose, delivered from the lust of result, is every way perfect.'[112] Crowley called this process of uncovering one's True Will the Great Work.[113] 'The Adventure of the Great Work is the only one worth while; for all others are but interludes in the sinister farce of Life and Death, which limits all human endeavour... Death makes life futile and fatuous.'[114]

The transmission of *The Book of the Law* also inaugurated the Aeon of Horus, which was deemed to have commenced that April in 1904. Thelemic lore divides human history into three Aeons; the Aeon of Isis, the Aeon of Osiris, and the Aeon of Horus, or those of Nuit,[115] Hadit,[116] and Ra-Hoor-Khuit[117] as they are identified in the text of *The Book of the Law* itself. The Aeon of Isis/Nuit, occurring in prehistory, was considered to have been

---

Vol II No I p 41.

112 *The Book of the Law*, I: 42-44.

113 The entirety of which is beyond simple summary for this book's purposes, though two essential components of the Great Work are 'knowledge and conversation of the Holy Guardian Angel' and 'crossing the Abyss'. 'The Single Supreme Ritual is the attainment of the Knowledge and Conversation of The Holy Guardian Angel. It is the raising of the complete man in a vertical straight line. Any deviation from this line tends to become black magic. Any other operation is black magic.' (Aleister Crowley, *Magick*, p 294). The Holy Guardian Angel is sometimes conceived of as one's 'higher self', sometimes an exterior being; whichever way one views it, a connection is crucial in unveiling the True Will. Crossing the Abyss involves a full and conscious transition across the void between the mundane and the non-corporeal, of 'the gap in thought between the Real, which is ideal, and the Unreal, which is actual.' Crossing the Abyss is an all or nothing affair; one either comes out on the other side into a mystical state of being where all is unity (becoming what Crowley termed 'a Babe of the Abyss'), or one descends into madness. Another and perhaps more straightforward explanation of The Great Work can be found in an undated letter from approximately 1941 from Crowley to Lady Frieda Harris, wherein he recommended that she 'interpret every phenomenon as a particular dealing of God with your soul... then, having embraced and loved the fact (however repugnant) you thereby transform it into holiness and beauty. This is the Great Work.'

114 Aleister Crowley, quoted in *Aleister Crowley in America* by Tobias Churton, p 30.

115 Equivalent to the Egyptian sky goddess Nut, and also referred to as the Queen of Space, the Queen of Heaven, and Our Lady of the Stars.

116 Consort of Nuit, comparable to Osiris, and referred to in *The Book of the Law* as 'the flame that burns in every heart of man, and in the core of every star.'

117 Equivalent to Horus, and child of Nuit.

matriarchal. The Aeon of Osiris/Hadit was patriarchal and defined by the monotheistic worship of male sky gods. The third Aeon, which had just begun in Crowley's view, was the Aeon of Horus/Ra-Hoor-Khuit, the child, and he posited that it would see the abandonment of one-god belief systems in favour of individual self-actualisation through magick.[118]

Further travels followed Crowley's departure from Cairo; initially to Europe then to India, Burma, Nepal, and China, before sailing to America by way of Japan and Canada. All the while he wrote prolifically, and continued his magical practice and drug intake, in particular of hashish which he found aided immeasurably in his occult activities and the use of which he detailed in the essay *The Psychology of Hashish*. In October 1906 he deemed himself to have completed the Abramelin magical operation begun at Boleskine House in 1900, attaining Knowledge and Conversation of the Holy Guardian Angel. 'I *did* get rid of everything but the Holy Exalted One, and must have held Him for a minute or two. I did. I am sure I did. I expected Rose to see a Halo round my head.'[119] Crowley admitted in his diary that his drug use and ritual performance had begun to blur together; in the final days of the Abramelin working he noted 'many strange illusions of sight, sense of proportion, locality, illusions of muscular distortion... the hashish enthusiasm surged up against the ritual enthusiasm; so I hardly know which phenomena to attribute to which.'[120]

In 1907 Crowley was contacted again by Aiwass, who gave him two further texts which became known as *Liber VII* and *Liber Cordis Cincti Serpente* in October and November of that year.

> They were not taken from dictation like *The Book of the Law* nor were they my own composition. I cannot even call them automatic writing. I can only say that I was not wholly conscious at the time of what I was writing, and I felt that I had no right to 'change' so much as the style of a letter. They were written with the utmost rapidity without pausing for thought for a single moment, and I have not presumed to revise them. Perhaps 'Plenary inspiration' is the only adequate phrase, and this has become so discredited that people are loth to admit the possibility of such a thing.[121]

---

118 One could of course see a loose analogue here between the Age of Taurus, Age of Pisces, and the dawning Age of Aquarius of classical astrology were one so inclined.

119 Aleister Crowley, diary, 10 October 1906. Emphasis in original.

120 Ibid., 9 October 1906. The second part of the quotation was a later addendum.

121 Aleister Crowley, *The Confessions of Aleister Crowley*, p 603.

Additional Thelemic texts followed; *Liber LXVI, Liber Porta Lucis, Liber Tau, Liber Arcanorum, Liber DCCCXIII vel Ararita, Sub Figura X,* and *Liber Trigrammaton.* Despite his initial doubts and concerns Crowley eventually came to accept Thelema and *The Book of the Law,* and that Aiwass was an external discarnate intelligence and not simply an aspect of his own subconscious;[122]

> *The Book of the Law* is not in any way my work... It is not inspired. It was dictated, and the only duty of a scribe is to take down accurately what is said. In this particular case, the scribe disagreed with a great deal of the material. This frequently happens in business offices. But I should not recommend you listen to the financial opinion of a girl who is transcribing the letters of J P Morgan at eighteen dollars a week.[123]

Crowley also grew to identify himself as Thelema's messenger tasked with inaugurating a new aeon. 'For the first time since the spring of 1904 I felt myself free to do my will... My aspiration to be the means of emancipating humanity was perfectly fulfilled. I had merely to establish in the world the Law which had been given me to proclaim.'[124]

In 1908 Crowley wrote – in five days – *The World's Tragedy,* containing his first (and much less-known) autobiography, which he deemed

> beyond all question the high-water mark of my imagination, my metrical fluency, my wealth of expression, and my power of bringing together the most incongruous ideas so as to enrich my matter to the utmost. At the same time, I succeeded in reaching the greatest height of spiritual enthusiasm, human indignation, and demoniac satire. I sound the gamut of every possibility of emotion from innocent faith and enthusiasm to experienced cynicism.[125]

---

122 Crowley wavered as to the true nature of Aiwass for much of his life, as he wavered as to the objective reality or otherwise of the other entities with which he worked. Sometimes he viewed them as exterior non-corporeal forms and sometimes as facets of his own subconscious mind, ultimately concluding that the matter was secondary to the result which ensued.

123 Aleister Crowley, quoted in *Perdurabo: The Life of Aleister Crowley* by Richard Kaczynski, p 129.

124 Aleister Crowley, *The Confessions of Aleister Crowley,* p 647.

125 Ibid., p 602.

Crowley still had a tremendously high opinion of his own literary ability:

> I had come to my full stature as a poet. My technique was perfect; it had shaken off from its sandals the last dust which they had acquired by walking in the ways of earlier masters. I produced lyric and dramatic poetry which shows an astounding mastery of rhythm and rime, a varied power of expression which had no equal in the history of the language, and an intensity of idea which eats into the soul of the reader like vitriol. I should have been assigned publicly my proper place among my peers of the past without difficulty had it not been for one fatal fact. My point of view is so original, my thoughts so profound, and my allusions so recondite, that superficial readers, carried away by the sheer music of the words, found themselves, so to speak, intoxicated and unable to penetrate to the pith. People did not realise that my sonorous similes possessed a subtle sense intelligible only to those whose minds were familiar with the subject. It is, in fact, necessary to study almost any poem of mine like a palimpsest. The slightest phrase is essential; each one must be interpreted individually, and the poem read again until its personality presents itself. People who like my poetry, bar those who are simply tickled by the sound of what they imagine to be the sense, agree that it spoils them for any other poetry.[126]

Despite the fact that Crowley had inherited the equivalent of somewhere in the region of £1,000,000 little more than a decade prior, by 1908 his funds were running low, having been spent on extensive travel and extravagant living and the publishing of his own books. He would never fully recover financially, and for much of the rest of his life wavered between comfortable and destitute. He was still an abundant writer of poetry, to which he added fiction and drama, though this provided only a meagre income. He refused to profit from the occult:

> It seemed to me that my first duty was to prove to the world that I was not teaching Magick for money. I promised myself always to publish my books on an actual loss on the cost of production – never to accept a farthing for any form of instruction, giving

---

126 Ibid., p 574.

advice, or any other service whose performance depended on my magical attainments. I regarded myself as having sacrificed my career and my fortune for initiation, and that the reward was so stupendous that it made the price pitifully mean, save that, like the widow's mite, it was all I had. I was therefore the wealthiest man in the world, and the least I could do was to bestow the inestimable treasure upon my poverty-stricken fellow men.[127]

He attracted a number of students keen to learn magick from him, among them a young English poet named Victor Neuberg[128] (or Newbugger as Crowley's wife Rose Kelly called him). Neuberg and Crowley would swiftly become close, maintaining a strong and sometimes sexual friendship until they fell out in 1914.

Crowley had for some time been dispirited with the Hermetic Order of the Golden Dawn, and together with friend and fellow-occultist George Cecil Jones[129] he formed the A∴A∴ in early 1909, an Order that lifted much of its structure and teachings from the Golden Dawn – which it was intended to supersede – and with all rites reworked and added to by Crowley and Jones. The A∴A∴ is commonly reported to stand for Argentium Astrum, the Latin for 'silver star', though it is more likely the Greek for 'silver star' – Astron Argon – that was intended (the true meaning is deemed an Order secret). Prominent early A∴A∴ members included Victor Neuberg, Austin Osman Spare,[130] barrister and psychic investigator Everard Feilding (1867-

---

127 Ibid., p 630.

128 Victor Neuberg (1883-1940) was an English author and poet. Educated at Trinity College Cambridge, where Crowley also studied, the two didn't meet until 1906, with Crowley later initiating him into the A∴A∴ as Frater Omnia Vincam. Following his parting of ways with Crowley in 1914 Neuberg served in the British army in the First World War. On his return to England he embarked on a successful career as an editor and publisher, which included him discovering the then-unknown Dylan Thomas.

129 George Cecil Jones (1873-1960) was an English occultist and chemist and Hermetic Order of the Golden Dawn member, a friend and tutor of Crowley's who had first introduced Crowley to that Order back in 1898.

130 Austin Osman Spare, born 1886 in London where he lived all his life, was an artist and occultist. He pioneered a number of magical techniques including sigilisation and automatic drawing and writing. He wrote and illustrated occult books including *Earth Inferno*, *The Focus of Life*, *The Anathema of Zos*, *The Book of Satyrs*, and *The Book of Pleasure*. He died in poverty in 1956 aged 70. Scarce-known during his lifetime aside from acclaim for his art, and all but forgotten upon his death, he is now regarded as one of the most important magical figures of the twentieth century. This is in large part down to occultist and author Kenneth Grant, who preserved and

1937), novelist George Raffalovich (1880-1958), writer Frank Harris,[131] palmist William John Warner, better known as Cheiro (1866-1936), and author and poet Ethel Archer (1885-1962) amongst others.

In November 1909 Crowley and Neuberg journeyed into the Algerian desert together for an extended sequence of invocations of the thirty Æethyrs of Enochian magick,[132] with Crowley experiencing a transcendent epiphany during ritual anal sex:

> I did not merely admit that I did not exist, and that all my ideas were illusions, inane and insane. I felt these facts as facts. It was the difference between book knowledge and experience. It seemed incredible that I should ever have fancied that I or anything else had any bearing on each other. All things were alike as shadows sweeping across the still surface of a lake – their images had no meaning for the water, no power to stir its silence.[133]

Despite the efficacy of their results Neuberg in particular felt as if they were venturing onto untrodden ground. 'We did something which has never been done before...' he later said. 'It's doubtful whether Dee himself ever called them. And since his day they have done nothing but lie on

---

promoted Spare's work and legacy, and the chaos magick movement which adopted a number of his approaches and techniques in the nineteen-seventies and carried them forward into the wider occult scene. Spare joined the A∴A∴ in July 1910 but his membership would prove brief and uneventful – he didn't make it past Probationer grade – and he soon moved on following a disagreement with Crowley regarding fees for artwork of Spare's solicited for *The Equinox*.

131 Frank Harris (1855-1931) was an Irish-American novelist best remembered for his five-volume memoir *My Life and Loves*, banned for its sexually explicit content, though he also worked as a journalist, editor, publisher, and author of short stories. *My Life and Loves*, illustrated with both photographs and drawings, was not published in full until some years after Harris' death. As well as frequent descriptions of his many purported sexual encounters, numerous contemporaries make an appearance, including Oscar Wilde, Robert Browning, Lord Randolph Churchill, Lord Salisbury, George Meredith, Joseph Chamberlain, Thomas Carlyle, Elizabeth Barrett Browning, Algernon Charles Swinburne, and Cecil Rhodes amongst others (though – surprisingly perhaps – not Crowley).

132 Systems and techniques of magick from the sixteenth century writings of Elizabethan occultist John Dee, purportedly revealed to Dee and his scryer Edward Kelley by angelic beings. Obscure for years, much of Dee and Kelley's material was rediscovered by the Hermetic order of the Golden Dawn in the eighteen-eighties, and incorporated into their system and teachings.

133 Aleister Crowley, *The Confessions of Aleister Crowley*, p 675.

dusty shelves. We called them. We didn't know what would happen."[134] The desert rites peaked on 6 December with the blood of three pigeons and a confrontation with the demon Choronzon, the Dweller in the Abyss, which Crowley considered one of the most potent workings of his magical career:

> Choronzon... is not really an individual. The Abyss is empty of being; it is filled with all possible forms, each equally inane, each therefore evil in the only true sense of the word – that is, meaningless but malignant, in so far as it craves to become real... Choronzon appeared in many physical forms... He took the form of myself, of a woman whom Neuburg loved, of a serpent with a human head, etc. He could not utter the word of the Abyss, because there is no word; its voice is the insane babble of a multitude of senseless ejaculations... His main object was to induce [Neuberg] to leave the circle, or to break into it; so as to obsess him, to live in his life... Choronzon, in the form of a naked savage, dashed through and attacked [Neuberg]. He flung him to the earth and tried to tear out his throat with froth-covered fangs. [Neuberg] invoked the names of God and struck at Choronzon with the Magical Dagger. The demon was cowed by this courageous conduct and writhed back into the Triangle... He tried to shake [Neuberg's] faith in himself, his respect for me, his belief in the reality of Magick, and so on... I had astrally identified myself with Choronzon, so that I experienced each anguish, each rage, each despair, each insane outburst. My ordeal ended as the last form faded; so, knowing that all was over, I wrote the holy name of BABALON in the sand with my magical ring and arose from my trance... The work had lasted over two hours and we were both utterly exhausted, physically and in every other way. I hardly know how we ever got back.[135]

The whole sequence of events was later written up and published as *The Vision and the Voice*, a text Crowley considered almost as Thelemically significant as *The Book of the Law*:

> I admit that my visions can never mean to other men as much as they do to me. I do not regret this. All I ask is that my results

---

134 Victor Neuberg, quoted in *The Magical Dilemma of Victor Neuberg* by Jean Overton Fuller, p 87.

135 Aleister Crowley, *The Confessions of Aleister Crowley*, p 677-678.

should convince seekers after truth that there is beyond doubt something worthwhile seeking, attainable by methods more or less like mine. I do not want to father a flock, to be the fetish of fools and fanatics, or the founder of a faith whose followers are content to echo my opinions. I want each man to cut his own way through the jungle.[136]

On 24 November 1909, after six years of marriage, Crowley and the by then alcoholic Rose Kelly divorced, Crowley citing his own infidelity as grounds though the true reason in his mind was her excessive drinking. There were two daughters of the union, Nuit Ma Ahathoor Hecate Sappho Jezebel Lilith Crowley (usually simply referred to as Lilith or sometimes Nuit) born 28 July 1904 who died 1 May 1906, and Lola Zaza Crowley,[137] born September 1906, who went to live with an uncle after the divorce, with Crowley ordered to pay £52 annually in support.[138]

---

136 Ibid., p 671.

137 Lola Zaza Crowley (1906-1990) was raised by Gerald Kelly, an artist of some repute and Rose Kelly's brother. Crowley saw little of her during her childhood, though noted in his diary following a 1921 visit when she was fifteen that 'I have just seen Gerald Kelly, annoyed & bewildered because Lion's daughters do not grow wool! Lola Zaza is unmanageable. She despises everybody, thinks she is a genius, is stupid, inaccurate, plain, ill-tempered, etc. etc. God! but it's good to be a Lion! For the first time in my life I taste the true pleasures of immortality. But the sheep are many, & their pressure may suffocate Lion cubs.' In later life Lola married, and distanced herself from her father. In 1929, curious about him, Gerald Kelly sent her some of Crowley's books; after reading them she wrote 'I have judged him by his own works and what could be fairer?... I really have no time to spare on a man so rude or conceited. His works are a part of him and I am very sorry for the other part. What a hash he has made of it.' Crowley did not see her again.

138 Perhaps unsurprisingly given how many sexual partners Crowley had throughout his life, Lilith and Lola were not his only children. He also fathered Anne Léa Crowley, also known as Poupée (20 February 1920-14 October 1920), with Leah Hirsig, Astarte Lulu Panthea Crowley (1920-2005) with Ninette Shumway, and Randal Gair, better known as Aleister Ataturk Crowley (1937-2002) with Patricia Doherty, though there were possibly others. This author doesn't don't count Amado Crowley (1930-2010), who claimed to be Crowley's son and to have knowledge of the true occult teachings that Crowley left out of his books. Crowley's extensive diaries and notebooks – which make mention of pretty much everybody he knew or met – carry no word of Amado at all. The only person who alleged that Amado was Crowley's offspring was Amado himself.

Crowley was still a fervent drug user, especially of hashish but also of peyote[139] (or anhalonium, the genus name, as it was then often called and as he referred to it). Magick-infused drug parties and trip sessions at Crowley's 124 Victoria Street, London residence became popular events and are known to have been attended by poet Meredith Starr (1890-1971), Everard Feilding, George Raffalovich, and naval officer and occult student Guy Marston (1871-1928)[140] among others. Readers more used to accounts of the use of peyote-alkaloid mescaline by the likes of Aldous Huxley[141] as related in his 1954 book *The Doors of Perception* might be surprised to learn that Crowley and friends were doing it fifty years earlier. That said, despite Crowley's claim that peyote was 'introduced by me to Europe'[142] he was not the first westerner to do so, though he was one of the first Europeans to methodically and regularly use it.[143]

In March 1910 Crowley was subject to legal proceedings from the Hermetic Order of the Golden Dawn, brought by his former initiator Mathers on the grounds that Crowley had reproduced, without permission, Order secrets and rituals in his publication *The Equinox*, a doorstop of

---

139 Peyote is a cactus native to Mexico and southern Texas, renowned for its psychoactive effects. It contains several such alkaloids, in particular mescaline. Its use by indigenous Americans dates back at least 5,700 years. The first scientific investigations into its effects took place in the eighteen-eighties, with mescaline isolated in 1897 by the German chemist Arthur Heffter, and synthetic mescaline following in 1919.

140 Who was of the belief that the sound of tom-toms could spontaneously induce 'shameless masturbation or indecent advances' (*The Equinox* Vol I No IX, p 53) in married English women. Sadly, what he thought their effect would be on single and non-English women is not recorded.

141 Though it is true enough that Crowley and Huxley met, in Berlin in 1930 – Crowley found him 'exceptionally charming' – that Crowley turned Huxley on to peyote at the time is a myth. Huxley's own psychedelic adventures would not commence until more than twenty years later, when he was introduced to mescaline by Dr Humphry Osmond in 1953.

142 In the article *Energised Enthusiasm*, published in *The Equinox* Vol I No IX, p 63.

143 Outside of it its use by indigenous Americans, western use of peyote dates back to at least the eighteen-eighties; beyond the early missionaries and anthropologists, John Raleigh Briggs was probably the first westerner to draw attention to its use in 1887, Louis Lewin – after whom Anhalonium Lewinii was named – was studying its effects by 1888, Havelock Ellis using it in 1896 and publishing reports of his findings, and Arthur Heffter and Silas Weir Mitchell among others were experimenting with mescaline that same decade. These notes are not exhaustive; for the full history of peyote and mescaline use the reader is pointed to *Mescaline: A Global History of the First Psychedelic* by Mike Jay.

a journal launched a year earlier as the biannual organ of the A∴A∴.[144] Crowley eventually won the case at a 21 March 1910 Court of Appeal hearing, though the ensuing media furore saw him tarred as a practitioner of the black arts, an allegation that has stuck to his name ever since. Crowley perhaps secretly appreciated the infamy despite this claim being untrue, though one publication in particular, *The John Bull*, took exception and would dog him for years, determined to publicly expose him.[145] It was in the meantime however all good promotion for the A∴A∴ and for Thelema, with new members attracted to the cause, 'some silly loafers looking for a new sensation, but many most sincere and sensible.'[146]

℘℞

Crowley makes no note of when he and Leila Waddell first met in his autobiography *The Confessions of Aleister Crowley*, despite a number of mentions of her therein. The first entry to cover her merely recounts that

> in the spring, on May 9 [1910], an invocation of Bartzabel, the spirit of Mars, so successfully as to demand description. My assistants were Commander Marston, RN, one of the highest officials of the Admiralty,[147] and Leila Waddell, an Australian violinist who I had just met and who appealed to my imagination. I began at once to use her as a principal figure in my work. In the first week of our intimacy I wrote two stories about her; *The Vixen* and *The Violinist*. *The Vixen* is about a girl, an heiress in a fox-hunting shire, who tortures and uses for black magic a girl friend. She has a lover, Lord

144 The first edition of which proclaimed, in its Crowley-written introduction, that 'With the publication of this review begins a completely new adventure in the history of mankind. Whatever knowledge may previously have been imputed to man, it has always been fenced in with conditions and restrictions. The time has come to speak plainly, and so far as may be in the language of the multitude.' *The Equinox* was lavishly produced, in hardcover and often running to more than 400 pages, and Crowley lost money with each issue.

145 It was *The John Bull* who famously proclaimed Crowley 'the Wickedest Man in the World', words that still attach to his name today and long after the demise of the journal itself; see the chapter *Love Alway Yieldeth: Love Alway Hardeneth (1914-1923)* later in this book.

146 Aleister Crowley, *The Confessions of Aleister Crowley*, p 685.

147 Crowley was for some reason frequently prone to exaggerating Marston's naval rank in his writings; Marston was – according to his service record – a navigation officer.

Eyre, whom she despises. She has some intimate relations with a phantom fox, who (to put it briefly) obsesses her. She yields to Eyre, who climbs into her room at night and finds that she is not a woman but a vixen. The effect is to turn him to a hound and he fastens his teeth in her throat. Hound and fox are found dead and nothing is ever heard again of Eyre and his mistress. *The Violinist* is about a girl who invokes, by means of her music, a demon belonging to one of the Elemental Watch Towers. She becomes his mistress. One day her husband returns to the house. He kisses her and falls dead. The demon has conferred this power upon her lips.[148]

Along with the lack of a date, precisely where Waddell and Crowley met was also not recorded, though as previously noted this was possibly at the Café Royal in London, where Crowley was a regular. Martin Booth, in his *A Magick Life: A Biography of Aleister Crowley*, notes in passing that the two 'had met, probably, in Paris',[149] though frustratingly the now-deceased Booth doesn't elaborate or provide a source; this author is also unable to find any record of either Crowley or Waddell spending time in Paris in spring 1910.

One occasional trick of Crowley's at this time was to visit the Café Royal (and elsewhere) in ceremonial attire, this by and large seeming to go unnoticed or at least unacknowledged by the other patrons, which he attributed to a form of magical invisibility he'd been practising:

I reached a point when my physical reflection in a mirror became faint and flickering. It gave very much the effect of the interrupted images of the cinematograph in its early days. But the real secret of invisibility is not concerned with the laws of optics at all; the trick is to prevent people noticing you when they would normally do so. In this I was quite successful. For example, I was able to take a walk in the street in a golden crown and a scarlet robe without attracting attention.[150]

The (perhaps apocryphal) story goes that upon one guest asking a Café Royal waiter who he was and why he was so dressed, the waiter remarked 'don't worry, that's just Mr Crowley being invisible.'[151]

---

148 Aleister Crowley, *The Confessions of Aleister Crowley*, p 685.

149 Martin Booth, *A Magick Life: A Biography of Aleister Crowley*, p 285.

150 Aleister Crowley, *The Confessions of Aleister Crowley*, p 198.

151 Crowley remained a patron of the Café Royal whenever he was in London until

Copy of the oath Leila signed upon being initiated in the A.·.A.·.
by Crowley, from Astrum Argenteum <https://www.astrumargenteum.
org/gallery/leila-waddell>

Though Crowley mentions the date of 9 May in his *Confessions of Aleister Crowley*, he and Waddell were already lovers by that point, she having been initiated by him into the A.·.A.·. on 1 April and assuming the magical title Soror Agatha. It is therefore likely that they met sometime in March 1910, while the Golden Dawn court proceedings were ongoing. Her

---

an incident in the late nineteen-thirties or early forties (precise date uncertain), when he and a party of friends ran up a bill in the region of £100 in a lavish evening of food and drink. At the end of the night Crowley – then living in poverty – is said to have excused himself, ostensibly to go to the bathroom, and exited the building without paying. He was not welcome again.

musical ability transfixed him, and he rapidly saw the possibilities for its use in magical ritual. Despite our not having a date or a location for Waddell and Crowley's first meeting, what does remain in the A∴A∴ archives is the certificate she signed following her initiation. Headed 'The Oath of the Probationer' and dated 1 April 1910, it reads:

> I, Leila Waddell, being of sound mind and body on this 1st day of April [Anno VI, ☉ in 10° of ♈] do hereby resolve: in the presence of Perdurabo a neophyte of the A∴A∴ To prosecute The Great Work: which is, to obtain a scientific knowledge of the nature and powers of my own being. May the A∴A∴ crown the work, lend me Its wisdom in the work, enable me to understand the work! Reverence, duty, sympathy, devotion, assiduity, trust do I bring to the A∴A∴ and in one year from this date may I be admitted to the knowledge and conversation of the A∴A∴'
>
> Witness my hand Leila Waddell [*signed*]
>
> Motto [Αγάθη]

Precisely what induced an internationally acclaimed professional touring musician to fall so swiftly in with a notorious occultist from the other side of the world is sadly lost to history. Crowley didn't specify, and if Waddell kept any kind of journal it hasn't survived. Though he evidently had his charms, and throughout his life never ceased to attract women, Crowley's opinion of the female sex was low:

> Every woman that I met enabled me to affirm magically that I had defied the tyranny of the Plymouth Brethren and the Evangelicals. At the same time women were the source of romantic inspiration; and their caresses emancipated me from the thraldom of the body. When I left them I found myself walking upon air, with my soul free to wing its way through endless empyreans and to express its godhead in untrammelled thought of transcendent sublimity, expressed in language which combined the purest aspirations with the most majestic melodies.... But, morally and mentally, women were for me beneath contempt. They had no true moral ideals. They were bound up with their necessary preoccupation, with the function of reproduction. Their apparent aspirations were camouflage. Intellectually, of course, they did not exist. Even the few whose minds were not completely blank had them furnished with Wardour Street Chippendale. Their attainments were those

of the ape and the parrot. These facts did not deter me. On the contrary, it was highly convenient that one's sexual relations should be with an animal with no consciousness beyond sex.[152]

One thing that is often overlooked in Waddell's story is that throughout her time with Crowley she continued to perform professionally, fulfilling concert commitments both in England and internationally. Just weeks after her A∴A∴ initiation she was once more at the now-renovated Shaftesbury Hall in Bournemouth, playing two two-hour shows each day at 3pm and 8pm from 25 to 30 April 1910. The posters prominently billed her; 'Welcome Return Visit of Miss Leila Waddell, the Queen of Australian Violinists.' The Bournemouth Daily Echo singled her out for mention in its review of the first of these shows:

> Her numerous musical admirers will be glad to hear the brilliant Australian violinist, Miss Leila Waddell, who, since her first appearance here, exactly one year ago, has travelled far and wide, both through Great Britain and on the Continent. Her playing of a Romance, by Reiss, and the Moto Perpetuo, by the same composer, proved that she has lost none of her old charm.[153]

She returned to Shaftesbury Hall two months later, performing twice daily at 3pm and 8pm between 4 and 9 July[154] and from 11 to 16 July, by then being billed as 'Australia's Finest Violinist.' She passed the period in between in London with Crowley, and his diary for 4 June noted an extended and trippy hashish session that night in Crowley's Victoria Street flat, with the two of them accompanied by Victor Neuberg and Charles Stansfield Jones.[155]

---

152 Aleister Crowley, The Confessions of Aleister Crowley, p 130-131.

153 The Bournemouth Daily Echo, 26 April 1910.

154 The Bournemouth Graphic newspaper was most-taken by her reappearance, writing on 7 July that 'the beautiful Australian, Miss Leila Waddell, has excited universal admiration from the double standpoint of artistic ability and personal charm.'

155 For a partial transcript of which, see Aleister Crowley: The Biography by Tobias Churton, p 153-155.

As noted, Waddell and Crowley – along with Neuberg[156] – spent a weekend at the home of Guy Marston, a Royal Navy officer and student of magick, at Rempstone in Dorset, where on 9 May 1910 they carried out an invocation of Bartzabel, a demon associated with the planet Mars. It is likely that there were prior magical workings of Crowley's that Waddell participated in, but this is the earliest account Crowley gives. In an interview with a New York journalist in 1914 Crowley claimed that this working predicted the advent of the First World War, still four years away.[157] It is worth quoting for the insight it provides into Crowley's approach to and techniques of practical magick:

Three of us – myself, a British naval officer of high rank, and a famous violinist – decided to evoke the spirit of Mars. By Mars we don't mean the planet in the sky, at all; we mean the hidden forces that possess the powers we attribute to Mars. Also we performed no sacrifice. In the old days when the Israelites went out to give battle they would sacrifice an animal, but nowadays it is not necessary to shed blood. You use the proper incense, and the beings you want materialise from the smoke.

As we were going to invoke the spirit of Mars I used a blood-red robe and wore the crown of the Uraeus serpent and armed myself with the sword and the spear. My two assistant Magi were clad in white and gold.

Around the altar we had traced a large circle, ample in size to contain the three of us. And then, following the ancient rites, we consecrated the spear, and then the sword, and then the altar, and lastly the magic circle itself. So long as we remained inside that circle no harm could come to us. Once we were secure we conjured the Dog of Evil, just as the minister exorcises the spirits of evil before laying the foundation stone of a church, and having done that we bound ourselves by a great oath to the purposes of the ceremony. That is one of the most important things.

---

156 Though Neuberg was definitely there that weekend – his presence is recorded in the ritual transcript – Crowley makes no mention of him in later accounts, instead referring just to himself, Waddell, and Marston being present. This is perhaps because Crowley and Neuberg fell out in 1914, and Crowley disowned him.

157 Which is perhaps less remarkable a prophecy than it might appear, with increasing tension among the European powers in the years before war broke out, and intimations of looming conflict being felt throughout the continent and beyond.

And as the clouds of incense rose from the altar we lifted up our voices and praised the God of Battle. We invoked the Egyptian God Horus and called upon Elohim Gebor to aid us. And then as I felt the power within me grow I commanded the blind spirit Bartzabel to come forth.

The dark clouds of incense slowly took form and, standing without the circle, a sexless ox-like form appeared, with dull, deceitful head and hideous human features suffused with blood. It stood panting, its heart beating violently, and in a deep hoarse voice said that there would be two wars, and predicted that the greatest of the two would end by the crushing of Germany.[158]

Though Crowley gives the impression here that Bartzabel physically manifested before them this is contradicted by the account found in *The Confessions of Aleister Crowley* and from reading a transcript of the working;[159] rather, Neuberg was possessed by Bartzabel and the demon spoke through him. 'In the Triangle was Frater Omnia Vincam [Neuberg], to serve as a material basis through which the spirit might manifest... The idea was to work up the magical enthusiasm through the exhilaration induced by music.'[160] This last line also indicates that Waddell soundtracked proceedings on violin.

Following the Bartzabel working – which the parties deemed a rousing success – between them they formulated at Marston's suggestion the idea for a new kind of musical ritual theatre in an effort at presenting the teachings of the A∴A∴ to a broader audience. Named the Rite of Artemis, this was conceived as a performance piece heavy with occult symbolism and correspondences wherein A∴A∴ members would personify different deities and elemental forces. Waddell's role was to be chiefly a musical one; Crowley found her antipodean accent unsuitable for the pronunciation of magical terms and entity names, and so she was set to perform on violin to accompany the poetry and drama. Crowley took to calling her Mother of Heaven in tribute to her assigned role in the planned rite, and was heard by friend and socialite Gwendoline Otter[161] (1876-1958) to declare 'Oh

158 Aleister Crowley, quoted in *Master Magician Reveals Weird Supernatural Rites*, Henry N Hall, *Fort Wayne Gazette*, 20 December 1914.

159 As published in *The Equinox* Vol I No IX.

160 Aleister Crowley, *The Confessions of Aleister Crowley*, p 685-686.

161 Otter's first name is sometimes spelled Gwendolyn or Gwendolen, though Gwendoline is most common. Ever-perceptive, around this time Otter was told by Victor Neuberg that she was lucky to have known Crowley for as long as she had

Mother, I wish you'd get rid of your Australian accent. It sounds so bad in the ceremonies,' which led to an insecure Waddell asking Otter 'Will you tell me when I sy anything in Austreyelian?'[162]

Later in May 1910 Crowley and Waddell travelled to Venice, where on the afternoon of 18 May during a peyote session he reported 'a faery flush of yellow and red over Venice on closing eyes.'[163] Stopping off at the hotel Pallanza in Lago Maggiore on the way home he wrote *Household Gods*, a short verse play published in 1912 in a slim volume dedicated to Waddell. Crowley described it as 'a poetical dramatic sketch. It is a sort of magical allegory, full of subtle ironies and mystifications; almost the only thing of its kind I have ever done – which perhaps accounts for my having a sneaking affection for it.'[164] The drama – written in rhyming verse – concerns the character Crassus and two women, his wife Adela and servant Alicia. The narrative is mostly uneventful. Crassus and Alicia converse on Crassus' estate, then walk among woods where a statue of Pan and a faun address them, and Crassus declares his feelings for Alicia. All the while they discourse on the essence of love. At the play's climax they catch Adela copulating with a swan – the god Jupiter in disguise – and in the struggle that ensues Alicia is revealed to be the goddess Ganymede. Crassus and Adela make up and renew their love for each other, their dalliances with the gods forgotten.

Back in London Waddell and Crowley worked together to prepare for the coming Rite of Artemis, he reading poems aloud against which she played music that echoed its tone, improvising or drawing from her extensive repertoire. Peyote likely informed these sessions, keen as Crowley was to see how the drug affected magical and creative undertakings; 'when LW and I played and read poetry against each other before the Lord, we got such wonderful spiritual results that we tried to reduce all to a rule.'[165] As Crowley later described it (giving a different account of the origin of the Rite and failing to credit Guy Marston's role in coming up with the idea),

---

without getting hurt, to which Otter replied 'How could he hurt me? I'm not in love with him, and I've never lent him money.'

162 Quoted in *Museum Piece: The Education of an Iconographer* by James Laver, p 117. Phonetic spelling in original.

163 Aleister Crowley diary, 18 May 1910.

164 Aleister Crowley, *The Confessions of Aleister Crowley*, p 685.

165 Aleister Crowley, quoted in *A Magick Life: A Biography of Aleister Crowley* by Martin Booth, p 286.

I happened to have a few friends in my room in the evening, among
them the celebrated Australian violinist, Miss Leila Waddell. It
struck me that we might pass the time by a sort of artistic dialogue;
I read a piece of poetry from one of the great classics, and she
replied with a piece of music suggested by my reading. I retorted
with another poem; and the evening developed into a regular
controversy. The others [present] were intensely interested enough
in this strange conflict, and in the silence of the room spiritual
enthusiasm took hold of us; so acutely that we were all intensely
uplifted, to the point in some cases of actual ecstasy, an intoxication
of the same kind experienced by an assistant at the celebration of
the Mass or the performance of Parsifal, but stronger because of
its naturalness and primitiveness. It was subsequently decided to
try and tune everybody up to some definite, prearranged emotion,
and we strung together a rough ceremony in honour of Artemis.[166]

Inspired, Crowley wrote the poems *Pan to Artemis* and *The Interpreter*,
both to Waddell, the first of numerous poetical works he composed about
or inspired by or dedicated to her over the next seven years. Both were
published in the Vol I No IV edition of *The Equinox* in September 1910, set
next to the famed photo of a robed Waddell in profile playing violin (which,
according to a note at the back of the journal, was taken at Dover Street
Studios, London).

The Interpreter

Mother of Light, and the Gods! Mother of Music, awake!
Silence and speech are at odds; Heaven and Hell are at stake.
By the Rose and the Cross I conjure; I constrain by the Snake and
the Sword;
I am he that is sworn to endure – Bring us the word of the Lord!

By the brood of the Bysses of Brightening, whose God was my sire;
By the Lord o the Flame and the Lightning, the King of the Spirits
of Fire;
By the Lord of the Waves and the Waters, the King of the Hosts of
the Sea,

---

166 Aleister Crowley, *The Rites of Eleusis: Their Meaning and Origin*, published in the
Bystander, 23 November 1910.

The fairest of all whose daughters was mother to me;

By the Lord of the Winds and the Breezes, the king of the Spirits of Air,
In whose bosom the infinite ease is that cradled me there;
By the Lord of the Fields and the Mountains, the King of the Spirits of Earth
That nurtured my life at his fountains from the hour of my birth;

By the Wand and the Cup I conjure; by the Dagger and Disc I constrain;
I am he that is sworn to endure; make thy music again!
I am Lord of the Star and the Seal; I am Lord of the Snake and the Sword;
Reveal us the riddle, reveal! Bring us the word of the Lord!

As the flame of the sun, as the roar of the sea, as the storm of the air,
As the quake o the earth – let it soar for a boon, or a bane, for a snare,
For a lure, for a light, for a kiss, for a rod, for a scourge, for a sword –
Bring us thy burden of bliss – Bring us the word of the Lord!

The Rite of Artemis was held on 23 August 1910 at A∴A∴ headquarters – and Crowley's then residence – at 124 Victoria Street, London, and was well-received, though the audience were unknowingly given fruit punch laced with peyote (and possibly also opium) to heighten the experience. Writer Ethel Archer, present in the crowd, reported feeling 'pepped up and lively'[167] after drinking what was described as a bitter-tasting concoction akin to rotten apples. An extensive write-up of the evening's proceedings, published in *The Sketch* on 24 August, noted under a photograph of Waddell seated in full ceremonial garb and holding her violin with the headline 'During A Ceremony to Invoke Artemis: the Lady of Mystery, the Violin Player', that

on another page of this issue will be found an article dealing with A New Religion. Apropos of this illustration of the lady who played the violin at Mr Aleister Crowley's At Home, at which

---

167 Ethel Archer, quoted in *The Magical Dilemma of Victor Neuberg* by Jean Overton Fuller, p 182.

an experiment was made in the effect of a ceremony to invoke Artemis... The lady in question, it may be recorded, is Miss Leila Waddell, who is very well-known in Australia and New Zealand.[168]

The *Sketch* article is worth quoting. It is remarkable for its detail, for how openly the Rite's ideas and methods were accepted, and for how its author demonstrates a basic understanding at least of the occult.[169]

Aleister Crowley's Rite of Artemis

Reviewed by Raymond Radclyffe.

A certain number of literary people know the name of Aleister Crowley as a poet. A few regard him as a magician. But a small and select circle revere him as the hierophant of a new religion. This creed Captain Fuller, in a book on the subject extending to 327 pages, calls 'Crowleyanity.' I do not pretend to know what Captain Fuller means. He is deeply read in philosophy, and takes Crowley very seriously. I do not quite see whither Crowley himself is driving; but I imagine that the main idea in the brain of this remarkable poet is to plant Eastern Transcendentalism, which attains its ultimate end in Samadhi, in English soil under the guise of Ceremonial Magic.

Possibly the average human being requires and desires ceremony. Even the simplest Methodist uses some sort of ceremony, and Crowley, who is quite in earnest in his endeavour to attain such unusual conditions of mind as are called ecstasy, believes that the gateway to Ecstasy can be reached through Ceremonial Magic. He has saturated himself with the magic of the East – a very real thing, in tune with the Eastern mind. He is well read in the modern metaphysicians, all of whom have attempted to explain the unexplainable.

---

168 *The Sketch*, 24 August 1910.

169 The article's author, journalist Raymond Radclyffe, was a friend of Crowley's; Crowley writes in *The Confessions Of Aleister Crowley* that Radclyffe, 'though utterly indifferent to Magick, was passionately fond of poetry and thought mine first-class, and unrivalled in my generation. He edited a high-class financial weekly and was rightly reputed as the most incorruptible, high-minded and shrewd critic of the city.' (Aleister Crowley, *The Confessions of Aleister Crowley*, p 696).

He abandons these. They appeal only to the brain, and once their jargon is mastered they lead nowhere; least of all to Ecstasy. He goes back upon ceremony, because he thinks that it helps the mind to get outside itself. He declares that if you repeat an invocation solemnly and aloud, 'expectant of some great and mysterious result,' you will experience a deep sense of spiritual communion...

I attended at the offices of the Equinox. I climbed the interminable stairs. I was received by a gentleman robed in white and carrying a drawn sword.

The room was dark; only a dull-red light shone upon an altar. Various young men, picturesquely clad in robes of white, red, or black, stood at different points around the room, illuminated by a tiny lamp hung high on the cornice.

A brother recited 'the Banishing Ritual of the Pentagram' impressively and with due earnestness. Another brother was commanded to 'purify the Temple with water.' This was done. Then we witnessed the 'Consecration of the Temple with Fire,' whereupon Crowley, habited in black, and accompanied by the brethren, led 'the Mystic Circumambulation.' They walked around the altar twice or thrice in a sort of religious precession. Gradually, one by one, those of the company who were mere onlookers were beckoned into the circle. The Master of Ceremonies then ordered a brother to 'bear the Cup of Libation.' The brother went around the room, offering each a large golden bowl full of some pleasant-smelling drink. We drank in turn. This over, a stalwart brother strode into the centre and proclaimed 'The Twelvefold Certitude of God'. Artemis was then invoked by the great ritual of the Hexagram. More libation. Crowley read us the *Song of Orpheus* from the Argonauts.

Following upon this song we drank our third Libation and then the brothers led into the room a draped figure, masked in that curious blue tint we mentally associate with Hecate. The lady, for it was a lady, was enthroned on a seat high above Crowley himself. By this time the ceremony had grown weird and impressive, and its influence was increased when the poet recited in solemn and reverent voice Swinburne's glorious first chorus from *Atalanta*, that begins 'when the hounds of spring.' Again a libation; again an invocation to Artemis. After further ceremonies, Frater Omnia

Vincam[170] was commanded to dance 'the dance of Syrinx and Pan in honour of our lady Artemis.' A young poet, whose verse is often read, astonished me by a graceful and beautiful dance, which he continued until he fell exhausted in the middle of the room, where, by the way, he lay until the end. Crowley then made supplication to the goddess in a beautiful and unpublished poem. A dead silence ensued. After a long pause, the figure enthroned took a violin and played – played with passion and feeling, like a master. We were thrilled to our very bones. Once again the figure took the violin, and played an Abendlied so beautifully, so gracefully, and with such intense feeling that in very deed most of us experienced that Ecstasy which Crowley so earnestly seeks. Then came a prolonged and intense silence, after which the Master of Ceremonies dismissed us in these words – 'By the power in me vested, I declare the Temple closed.'

So ended a really beautiful ceremony – beautifully conceived and beautifully carried out. If there is any higher form of artistic expression than great verse and great music I have yet to learn it. I do not pretend to understand the ritual that runs like a thread of magic through these meetings of the AA. I do not even know what the AA is. But I do know that the whole ceremony was impressive, artistic, and produced in those present such a feeling as Crowley must have had when he wrote:

So shalt thou conquer space, and lastly climb
The walls of Time;
And by the golden path the great trod
Reach up to God![171]

---

170 The A∴A∴ name for Victor Neuberg.
171 *The Sketch*, 24 August 1910.

LEILA AS 'THE GODDESS'. *THE RITES OF ELEUSIS*, PRIVATELY PUBLISHED, PRINTED BY CHISWICK PRESS: CHARLES WHITTINGHAM AND CO., LONDON, 1910, P. 5. CARL HENTSCHEL PH. LC.

Not every review was so sympathetic. Under the header 'Are You Foolish? Then Start a New Religion in London: Do Not Delay' (and with the article again illustrated with the photo of a seated violin-wielding Waddell), Fred L Boalt[172] wrote for *The Cleveland Plain Dealer:*

You are in search of Ecstasy. Why not? When your state of mind is ecstatic, you are enraptured. Exultation is yours. You experience a diminished consciousness and a joy that is not of earth.

So – on with the adventure! – You climb interminable stairs – a bad start. You arrive at the top landing, wiping the sweat from your brow and wondering why London landlords don't put in elevators.

A door opens silently. You are received by a gentleman in a white robe carrying a drawn sword. Be not afraid; the sword is not a shortcut to ecstasy.

The room is dark, but a dull-red light shines upon an altar. There are several gentlemen standing about, some in white robes, some in red, some in sombre black.

A few carry swords. Never mind why. You wouldn't understand...

Enters Aleister Crowley, poet. Aleister is good, but Aleister jars. The poet ought to change his name or quit the game. Who wants to follow a Crowley – or, for that matter, a Simpkins or a Snobgrass – when one is on the trail of ecstasy.

Crowley is habited in black. Accompanied by the brethren, he leads the 'Mystic Circumambulation';..

A black-robed brother glides away and vanishes in shadow, to reappear a moment later, bearing in his hands a golden bowl filled with sweet-scented wine. You drink in turn... You begin to feel that Ecstasy would be a cinch if only the cup were larger...

A draped figure. You wonder where it came from. It is there, before you. The draperies are not black, but blue-black.

By the dim light from the altar you see it is the figure of a lady, a very pretty lady, in bare feet. She moves slowly, noiselessly over the floor. She carries a violin.

The poet meets her and escorts her to the throne; then reclines at her feet..

172 Whether Boalt actually attended the Rite of Artemis, or merely based his report on the accounts of others, is unclear, though he was in London at the time, working as a correspondent for United Press.

'Frater Omnia Vincam,' commands Crowley, 'dance the dance of Syrinx and Pan in honour of our Lady Artemis.'

It's a little puzzling. The lady isn't Artemis really but Miss Leila Waddell, a violinist of wonderful promise who won so much praise in Australia and New Zealand that she has come to London to take the capital of the world by storm.

Frater Omnia Vincam, who, like Crowley, writes poetry when he isn't pursuing ecstasy, advances to the middle of the floor, where he performs a really beautiful dance which continues until he falls exhausted.

Crowley, standing over the prostrate brother-poet, makes supplication to the enthroned goddess in original verse. A dead silence ensues.

Evidently the goddess is touched. She plays – plays with feeling and passion, like a master. Ecstasy evades you. The music halts abruptly, and the goddess' head drops upon her breast.

Once more she takes up the violin and plays *Abend Lieb*, and the sounds that spring from the quivering strings are like a human voice of wondrous purity – singing and sighing in tenderest cadences.

In the face of Crowley, in the face of Frater Omnia Vincam, in the faces of the brethren shines an expression of unearthly joy.

This – this – is Ecstasy!

The brethren call themselves the AA. No one outside the cult knows what the AA is or stands for.

Crowley calls it a the 'New Religion'. This is not a good name. It suggests the mundane. One speaks of the newest thing in safety razors, but one does not speak of the newest thing in religions.

Crowley is the inventor of it. He does not call himself a prophet, or a second Messiah, or anything of the sort. He's the inventor. His main idea is to plant in the Occident the Eastern Transcendental Buddhism under the guise of ceremonial magic. He believes that the human mind is most easily raised to ecstasy by beauty, mystery, and ceremony.

This is the silly season in London religious circles.[173]

News of Waddell's sudden occult involvement even made it as far as the Australian newspapers:

---

173 *Cleveland Plain Dealer*, 18 September 1910.

Leila Waddell, a Bathurst girl, who was a pupil of Henri Staell's
for the violin, and after a successful career as an amateur, went to
England three years ago in search of professional fame, has come
out in a new character as a high priestess of a new religion. She is
the star of the Crowleyites – Aleister Crowley has started a creed
of Eastern Buddhism in England. The ceremonies are very weird.
Every one is clothed in a one-piece robe of white, red, or black; feet
are bare. The doorkeeper wears a white robe, and is armed with
a drawn sword. After much mystic business and invocation, each
drank in turn from a golden goblet, and then three brethren led in
a draped woman, who was enthroned on a seat higher than even
Crowley. Swinburne's chorus from *Atalanta*, beginning *When the
Hounds of Spring*, was recited by Crowley, and then a young man
danced a weird sort of dance till he fell exhausted in the middle of
the room. Crowley then made supplication to the enthroned blue-
robed lady, who, after a pause, lifted her violin and played. I've
seen a portrait of Leila the Priestess sitting in a stiff attitude, with
her knees and feet tightly together. Her robe is a neck to toe affair,
something like a surplice, and as her feet are bare her ten toes are
a feature of the landscape. On her head is a huge helmet, and she
holds her violin and bow. Leila is dubbed the Lady of Mystery.
She is coming to Australia, probably as a rival to that esoteric lady
Annie Besant.[174]

If anything, a sense of pride in their national export and not one of
disapproval can be found in the Australian coverage, with *The Sydney
Evening News* writing on 3 December of

the success of Miss Leila Waddell in London. She has been playing in
those revivals of antique ceremonies in various old religions, which
have at present got London by the nose. Miss Waddell played in the
ceremony to invoke Artemis 'with fire and passion like a master.'[175]

---

174 *The Truth* (Brisbane), 9 October 1910. Similar articles can be found throughout
the Australian press of this period; this one has been chosen as representative.
  Annie Besant (1847-1833) was a prominent Theosophist, socialist, and activist
for numerous causes, from Indian and Irish self-rule to women's rights to atheism to
Marxism to birth control. She authored hundreds of books and pamphlets in support.
In her capacity as a Theosophist she was friends with Helena Blavatsky and travelled
and lectured widely, propagating the subject and its teachings.
175 Quoted from Raymond Radclyffe's 24 August 1910 *Sketch* article, which the

The spirit of mystery and abandon that is the dominant factor in these queer ceremonies give tremendous scope to the artist, and it is satisfactory to think that the girl who used to be such a familiar figure in all musical things, was a pupil of Mr Staell, and got all her artistic training and culture in Sydney.[176]

Enthused by the success of the Rite of Artemis, Crowley and Waddell expanded upon the idea, evolving it into the Rites of Eleusis. A more ambitious undertaking, there were seven Rites of Eleusis in all,[177] centred on the seven planets of classical astrology: Saturn, Jupiter, Mars, the Sun (or 'Sol'), Venus, Mercury, and the Moon (or 'Luna'). Each was dramatised with poetry and dance and with original music composed by Waddell to correspond to the energies invoked at that specific working. Sadly, none of Waddell's scores for the Rites of Eleusis have survived, but it is known that the titles included *Samadhliedi* or *Samadhi Song*, *Marche Funébre*, and *Mort d'Adonis*. She also performed the work of other composers at the Rites; Wieniawski and Vieuxtemps, Bach's *Aria for G String*, and Paganini's *Witches' Dance*, along with selections from Brahms, Mendelssohn, Schumann, Tchaikovsky, Beethoven, Hauser, Ries, Bohm, Thomé, Bruch, Wagner, D'Ambrosio, and Saint-Saëns. The texts for each Rite were chiefly written by Crowley, and included pieces by Swinburne with additional material by novelist and A∴A∴ initiate George Raffalovich. Such was the significance of Waddell's contribution in Crowley's mind that the programme for the Rites gave joint credit to 'Miss Leila Waddell and Mr Aleister Crowley with distinguished assistance.' The Rites were staged at Caxton Hall, Westminster, London in October and November 1910, with the first – Saturn – on Wednesday 19 October and the remainder following each Wednesday weekly.[178] Again Waddell played an active role as a

---

Sydney Evening News writer had evidently read.

176 *The Evening News* (Sydney), 3 December 1910.

177 The texts of the Rites of Eleusis were published in Vol I No VI of *The Equinox* as *The Rites of Eleusis as Performed at Caxton Hall Westminster in October and November 1910 by Miss Leila Waddell and Mr Aleister Crowley with Distinguished Assistance*, dedicated 'To my friend Commander G M Marston, RN to whose suggestion these rites are due'. They were republished much later as *The Rites of Eleusis: as Performed at Caxton Hall* by Mandrake Press in 1990, and are also widely available online. There have been a number of modern performances and recreations by Ordo Templi Orientis lodges, sometimes with additional texts and musical accompaniment added.

178 The full schedule of dates was: 19 October, the Rite of Saturn; 26 October, the Rite of Jupiter; 2 November, the Rite of Mars; 9 November, the Rite of Sol; 16 November,

musician on violin, alongside Victor Neuberg dancing and others of the A∴A∴, and Jeanne Heyse (1890-1912), also known as Joan Hayes or Ione de Forest – the latter being her stage name – who participated as a dancer. Heyse, soon to be a lover of Neuberg's,[179] was not a member of the A∴A∴ and had little interest in magick, having merely replied to an advert in *The Stage* newspaper, but both Crowley and Neuberg were evidently impressed by her talent and beauty and included her.

The Rites of Eleusis borrowed their name from the Eleusinian Mysteries, rituals of initiation held annually in ancient Greece in honour of Demeter and Persephone, that took place at the Sanctuary of Eleusis in West Attica. Of considerable antiquity, they may possibly predate ancient Greece itself, dating back to an agrarian cult of the Mycenaean era. Little is known as to precisely what form they took as details were kept a closely held secret. A symbolic rebirth likely played a part, as did a libation known as the kykeon, and modern scholarly speculation is that some form of psychoactive drug may have been involved. These rites were frequently spoken of as life-transforming.

Waddell's and Crowley's Rites of Eleusis were advertised as 'a series of symbolical ceremonies... to illustrate the magical methods followed by a mystical society which seeks for illumination by ecstasy'.[180] Though audience participation wasn't encouraged, spectators were asked to dress in colours appropriate to the celestial form being worked with; black or very dark blue for Saturn, violet for Jupiter, scarlet or russet brown for Mars, orange or white for Sol, green or sky-blue for Venus, shot silk and mixed colours for Mercury, and white, silver, or pale blue for Luna. Semi-darkness was maintained in the hall throughout proceedings. It is unrecorded whether the crowd – who numbered approximately one hundred at each event – were surreptitiously dosed with peyote as at the Rite of Artemis; it would appear not. Admission was a very pricey five guineas (the equivalent today of more than £500) for the whole series of performances, each of which commenced at 9pm and lasted one and a half to two and a half hours.

What is of note is how far news of the Rite of Artemis and the Rites of Eleusis spread, with features in *The Sun of Sydney* (1 October 1910), *The Cincinnati Enquirer* (5 October 1910), *Truth of Brisbane* (9 October 1910), *The Straits Times of Singapore* (2 November 1910), *The Australasian of Melbourne* (5 November 1910), *The Boston Sunday Post* (6 November 1910), *The New*

---

the Rite of Venus; 23 November, the Rite of Mercury; 30 November, the Rite of Luna.

179 As well as Neuberg, Heyse also won the heart of poet Ezra Pound; his works *Dance Figure* and *Dead Ione* are addressed to her.

180 The Rites of Eleusis flyer.

York Times (13 November 1910) and elsewhere. More than one used the photograph of a seated Waddell in ceremonial attire and holding her violin.

The public reception to the Rites of Eleusis wasn't as good as it had been to the Rite of Artemis (perhaps due to the lack of peyote). *The Morning Leader* for example wrote on 20 October that

> The first Rites of Eleusis was held at Caxton Hall last night by the mystical society of which Mr Crowley... is the chief. It was the rite of Saturn. The rites of Jupiter, Mars, Sol, Venus, Mercury, and Luna follow on successive Wednesdays, and unless a more cheerful tone is imparted than Saturn gave, the people who have paid five guineas for the whole lot will have committed suicide before they reach Luna.[181]

> *The Hawera & Normandy Star* reported that

> an atmosphere heavily charged with incense, some cheap stage effects, an infinity of poor reciting of good poetry, and some violin playing and dancing are the ingredients of the rite... Positively the only relief in a dreary evening was afforded by a neophyte falling off his stool, which caused mild hilarity among a bored and uncomfortable audience, most of whom were perched on small wooden stools a foot from the floor. Mr Crowley says that the end aim of his rites is ecstasy. Somebody ought to tell him that ecstasy of any kind is impossible when your foot has gone to sleep.[182]

The John Bull – which would in time become Crowley's nemesis – noted in their review on 5 November that

> A new 'religion' is usually viewed with suspicion in this country, but Mr Crowley is just the person for such an enterprise. He is a man of good birth and education, with distinguished, almost pontifical manners. He has travelled all over the unusual parts of the world and investigated fantastic things with zeal, if not with discretion. He has probed the secret recesses of most oriental religions and has made a special study of all the endless literature of magic and mysticism... His work, however, is spoiled by the intrusion of wild,

---

181 *The Morning Leader*, 20 October 1910.
182 *Hawera and Normandy Star*, 15 December 1910.

erotic, and disgusting images and startling blasphemies, which restricts his writings to private circulation, though it possesses an artistic enchantment quite apart from its appeal to pruriency and debauchery.

His present 'mission' was heralded in March last year by a portly publication called *The Equinox*. The idea, evidently, is to attract the public to the teachings of medieval alchemists and magicians. The propaganda consists in assembling a number of ladies and gentlemen in a dark room where poems are recited and a violin is played with considerable expression amid choking clouds of incense, varied by barbaric dances, sensational interludes of melodrama, blasphemy and erotic suggestion...

I was able to get admission into the chamber of mysteries... In the corridor there stood none other than Aleister Crowley himself – a man of fine physique with all the appearance of an actor – in a long white garment which reminded one of a cassock one moment and a Roman tunic the next, though undoubtedly it was neither the one nor the other. He vanished as mysteriously as he had appeared. Then there came among us, for a few brief seconds, a woman with strong features set in a deathly pale face. Someone said, 'That is Leila Waddell. She plays the violin and takes the chief part in the mystic seance'...

The room was in semi-darkness, a bluish light hanging from the ceiling at the far end, a heavy smell of incense pervading the air, while the solemn stillness and hushed voices helped to enhance the weirdness of the place... Presently the door was closed and locked, the low blue light fell pale and mystical upon a male figure sitting behind a cauldron, with a drum between his knees; he beat the drum with his hands, paused, and then resumed the beating, and from a small door behind him entered a number of male and female figures, ten or twelve... He ceased to beat the drum, and one of the male figures then performed the vanishing [*sic.*] ritual of the Pentagram, which is designed to keep away evil influences. He then lighted a fire in the cauldron, and crouching behind, recited. Next, he joined with the brethren in an endeavour to arouse someone whom they called the 'Master of the Temple'. I could not refrain from a feeling of envy at his ability to slumber through such a din! They failed to wake him, and the same brother appealed to the 'Mother of Heaven'. She appeared in the person of Leila Waddell, played an invocation, and the 'Master of the Temple' was at last aroused. I was not surprised!

He came forward, crouching behind the cauldron, and recited a most blood-curdling composition... Suddenly he lifted what looked like a tin of Nestlé's milk, and pouring the contents on the flame, extinguished the fire, declared that 'there is no God,' that everybody was free to do just as he or she liked, and left the audience in utter darkness! Not the slightest ray of light entered the room, and the atmosphere seemed heavier and more oppressive than ever. There was a sound as of people moving quietly about which added to the uncanniness...

The next moment the blue light appeared. The mystical figures were moving before me, and I watched, fascinated. The presence of a traitor amongst them was suspected, and a man clad in white, sword in hand, sought this traitor amongst the crouching figures. What a weird picture it was! With an unearthly scream he fell upon one of the male figures, and, dragging him forth, 'slew' him before our eyes. After this there was more violin music, and a wild barbaric dance in the misty, smoky blue light. One little scene that chilled my blood occurred when the lights were extinguished. In the utter darkness, and after a long pause, in which one could hear one's own heart beat, a male voice, a terrible voice, called out: 'My brethren, are the dead men fed?' 'Yes, verily the dead men are fed,' came the reply. 'My brethren, upon what have the dead men fed?' 'Upon the corpses of their children,' was the horrible answer. I had had enough, and was most heartily glad when it was all over.[183]

Crowley, in his *Confessions of Aleister Crowley*, laid the blame for the relative lack of success of the Rites of Eleusis on insufficient preparation:

I throw myself no bouquets about these Rites of Eleusis. I should have given more weeks to their preparation than I did minutes. I diminished the importance of the dramatic elements; the dialogue and action were little more than a setting for the soloists.[184]

He did praise Waddell's violin solos, though took credit for his magick making her the skilled player she was:

183 *The John Bull*, 5 November 1910.
184 Aleister Crowley, *The Confessions of Aleister Crowley*, p 693.

My new methods of Magick were so successful that we became more ambitious every day. I wrote a ritual for invoking the moon. The climax of the ceremony was this; Leila Waddell was to be enthroned as a representative of the goddess and the lunar influence invoked into her by the appropriate lyrics. (I wrote *The Interpreter* and *Pan to Artemis*). The violinist was to reply by expressing the divine nature through her art. She was a rough, ill-trained executant, and her playing coarse, crude, with no touch of subtlety to interpret or passion to exalt the sequence of sound. The most cynical critics present were simply stunned at hearing this fifth-rate fiddler play with a genius whose strength and sublimity was equal to anything in their experience... Magick, properly understood, performed and applied, is capable of producing results of quite practical kinds. More yet, these results involve no improbable theories. We can explain them in terms of well-known laws of nature. I have always been able to loose the genius which dwells in the inmost self of even the most imperfect artist, by taking the proper measures to prevent the interference of his conscious characteristics.[185]

This is a remarkable statement; Waddell had been performing professionally for eight years by this point and was acclaimed for the skill of her playing both in her homeland and internationally long before she met Crowley.

What also likely rankled with observers to the Rites of Eleusis was their non-Christian content and sexual symbolism, which though decidedly tame by twenty-first century standards did not go down well in Georgian London, especially the point during one performance when Waddell knelt on Crowley's chest. The police were notified, and one London superintendent later stated that

[Crowley] came under [police] notice in November 1910 when he held a series of meetings at Caxton Hall... It was alleged at the time that he was addicted to sodomitical practices. Observations were kept by the Police at these meetings, but although the proceedings were of a blasphemous character, no open act of indecency was witnessed.[186]

---

185 Ibid., p 688-689.

186 Quoted in *Aleister Crowley: The Beast Demystified* by Roger Hutchinson, p 122-123.

Attendance at the Rites dropped as a result of poor publicity, with tickets being sold to separate performances to cover costs.

One critic in particular – West de Wend Fenton, editor of the journal *The Looking Glass* – took exception to the Rites of Eleusis. Under the header 'An Amazing Sect', an article in its 29 October 1910 issue set out to

place on record an astounding experience which we have had lately in connection with a sect styled the Equinox, which has been formed under the auspices of one Aleister Crowley.... We had previously heard a great many rumours about the practices of this sect, but we were determined not to rely on any hearsay evidence, and after a great deal of manoeuvring we managed to secure a card of admission... We arrived at Caxton Hall [and]... were conducted by our guide to the door, at which stood a rather dirty looking person attired in a sort of imitation Eastern robe,[187] with a drawn sword in his hand, who, after inspecting our cards, admitted us to a dimly lighted room heavy with incense... At the extreme end of the room was a heavy curtain, and in front of this sat a huddled-up figure in draperies, beating a kind of monotonous tom-tom... After a while more ghostly figures appeared on the stage, and a person in a red cloak, supported on each side by a blue-chinned gentleman of some sort of Turkish bath costume, commenced to read some gibberish, to which the attendants made responses at intervals... More Turkish bath attendants then appeared, and executed a kind of Morris dance round the stage. Then the gentleman in the red cloak, supported by brothers Aquarius and Capricornus – the aforesaid blue-chinned gentlemen – made fervent appeals to Mother of Heaven to hear them, and after a little while a not unprepossessing lady appeared,[188] informed them that she was the Mother of Heaven, and asked if she could do anything for them... They beg her to summon the Master, as they wish to learn from him if there is any God, or if they are free to behave as they please. The Mother of Heaven thereupon takes up the violin and plays not unskilfully for about ten minutes, during which time the room is again plunged in complete darkness. The playing is succeeded by a loud hammering, in which all the robed figures on the stage join, and after a din sufficient to wake the Seven Sleepers the lights are

---

187 Which would have been Victor Neuberg.

188 Leila Waddell.

turned up a little and a figure appears from the recess and asks what they want. They beseech him to let them know if there is really a God, as, if not, they will amuse themselves without any fear of the consequences. The Master promises to give the matter his best attention, and, after producing a flame from the floor by the simple expedient of lifting a trap-door, he retires with the Mother of Heaven for 'meditation', during which time darkness again supervenes. After a considerable interval he returns, flings aside a curtain on the stage, and declares that there is no God. He then exhorts his followers to do as they like and make the most of life. There is no God, no hereafter, no punishment, and no reward. Dust we are, and to dust we will return. This is his doctrine, paraphrased.... There is more meditation, followed by an imitation Dervish dance by one of the company,[189] who finally falls to the ground, whether in exhaustion or frenzy we are unable to say. There is also at intervals a species of Bacchie revel by the entire company on the stage, in which an apparently very young girl,[190] who is known as the Daughter of the Gods, takes part... We leave it to our readers, after looking at the photographs – which were taken for private circulation only, and sold to us without Crowley's knowledge or consent, and of which we have acquired the exclusive copyright – and after reading our plain, unvarnished account of the happenings of which we were an actual eye-witness, to say whether this was not a blasphemous sect whose proceedings conceivably lend themselves to immorality of the most revolting character. Remember the doctrine which we have endeavoured to faintly outline – remember the periods of complete darkness – remember the dances and the heavy scented atmosphere, the avowed object of which is to produce what Crowley calls 'ecstasy' – and then say if it is fitting and right that young girls and married women should be allowed to attend such performances under the guise of the cult of a new religion. New religion indeed! It is as old as the hills. The doctrines of unbridled lust and licence, based on the assumption that there is no God and no hereafter, have been preached from time immemorial, sometimes by hedonists and fanatics pure and simple, sometimes by charlatans whose

---

189 Neuberg once more.

190 Likely Jeanne Heyse, who having been born in 1890 was – at twenty – definitely the youngest of the participants in the Rites.

one thought is to fill their money-bags by encouraging others to gratify their depraved tastes.[191]

Crowley was perhaps more bemused than anything upon reading this, though *The Looking Glass* would not go away, digging deep into his past (probably being fed information by a still-disgruntled Samuel Liddell MacGregor Mathers) and running further critical articles in November and December 1910, including mention of Crowley's numerous affairs, his drug use, his divorce, and allegations of 'unmentionable immoralities' – gay sex, then illegal – between Crowley and his former tutor Allan Bennett, described as 'the rascally sham Buddhist monk.'[192] There were also intimations of a sexual relationship between Crowley and his friend and A∴A∴ co-founder George Cecil Jones. Bennett, then resident in India, was likely not even aware of the claims against him, though Jones – married and with four children – objected via solicitors' letter and subsequently sued for libel, losing the case in court in April 1911. The proceedings, which were over in two days, centred more on the character of Crowley and Jones' association with him than with Jones himself, with Mathers being called to testify and the judge, Mr Justice Scrutton, stating that 'it has been shown that [Crowley] wrote, published and advertised literature of the most disgusting character and conduct.' Crowley – though present in court as a spectator throughout – was not called upon at all in Jones' defence, Jones was condemned more because of his association with such a reprehensible character than any evidence, and the allegations against him were not found to be damaging; anybody who kept such poor company clearly didn't have a reputation to lose. In Crowley's eyes the case would have been won if he had testified; 'The intensity of my enthusiasm, my candour and my sheer personality would have dominated the court. They would have been bound to understand that even my follies and faults testified to my good faith, high-mindedness and honour.'[193] Jones and Crowley's friendship was effectively at an end, and Jones kept his distance from then on. The resulting poor publicity from the case also reflected badly on the A∴A∴, and only three new members would apply to join in 1911.

Along with Crowley falling for her, Waddell evidently also made an impression on Victor Neuberg (though there is nothing to indicate that anything occurred between them); Neuberg dedicated the poem *The Muse*

---

191 *The Looking Glass*, 29 October 1910.

192 Ibid., 26 November 1910.

193 Aleister Crowley, *The Confessions of Aleister Crowley*, p 699.

from his book *The Triumph of Pan*, published by The Equinox in December 1910, to her.[194]

The Muse

Night and shadow go trembling over
The dewy grass and the purple clover.

The hills are darkened, and day is sent
To the long low land of her banishment.

Dewy sprays from the gray-cloud skies
Linger, linger before my eyes.

And I think I see, as I linger here,
Shadowy feet go across the mere.

I fancy I hear, as the night falls slow,
The shadowy footfalls of long ago.

And the queen of the marshes in her crown
Of dewy dusk floats over the down.

Silence falls in the hush of dusk,
Rainy earth and dew and musk.

Here I halt by the wayside hedges,
As night creeps over the earth's dark edges.

Wonderment calm of the afterglow
Of daylight, – I knew thee how long ago!

Once I found thee, alone, forlorn,
Waiting the call of the windy morn.

Now I dream of an olden sea,
And sea-birds twittering melody.

194 Not that Neuberg was in any way exclusive in his dedications; the book also contains poems dedicated to Crowley, Austin Osman Spare, Guy Marston, Jeanne Heyse, Ethel Archer, George Raffalovich, and numerous others.

Once I found thee, O sister mine,
Rising, re-born, from the foam-flecked brine -

Thee! My Night, my mother obscene,
Gentle and curling and dark and green.

Mother of slime, and the things of dust;
Wonder in pain and joy and lust-

Mother of all men, queen of love's star,
I tread in the wake of thy fairy car.

Methought I had left you to die, to drown,
To burn, to fade, in the bright-lit town.

"Nay," you whisper; "the way to death
Lies through the river that gave me breath.

"Old, forgotten, Lethean, dumb,
I wonder if thou in the night be come."

Silence calls from the wind-swept mere,
An enchanted lyre in the hemisphere.

"O windy moon! O pure pale curse!
Lady-love of the universe!

"O rose-lipped daughter of foam and fire,
Faded, paled, in thy lost desire!

"O silence informed by the secret rune
Writ of old at the set o' the moon!

"Hush! for the wind goes sailing by
Under the dome of the red, blind sky."

"Tell me, tell me before I go,
Lady mine was it ever so?

"Ever since first thou cam'st from the sea,
And didst bear in thine eyes her mystery?"

"Nay, or thou hadst not found me now,
Stalking the marshes with gray-starred brow.

"I came wrought, ere thou wast born,
Into the land of wine and corn.

"I came unknown from the sea's glad grace,
But I bore her sorrows upon my face.

"I sprang from the loins of the god of fire,
And I bore the lust of my lusty sire.

"So to thee am I all unknown;
So to thee do I sing alone.

"I am forgotten, child of grace,
Wandering over the heaven's face.

"The darkest place in the aching tide
Is the bridal-bed of the wondrous bride.

"Catch me and hold me, at last, at last;
Let me lie in thine arms asleep from the past.

"Let me feel thy kisses sink down on me,
Like the silver rain that falls on the sea.

"Make me thine own, O singer of flame;
Let me nestle close; from the skies I came."

So she sleeps in my arms, and I
Wake all lonely, under the sky.

From under the sky she has flown, and I
Know not wither under the sky.

So the came from the storied past,
But I shall know her at last, at last![195]

Just as Crowley claimed that Waddell had blossomed as a violinist only under his guidance and magical influence, he also took credit for the best of Neuberg's poetry:

> When I met him he was writing feeble verses of hardly more than undergraduate merit. Under my training he produced some of the most passionate, intense, musical and lofty lyrics in the language. He left me [in 1914]; the dog hath returned to his vomit again, and the sow that was washed, to her wallowing in the mire. His latest work is as lifeless and limp as it was before I took hold.[196]

1910 concluded with one final snipe at Crowley from *The Looking Glass* in their 17 December issue as he departed England for Algeria, albeit they got his destination wrong in the article:

> We understand that Mr Aleister Crowley has left London for Russia. This should do much to mitigate the rigour of the St Petersburg winter. We have to congratulate ourselves on having temporarily extinguished one of the most blasphemous and cold-blooded villains of modern times. But what were Scotland yard about to let him depart in peace?[197]

---

195 *The Triumph of Pan* was belatedly reviewed in July1912 for the journal *Rhythm* by Leila Waddell's friend Katherine Mansfield. In what may be a veiled dig at Crowley – of whom Mansfield was not fond – she writes that '[Neuberg] has something of the poet's vision in simplicity and sensuality which is born of passionate admiration.... But there is another side... He appears to take strange delight in mysticism, which is never anything but second-hand. Mysticism is perverted sensuality. It is 'passionate admiration" for that which has no reality at all. It leads to the annihilation of any true artistic effort. It is a paraphernalia of clichés. It is a mask through which the true expression of the poet can never be discerned. If he rejects this mask Mr Neuberg may become a poet.'

196 Aleister Crowley, *The Confessions of Aleister Crowley*, p 689.

197 *The Looking Glass,* 17 December 1910.

I love LAYLAH.
I lack LAYLAH.
'Where is the Mystic Grace?' sayest thou?
Who told thee, man, that LAYLAH is not Nuit, and I Hadit?
I destroyed all things; they are reborn in other shapes.
I gave up all for One; this One hath given up its Unity for all?
I wrenched DOG backwards to find GOD; now GOD barks.
Think me not fallen because I love LAYLAH, and lack LAYLAH.
I am the Master of the Universe; then give me a heap of straw in a
hut, and LAYLAH naked! Amen.

'Margery Daw', Aleister Crowley
Liber CCCXXXIII: The Book of Lies, Wieland and Co.,
London, 1913, p. 80.

LAYLAH, MY NIGHT
(1911)

Crowley spent the beginning of 1911 in Algeria once more with Victor Neuberg, though the trip was not a success. The intention had been for further Enochian workings in the same vein as the 1909 sequence, but things did not go to plan and Neuberg became ill. Crowley left him behind, returning alone to London by way of Paris. The excursion was not a complete failure however, Crowley completing a body of new poems, essays, and plays along the way. Of note is *On the Edge of the Desert*, written in January 1911 for Waddell. It was one of three Waddell-inspired poems Crowley composed in Algeria, the others being *Return*, and *Prayer at Sunset*, with *The Pilgrim* being written for her on the return journey.

On The Edge Of The Desert

You come between me and the night
    That was my queen till you arose;
You come between me and the light;
    You come between me and the snows.
The sun, the sands, the horizon:
Since you are come, all these are gone.

Leave me some love of flower and tree,
    Some passion for the moon and stars,
Some ache of spring, some sigh of sea,
    Some echo in love's ancient scars,
To witness ere your reign began
That among men I was a man.

No voice in life allures but yours;
    Nor sight nor sleep allays mine eyes;
Night sways my dull distemperatures
    Till light renews my scale of sighs.
Half a man's span I have lived. In sooth
You have found the elixir that gives youth!
From the most austral East you drove

On the most fortunate wind that blows,
A galleon piled with treasure trove,
  The sun's gold, silver of the snows,
All jewels, all virtue far above –
O tall ship laden with true love!

You strode majestical and fierce,
  Armed, an avenging Amazon,
A warrior maiden mad to pierce
  With unfleshed steel man's morion.
You thrust the rapier of your art,
Singing for rapture, through my heart.

I died: and you by death refreshed,
  Washed in my blood, gave up my soul
To Love, who, seeing us enmeshed,
  Wept, and with one smile made us whole:
Whence you have all life's gold for gain
And I am grown a boy again.

I am a thousand worlds withdrawn
  From these lone leagues of sand and sun.
I am with you in the windy dawn;
  I am with you when night's fingers run
Over the desert, when the dunes
Lift up their faces to the moon's.

I am blind to these: my life's one ache.
  My tongue is swollen; my lips are burnt;
My body shivers for your sake,
  For this last lesson I have learnt
(Laylah, my Night!) tragic and true:
I never loved till I loved you.

For you have fixed the boyish dream,
  And saved the man from 'love's a wraith.'
Your love rekindled hope's blue gleam,
  And hope fulfilled requickened faith,
And faith confirmed renewed the birth
Of a new heaven and a new earth.

Mine is the only star that ever
   Left the lone Cross to blend its ray
With my Lion's Heart in dear endeavour
   To knell the night and dim the day.
Mine is the only maiden worth
The wooing ever won on earth.

Laylah, my night! Enshadow me:
   Draw down mine eyelids; bid me sleep
And dream of thee, and dream of thee,
   Or wake and weep, or wake and weep.
I care not which, so thee I find
(Present or absent) in my mind.

This poem is notable for containing the first reference by Crowley this author can find to Leila Waddell as Laylah. Laylah, Arabic for *night*, was to his mind 'the ultimate feminine principle',[198] 'the subtle and supreme septenary in its mature magical manifestation through matter',[199] and numerologically can be rendered as 77, Crowley's number for her. It would rapidly become his pet name for her.

Also penned by Crowley on that voyage back to England from Algeria was the play *The Scorpion*, which featured a primary character named Laylah:

> I left Neuburg in Biskra to recuperate and returned to England alone. No sooner had I settled in my compartment than I was seized by an irresistible impulse to write a play dealing with the Templars and the Crusades. I had had with me in the desert the rituals of freemasonry, those of the Scottish, Memphis and Mizraim Rites... The ritual of the 30° had taken hold of my imagination. The idea of my proposed play, *The Scorpion*, sprang into life full-armed. I have always found that unless I jump on such inspiration like a tiger, I am never able to 'recapture the first fine careless rapture'. I accordingly jumped out of the train at El Kantara and wrote it that evening and next day.[200]

---

198 Aleister Crowley, *The Book of Lies*, p 67.

199 Ibid., p 164.

200 Aleister Crowley, *The Confessions of Aleister Crowley*, p 716.

Unfortunately, it can't be said that the short four-scene play that followed is especially inspiring or inspired. The language is archaic, the drama stilted, and naming aside the character Laylah – a woman wrongly condemned and executed as a witch – bears little similarity to Waddell.

During a stop-off in Paris Crowley wrote the short story *The Ordeal of Ida Pendragon,* Ida being one of Waddell's middle names. It was published in *The Equinox* Vol I No VI in September 1911 under the pseudonym Martial Nay. As Crowley explained,

> The hero, Edgar Rolles, meets a girl at the Taverne Panthéon (where I wrote the story) and takes her to a fight between a white man and a Negro, the latter suggested by Joe Jeannette, whom I had just seen and much admired for his physical beauty. He takes her to his studio and recognizes her as a member of the order. He proposes to put her through the ordeal of crossing the Abyss. She fails and they part. Ida meets the Negro, who loves her. Rolles and Ninon... lunch with them. Ida takes pleasure in torturing the Negro and begs him to 'respect her modesty' – which she has not got. The Negro suddenly understands that she is heartless and sinks his teeth in her throat. Rolles kills him with a kick. He then consults one of the Secret Chiefs,[201] who advises him to take Ida away. He tells Rolles that she has passed through the Abyss after all. The formula is that perfect love is perfect understanding. He marries her and a year later she dies in childbirth, saying that she has given herself three times, once to the brute, once to the man and now to God. Her previous failure had been to surrender herself. She wanted to get everything and give nothing. This story marks a stage in my own understanding of the formula of initiation. I began to see that one might become a Master of the Temple without necessarily knowing any technical Magick or mysticism at all.[202]

Despite this creative outpouring inspired by his love for Waddell, Crowley met another woman while in Paris, Jane Chéron, with whom he had a brief affair. Chéron, fond of opium, would become an occasional

---

201 Transcendent spiritual beings said to be responsible for the operation of the cosmos, their names and forms and role varying from system to system. In some they are even of earthly form and gathered or scattered in the hidden places of the world. A number of occultists claim to have had communication with them, including Crowley, and the founders of the Hermetic Order of the Golden Dawn.

202 Aleister Crowley, *The Confessions of Aleister Crowley,* p 718.

paramour of Crowley's whenever he was in the city.[203] Though we don't know Waddell's thoughts on the matter, Crowley was clear that he did not believe in monogamy:

> The social system of England makes it impossible for a young man of spirit and intelligence to satisfy his nature with regard to sex in any reasonable way. The young girl of position similar to his own is being fattened for the market. Even when his own situation makes it possible for him to obtain her he has to pay an appalling price; and it becomes more difficult than ever for him to enjoy female companionship. Monogyny is nonsense for any one with a grain of imagination. The more sides he has to his nature, the more women he needs to satisfy it. The same is, of course, true, mutatis mutandis, of women. A woman risks her social existence by a single experiment. A young man is compelled by the monogamic system to develop his character by means of corrupt society vampires or women of the lower classes, and though he may learn a great deal from these sources, it cannot but be unfortunate that he has no opportunity to learn from women of his own birth, breeding, education and rank in society.[204]

Crowley was also adamant that, as much as he professed to love some of the women with whom he was involved, including Waddell, he would not let it get in the way of the Great Work.

> I knew... that I was immune. I might dally with Delilah as much as I liked and never risk the scissors. Love, who binds other Samsons, blinds them and sets them to serve the Philistines, to be their scorn and sport, would be to me my Light and lead me in the way of liberty. The secret of my strength was this, that love would always stand a shining symbol of my truth, that I loved spiritually the soul of mankind. Therefore each woman, be she chaste or wanton, faithful or false, inspiring me to scale the summits of song or whispering me to wallow in the swamps of sin, would be to me no more than a symbol in whose particular virtue my love could find the bread and wine of its universal eucharist. Time has

---

203 Chéron's apartment was the location of Crowley's famed Paris Working in early 1914; see the chapter *Love Alway Yieldeth Love Alway Hardeneth (1914-1923)* later in this book.

204 Aleister Crowley, *The Confessions of Aleister Crowley*, p 94-95.

confirmed this claim: I have loved many women and been loved. But I have never wavered from my Work; and always a moment has come when the woman had to choose between comradeship and catastrophe. For in truth, there was no Aleister Crowley to love; there was only a Word for the utterance of which a human form had been fashioned. So the foolish virgins, finding that love and vanity could not live together, gave up a man for a mirror; but the wise, knowing that man is mortal, gave up the world for the Work and thereby cheated satiety, disillusionment and death.[205]

When Crowley finally arrived in England from France, he expected a telegram from Waddell which did not come, inspiring *The Earth*, an abstract prose rendering of his feelings for her, and *The Electric Silence*, an allegorical autobiography; 'I waited for news that my heart beat. The severing night was between me and my love. There was no god of sleep; sleep were traitor. I sought to praise my love, and to lament the hours that divided us; and I could not. Therefore I wrote down the story of my life.'[206] Both were published in *The Equinox* Vol I No VI, the former under the pseudonym Francis Bendick. Back 'to my inamorata in London',[207] Crowley wrote the play *Snowstorm* with a part intended for Waddell, but changed his mind and switched the acting role to a musical one. In the customary fashion of his *Confessions of Aleister Crowley* it was her fault that he had to do so; 'This is a play in three acts, but once again I have tried to introduce a new artistic form. Leila Waddell was to play the part of the heroine, but as she was incapable of speaking on the stage, I had to write her part as a series of violin solos.'[208] *Snowstorm* was never publicly performed, with Waddell or with anybody else, though the text did appear in Vol I No VII of *The Equinox* in March 1912. The part created for Waddell is listed as 'Nerissa, a Violinist', Nerissa being one of her middle names. The role does have some spoken lines in the text as it survives today, albeit short ones.

కఠ

Despite the Thelemic maxim that 'Every man and every woman is a star', Crowley, it will be recalled from the previous chapter, did not have a

205 Aleister Crowley, *The Confessions of Aleister Crowley*, p 228-229.
206 Aleister Crowley, *The Electric Silence*, published in *The Equinox* Vol I No VI p 55.
207 Aleister Crowley, *The Confessions of Aleister Crowley*, p 717.
208 Ibid., p 718.

high opinion of women, deeming them moral and intellectual inferiors but finding them useful for sex and for providing magical and poetic inspiration. The women who best exemplified these qualities were referred to as Scarlet Women, acting as a kind of simultaneous seer and muse and channel and lover and allowing his imagination to soar and his magical endeavours to flourish.

The Scarlet Woman is the earthly manifestation of the Thelemic goddess Babalon and is directly referenced in *The Book of the Law*; 'Now ye shall know that the chosen priest and apostle of infinite space is the prince-priest the Beast; and in his woman called the Scarlet Woman is all power given.'[209] Babalon herself is a godly personification of unbridled female sexual desire, and the Scarlet Woman her avatar. 'And I believe in one Earth, the Mother of us all, and in one Womb wherein all men are begotten, and wherein they shall rest, Mystery of Mystery, in Her name Babalon.'[210] Both were mentioned in *The Vision and The Voice*, which Crowley wrote immediately following the Enochian workings with Victor Neuberg in the Algerian desert in 1909:

> Glory unto the Scarlet Woman, Babalon the Mother of Abominations, that rideth upon the Beast, for she hath spilt their blood in every corner of the earth and lo! she hath mingled it in the cup of her whoredom... Beautiful art thou, O Babylon, and desirable, for thou hast given thyself to everything that liveth, and thy weakness hath subdued their strength. For in that union thou didst understand. Therefore art thou called Understanding, O Babylon, Lady of the Night![211]

Babalon and the Scarlet Woman can be identified with the Whore of Babylon of the Biblical *Book of Revelation*, with which Crowley would have been familiar from his Plymouth Brethren upbringing;

> And he carried me away in the Spirit into a wilderness, and I saw a woman sitting on a scarlet beast that was full of blasphemous names, and it had seven heads and ten horns. The woman was arrayed in purple and scarlet, and adorned with gold and jewels and pearls, holding in her hand a golden cup full of

---

209 *The Book of the Law*, I.15.
210 Aleister Crowley, *The Gnostic Mass*.
211 Aleister Crowley, *The Vision and the Voice*, p 82-83.

abominations and the impurities of her sexual immorality. And on her forehead was written a name of mystery: 'Babylon the great, mother of prostitutes and of earth's abominations.'[212]

An equivalent is also found in the Enochian magick of John Dee and Edward Kelley;

I am the daughter of Fortitude, and ravished every hour from my youth. For behold I am Understanding and science dwelleth in me; and the heavens oppress me. They cover and desire me with infinite appetite; for none that are earthly have embraced me, for I am shadowed with the Circle of the Stars and covered with the morning clouds. My feet are swifter than the winds, and my hands are sweeter than the morning dew. My garments are from the beginning, and my dwelling place is in myself... Happy is he that embraceth me: for in the night season I am sweet, and in the day full of pleasure. My company is a harmony of many symbols and my lips sweeter than health itself. I am a harlot for such as ravish me, and a virgin with such as know me not. For lo, I am loved of many, and I am a lover to many; and as many as come unto me as they should do, have entertainment.[213]

Crowley described the role of the Scarlet Woman in one of his *Book of the Law* commentaries;

I, the Beast 666, am called to shew this worship and to send it forth into the world: By my Woman called the Scarlet Woman, who is any Woman that receives and transmits my Solar Word and Being, is my Work achieved; for without Woman man has no power. By Us let all men learn that all that may be is their Way of Joy for them to go, and that all souls are the Soul of True Light.[214]

212 Revelation 17: 3-5

213 Quoted from *A True and Faithful Relation of What Passed for Many Years Between Dr. John Dee and Some Spirits*, online edition, originally published in 1599, p. 401. <https://archive.org/details/truefaithfulrela00deej>

214 Aleister Crowley, *Magical and Philosophical Commentaries on the Book of the Law*, p 307.

The position of Scarlet Woman was not fixed and was transferable from one woman to another:

> It is necessary to say here that The Beast appears to be a definite individual; to wit, the man Aleister Crowley. But the Scarlet Woman is an officer replaceable as need arises. Thus to this present date of writing, Anno XVI, Sun in Sagittarius, there have been several holders of the title.[215]

Love or sentiment were not considered necessary components of the relationship between Crowley and Scarlet Woman, though 'the attraction should be spontaneous and irresistible... the machinery should be constructed on similar principles. The psychology of the one should be intelligible to the other."[216]

There is debate amongst Crowley scholars as to whether Leila Waddell can or should be deemed one of his Scarlet Women. Though she fits the bill in many respects few authors include her, perhaps since she lacked the spark of magical inspiration that a Scarlet Woman typically provided for him. In her favour for consideration for Scarlet Womanhood – aside from her inspiring a great deal of poetry and literature in him, as women were wont to do – is her participation in numerous of Crowley's rites and the influence she had in the writing of *Book 4* and *The Book of Lies*, two of his most significant literary achievements, and which will be discussed later in this chapter and the next.

There is also the question of how magically inclined or capable Waddell was in her own right, or whether she even had any aptitude for it. According to Crowley she didn't – 'Striking too as her success had been in the Rites of Eleusis, it soon became clear that its source was the impulse of my personality. I could invoke the gods into her; I could not teach her how to invoke them herself.'[217] The truth of the matter though is that we don't know and should be wary of relying solely on Crowley's pronouncements. He was consistently disparaging of Waddell in *The Confessions of Aleister Crowley* and untangling what is truth and what is after-the-event bitterness is a difficult and perhaps impossible task. The only clue we have from Waddell

215 Aleister Crowley, *Liber AL* I:15, online edition. <https://nofaithinthehumanrace. com/legis/?chapter=1&verse=15>

216 Aleister Crowley, *Commentaries to Liber AL Vel Legis*, online edition. <https:// www.tarrdaniel.com/documents/Thelemagick/essay/english/Commentaries_to_ Liber_AL_vel_Legis.html>

217 Aleister Crowley, *The Confessions of Aleister Crowley*, p 753.

herself is that it is said that she complained to friend Gwendoline Otter early in the relationship that Crowley 'wants me to devote my life to magic, but I don't think I want to.'[218]

A further indication as to how Crowley saw Waddell fitting into his magical and poetic ideals was provided in 1933, long after their relationship had ended. He set out the three categories into which he thought the women in his life could be divided, defined by his own 'complexes':

No 1. My vanity complex – petite, passionate, decorative; to be used to shew off, to insult other men, arouse their envy etc.

No 2. Masochist pederasty-complex. Big, strong, heavy, muscular women preferably with moustaches and other masculine stigmata. Use – pleasure of abasement, suffering; ideas of complicity in crime.

No 3. Poet complex. Classically beautiful, spiritual, preferably intelligent and educated enough to understand me. Use – inspiration of ideally noble work. 'Wish-phantasm' of age of chivalry.

Any of these might within obvious limits satisfy need of friendship, companionship, specially No 3.[219]

Waddell fell into the third category, which should perhaps qualify her as a Scarlet Woman, especially when her influence in the writing of two of his most significant books is taken into consideration. That said, when Crowley compiled a retrospective list of those he deemed to have been Scarlet Women in 1923 he did not include her. He did admit that he loved and was inspired by her, writing in 1920

when was I last in love to the point of inspiration? Leila Waddell, for her fiddle; Jane Chéron, for her opium soul; and so on... Back, soul! Reach Rose,[220] whom I idealised and loved for herself, the only one besides Leila Waddell of whom I can say this... In both

218 Quoted in *Museum Piece: The Education of an Iconographer* by James Laver, p 117.
219 Quoted in *Aleister Crowley: The Biography* by Tobias Churton, p 285.
220 Rose Kelly, Crowley's first wife; see the previous chapter.

cases, the soul was capable of inspiring me with romantic love which is what makes me sing.[221]

If such was the case, why was she not on the 1923 list of Scarlet Women? That list is an interesting read, in part for who makes it and who doesn't; some of the inclusions had far less of an impact on Crowley's life and work than Waddell certainly did.

1. Rose Edith Crowley née Kelly my wife. Put me in touch with Aiwass... Failed as elsewhere on the record.

2. A doubtful case. Mary d'Este Sturges née Dempsey. Put me in touch with Ab-ul-Diz; hence helped with *Book 4*. Failed from personal jealousies.

3. Jeanne Robert Foster née Olivier. Bore the 'child' to whom this book [*The Book of the Law*] refers later. Failed from respectability.

4. Roddie Minor. Brought me in touch with Amalantrah. Failed from indifference to the Work.

5. A doubtful case. Marie Röhling née Lavroff. Helped to inspire *Liber CXI*. Failed from indecision.

6. A doubtful case, Bertha Almira Prykryl née Bruce. Delayed assumption of duties, hence made way for No 7.

7. Leah Hirsig. Assisted me in actual initiation; still at my side.'[222]

The reader is directed to the previous chapter *Agatha and Perdurabo (1910)* concerning Rose Kelly. Mary d'Este Sturges, better known as Mary Desti, whose tenure as Scarlet Woman was brief, will shortly be discussed in this chapter. Jeanne Foster was a New York poet and Theosophist who met Crowley in 1915; details of their relationship can be found in the

221 Aleister Crowley, *The Magical Record of The Beast 666*, p 137-138.
222 As quoted in Aleister Crowley, *Magical Diaries of Aleister Crowley*, Tunisia 1923, p 61.
    This note only runs up to 1923 when it was written, and is not a complete list of all Scarlet Women in Crowley's life; for those post-Hirsig, see the chapter *Love Alway Yieldeth: Love Alway Hardeneth (1914-1923)* later in this book.

chapter *Love Alway Yieldeth: Love Alway Hardeneth (1914-1923)*, along with accounts of Roddie Minor, Marie Röhling, and Leah Hirsig. Bertha Prykryl was a member of the Detroit branch of the Ordo Templi Orientis, magical name Soror Almeira, and her time with Crowley was also short, in late 1918, though Crowley was purportedly so fond of her that she was under serious consideration as a potential longer-term Scarlet Woman over Hirsig.

So, should Leila Waddell count as a Scarlet Woman? That the likes of Jeanne Foster, Marie Röhling, and Bertha Prykryl made Crowley's list and not Waddell is telling of his then-attitude towards her. As the reader will later see, it is this author's suspicion that he harboured a bitterness towards her by the nineteen-twenties which led to her exclusion as a Scarlet Woman, and to her subsequent exclusion by Crowley scholars since.

Though Crowley did not classify Leila Waddell as a Scarlet Woman, he did identify her with Babalon.

> Behold! I have lived many years, and I have travelled in every land that is under the dominion of the Sun, and I have sailed the seas from pole to pole. Now do I lift up my voice and testify that all is vanity on earth, except the love of a good woman, and that good woman LAYLAH. And I testify that in heaven all is vanity (for I have journeyed oft, and sojourned oft, in every heaven), except the love of OUR LADY BABALON.[223]

He described her as 'SHE that was LAYLAH, and BABALON and NUIT.'[224] He regarded Waddell's number to be 77 and that 'Seven letters hath Her holiest name, and it is Babalon.'[225] It may seem contradictory to the reader, as it does to this author, that Crowley deemed Waddell a personification of Babalon but not a Scarlet Woman, yet at the same time considered the Scarlet Woman to be Babalon's earthly avatar, but such would appear to be the case.

Crowley had several names for Waddell, including Mother Of Heaven (after her role in the Rites of Eleusis; see the previous chapter) and Sister Cybele (as she is identified in the novel *Moonchild*; see the chapter *Love Alway Yieldeth Love Alway Hardeneth (1914-1923)*), but perhaps the best-known of his names for her was Laylah.

---

223 Aleister Crowley, *The Book of Lies*, p 190. Capitalisation in original.
224 Ibid., p 190. Capitalisation in original.
225 Ibid., p 108.

As noted, Laylah is Arabic for night ('but "night" only means LAYLAH and Unity and GOD are not worth even her blemishes'),[226] is identified with Nuit ('Who told thee, man, that LAYLAH is not Nuit, and I Hadit?'),[227] and can be numerically rendered as 77. Crowley frequently referred to Waddell as Laylah in his notebooks, and in the later *Book of Lies* from spring 1912 (see the next chapter) wrote 'Love Alway Yieldeth: Love Alway Hardeneth', which besides containing the word Laylah in acrostic form, 'the name of the Beloved',[228] perhaps gives us an insight into the ambivalence with which he approached the matter of love.

It is sometimes said that following the scandal and negative publicity of the Rites of Eleusis Waddell found it difficult to procure work as a professional musician, though the evidence of the historic record does not bear this out; she performed extensively throughout 1911 and beyond. By January of that year she was booked by theatre manager George Edwardes to lead The Viennese Ladies' Orchestra in a production of *A Waltz Dream* at Daly's Theatre in Leicester Square, London. Reviews of the show were good, with *Reynolds's Newspaper* noting on 8 January 1911 that 'the music throughout is instinct [*sic*] with suave charm and most artistically orchestrated.'[229] The show also played at the Palladium and the Coliseum theatres before touring Germany, France, Russia, and elsewhere. Though a precise concert itinerary is now lost to us it is likely that Waddell was away for much of 1911 performing.

Her health was poor that year, according to Crowley; 'I may mention the year 1911. At the time I was living, in excellent good health, with the woman whom I loved. Her health was, however, variable, and we were both constantly worried.'[230] It is of note here that Crowley stated that the two were cohabiting, presumably at his 124 Victoria Street residence in London; they were even engaged by late 1910 or early 1911, although no marriage would follow.

1911 was reportedly a glorious summer in Europe, and when Waddell wasn't performing, she and Crowley divided their time between Paris and Fontainebleau in north-central France where they stayed a while in a house on the edge of the forest at Montigny-sur-Loing:

---

226 Ibid., p 142. Capitalisation in original.

227 Ibid., p 136. Capitalisation in original.

228 Ibid., page 63.

229 *Reynolds's Newspaper*, January 8 1911.

230 Aleister Crowley, *Energised Enthusiasm*, published in *The Equinox* Vol I No IX, page 20.

By the end of the summer I knew every tree by name, as one might say. I had acquired a boundless love for that incomparable woodland, whose glorious beauty is still further hallowed by the romance which lurks in every glade. It was tame indeed in comparison with a hundred other jungles which I had known, but for all that it possesses an individual charm which endears it to me beyond any words of mine to utter.[231]

His literary output was prodigious that summer, producing numerous works of fiction and poetry and nineteen magical texts. By 10 August, Waddell's thirty-first birthday, she had returned to England to fulfil further concert commitments with The Viennese Ladies' Orchestra and *A Waltz Dream*, and Crowley, alone in France, commemorated the anniversary by writing the poem *A Birthday* for her. He comes across as utterly love-struck here and missing her deeply. Though the poem is lengthy it is worth reproducing as it shows a smitten Crowley at odds with the sniping and critical attitude towards her he displayed in his later *Confessions of Aleister Crowley* written in the nineteen-twenties.

A Birthday

Full moon to-night; and six and twenty years
Since my full moon first broke from angel spheres!
A year of infinite love unwearying -
No circling seasons, but perennial spring!
A year of triumph trampling through defeat,
The first made holy and the last made sweet
By this same love; a year of wealth and woe,
Joy, poverty, health, sickness – all one glow
In the pure light that filled our firmament
Of supreme silence and unbarred extent,
Wherein one sacrament was ours, one Lord,
One resurrection, one recurrent chord,
One incarnation, one descending dove,
All these being one, and that one being Love!

You sent your spirit into tunes; my soul
Yearned in a thousand melodies to enscroll

---

231 Aleister Crowley, *The Confessions of Aleister Crowley*, p 725.

Its happiness: I left no flower unplucked
That might have graced your garland. I induct
Tragedy, comedy, farce, fable, song,
Each longing a little, each a little long,
But each aspiring only to express
Your excellence and my unworthiness -
Nay! but my worthiness, since I was sense
And spirit too of that same excellence.

So thus we solved the earth's revolving riddle:
I could write verse, and you could play the fiddle,
While, as for love, the sun went through the signs,
And not a star but told him how love twines
A wreath for every decanate, degree,
Minute and second, linked eternally
In chains of flowers that never fading are,
Each one as sempiternal as a star.

Let me go back to your last birthday. Then
I was already your one man of men
Appointed to complete you, and fulfil
From everlasting the eternal will.
We lay within the flood of crimson light
In my own balcony that August night,
And conjuring the aright and the averse
Created yet another universe.

We worked together; dance and rite and spell
Arousing heaven and constraining hell.
We lived together; every hour of rest
Was honied from your tiger-lily breast.
We – oh what lingering doubt or fear betrayed
My life to fate! – we parted. Was I afraid?
I was afraid, afraid to live my love,
Afraid you played the serpent, I the dove,
Afraid of what I know not. I am glad
Of all the shame and wretchedness I had,
Since those six weeks have taught me not to doubt you,
And also that I cannot live without you.

Then I came back to you; black treasons rear
Their heads, blind hates, deaf agonies of fear,
Cruelty, cowardice, falsehood, broken pledges,
The temple soiled with senseless sacrileges,

Sickness and poverty, a thousand evils,
Concerted malice of a million devils; -
You never swerved; your high-pooped galleon
Went marvellously, majestically on
Full-sailed, while every other braver bark
Drove on the rocks, or foundered in the dark.

Then Easter, and the days of all delight!
God's sun lit noontide and his moon midnight,
While above all, true centre of our world,
True source of light, our great love passion-pearled
Gave all its life and splendour to the sea
Above whose tides stood our stability.

Then sudden and fierce, no monitory moan,
Smote the mad mischief of the great cyclone.
How far below us all its fury rolled!
How vainly sulphur tries to tarnish gold!
We lived together: all its malice meant
Nothing but freedom of a continent!

It was the forest and the river that knew
The fact that one and one do not make two.
We worked, we walked, we slept, we were at ease,
We cried, we quarrelled; all the rocks and trees
For twenty miles could tell how lovers played,
And we could count a kiss for every glade.
Worry, starvation, illness and distress?
Each moment was a mine of happiness.

Then we grew tired of being country mice,
Came up to Paris, lived our sacrifice
There, giving holy berries to the moon,
July's thanksgiving for the joys of June.

And you are gone away – and how shall I
Make August sing the raptures of July?
And you are gone away – what evil star
Makes you so competent and popular?
How have I raised this harpy-hag of Hell's
Malice – that you are wanted somewhere else?
I wish you were like me a man forbid,
Banned, outcast, nice society well rid
Of the pair of us – then who would interfere
With us? – my darling, you would now be here!

But no! we must fight on, win through, succeed,
Earn the grudged praise that never comes to meed,
Lash dogs to kennel, trample snakes, put bit
In the mule-mouths that have such need of it,
Until the world there's so much to forgive in
Becomes a little possible to live in.

God alone knows if battle or surrender
Be the true courage; either has its splendour.
But since we chose the first, God aid the right,
And damn me if I fail you in the fight!
God join again the ways that lie apart,
And bless the love of loyal heart to heart!
God keep us every hour in every thought,
And bring the vessel of our love to port!

These are my birthday wishes. Dawn's at hand,
And you're an exile in a lonely land.
But what were magic if it could not give
My thought enough vitality to live?
Do not then dream this night has been a loss!
All night I have hung, a god, upon the cross;
All night I have offered incense at the shrine;
All night you have been unutterably mine,
Mine in the memory of the first wild hour
When my rough grasp tore the unwilling flower
From your closed garden, mine in every mood,
In every tense, in every attitude,
In every possibility, still mine

While the sun's pomp and pageant, sign to sign,
Stately proceeded, mine not only so
In the glamour of memory and austral glow
Of ardour, but by image of my brow
Stronger than sense, you are even here and now
Miner, utterly mine, my sister and my wife,
Mother of my children, mistress of my life!

O wild swan winging through the morning mist!
The thousand thousand kisses that we kissed,
The infinite device our love devised
If by some chance its truth might be surprised,
Are these all past? Are these to come? Believe me,
There is no parting; they can never leave me.
I have built you up into my heart and brain
So fast that we can never part again.
Why should I sing you these fantastic psalms
When all the time I have you in my arms?
Why? tis the murmur of our love that swells
Earth's dithyrambs and ocean's oracles.

But this is dawn; my soul shall make its nest
Where your sighs swing from rapture into rest
Love's thurible, your tiger-lily breast.

A Birthday was later published in the Vol 1 No VII edition of *The Equinox* in March 1912. This poem bears a closer look, since it gives an insight into the first year of the couple's relationship – at least from Crowley's perspective – that we don't find in any other account. He describes 'a year of triumph trampling through defeat', and 1910 had indeed been a difficult one for Crowley particularly, with the *Looking Glass* press coverage and subsequent court case. 'Thus we solved the earth's revolving riddle: / I could write verse, and you could play the fiddle' perhaps alludes to the Rites of Artemis and Eleusis and Waddell's incorporation of music into Crowley's magical workings, as do the later lines 'we worked together; dance and rite and spell / Arousing heaven and constraining hell.' Going 'back to your last birthday' takes the reader to August 1910, when the two would have been a couple for about five months, he already her 'one man of men / Appointed to complete you'. They spent that birthday in London if the poem is to be believed, on the balcony of Crowley's London flat 'within the flood of crimson light'. It is not clear precisely what Crowley means by 'conjuring the aright and the averse / Created yet another universe'; perhaps they took peyote or similar that evening.

We don't know the reason why Crowley and Waddell briefly parted in that first year of their union; this poem is the only record we have of it. It evidently occurred before the Easter of 1911, around the time of the *Looking Glass* trial. The only reason Crowley gives is that 'I was afraid, afraid to live my love, / Afraid you played the serpent, I the dove, / Afraid of what I know not.' The separation lasted six weeks, which 'have taught me not to doubt you, / And also that I cannot live without you.' Reunited, the two travelled to France and to Fontainebleau, 'the forest and the river that knew / The fact that one and one do not make two. / We worked, we walked, we slept, we were at ease, / We cried, we quarrelled.' But despite their feuds and their worries, 'starvation, illness and distress', their 'each moment was a mine of happiness.'

Tired of the forest they returned to Paris for June and July before Waddell departed France at the start of August, leaving Crowley alone. 'And you are gone away – and how shall I / Make August sing the raptures of July?' He even seems jealous of her musical talent for making her 'so competent and popular' and depriving him of her company, for without it 'my darling, you would now be here!' So, he sits up until dawn dreaming on her and writing and finds that 'All night you have been unutterably mine, / Mine in the memory of the first wild hour.' and 'Mother of my children, mistress of my life.' His love for her swells, building her 'up into my heart and brain / So fast that we can never part again.'

Crowley states in *The Confessions of Aleister Crowley* that 10 August 1911 was Waddell's twenty-sixth birthday, and from the first line of the poem he clearly thought as much. This is incorrect; being born in 1880, she was thirty-one. It is apparent that Waddell had lied about her age to him, making herself out to be five years younger than she was. This untruth extended further than Crowley; her age was also often listed as being younger than she was on the passenger manifests of ships she travelled on, and had been since she first departed Australia in 1908.

With Waddell busy with concert engagements Crowley returned alone to London, where he met a woman named Mary Desti[232] on 11 October, at a

---

232 Born 1871 in Quebec, also known as Mary Estelle Dempsey or as Mary d'Este Sturges, and mother of Hollywood film director and screenwriter Preston Sturges. As well as her role as Scarlet Woman, for a brief period from March 1912 to September 1913 she was named as editor of *The Equinox* (though how involved she actually was in this capacity is moot). In later life she ran a successful perfumery, Maison Desti.

fortieth birthday party in her honour hosted by dancer and choreographer
Isadora Duncan (1877-1927) and held at the Savoy Hotel on The Strand.
Despite the sentiments so recently expressed towards Waddell in the
birthday poem he was much taken with Desti, finding her as 'a magnificent
specimen of mingled Irish and Italian blood, possessed of a most powerful
personality and a terrific magnetism which instantly attracted my own.
I forgot everything. I sat on the floor like a Chinese god, exchanging
electricity with her.'[233] Within weeks the two began an affair, travelling to St
Moritz together by way of Montparnasse and Zurich.

Though Mary Desti's association with Crowley would prove to be brief
and tumultuous, it was of great significance. Not long divorced and five
years older than he, she had no background in the occult; her interests were
more artistic, having sung and written for the stage and being a close friend
of Isadora Duncan. Nonetheless Desti would soon become Soror Virakam
of the A∴A∴, and a Scarlet Woman.

In November and December 1911 Desti and Crowley performed a
series of ritual workings together at which an entity named Ab-ul-Diz,[234]
purportedly one of the Secret Chiefs, spoke through her. It began on the
night of 21 November while the two were in Zurich. As Crowley writes,

> I... was aroused [from sleep] by Virakam being apparently seized
> with a violent attack of hysteria, in which she poured forth a
> frantic torrent of senseless hallucination. I was irritated and tried
> to calm her. But she insisted that her experience was real; that she
> bore an important message to me from some invisible individual.
> Such nonsense increased my irritation. But – after about an hour
> of it – my jaw fell with astonishment. I became suddenly aware of
> a coherence in her ravings, and further that they were couched in
> my own language of symbols. My attention being thus awakened,
> I listened to what she was saying. A few minutes convinced me
> that she was actually in communication with some intelligence
> who had a message for me... The man in her vision, Ab-ul-Diz, was
> acquainted with my system of hieroglyphics, literal and numerical,

---

She outlived almost everybody else in the Aleister Crowley saga, dying in 1971 at the
remarkable age of 100.

233 Aleister Crowley, *The Confessions of Aleister Crowley*, p 737.

234 Sometimes rendered Abuldiz.

and also with some incidents in my magical career. Virakam herself certainly knew nothing of any of these.[235]

The entity calling itself Ab-ul-Diz instructed Crowley to contact it a week later, when further information would be given. Desti's subsequent sex- and champagne- and drug-stoked pronouncements while in trance would lead Crowley to the writing of *Book 4*, one of his most significant texts, though despite the importance with which Crowley held these workings he found Desti a most unsuitable channel:

> She was very unsatisfactory as a clairvoyant... She was a quick-tempered and impulsive woman, always eager to act with reckless enthusiasm. My cold scepticism no doubt prevented her from doing her best. Ab-ul-Diz himself constantly demanded that I should show "faith" and warned me that I was wrecking my chances by my attitude. I prevailed upon him, however, to give adequate proof of his existence and his claim to speak with authority. The main purport of his message was to instruct me to write a book on my system of mysticism and Magick, to be called *Book Four*, and told me that by means of this book, I should prevail against public neglect. I saw no objection to writing such a book; on quite rational grounds, it was a proper course of action. I therefore agreed to do so. But Ab-ul-Diz was determined to dictate the conditions in which the book was to be written; and this was a difficult matter. He wanted us to travel to an appropriate place. On this point I was not wholly satisfied with the result of my cross-examination. I know now that I was much to blame throughout. I was not honest either with him, myself, or Virakam. I allowed material considerations to influence me, and I clung – oh triple fool! – to my sentimental obligations towards Laylah.[236]

Laylah of course being Leila Waddell, though any 'sentimental obligations' Crowley felt for her hadn't curbed him from eloping to a St Moritz hotel with another woman, nor did they stop him then embarking for Milan with her on a discarnate entity's say so. In Milan Ab-ul-Diz appeared through Desti again, telling Crowley that he should 'go to Rome

235 Aleister Crowley, *The Confessions of Aleister Crowley*, p 738.
236 Ibid., p 739.

and beyond Rome, though he refused to name the exact spot. We were to take a villa and there write *Book Four.*'[237]

Crowley and Desti did so, settling at the Villa Caldarazzo in Posillipo near Naples where he dictated the first two parts of the book with her transcribing. They were a terrible couple, each unsuited to the other, and when not having sex they were usually arguing. He also took exception to her thirteen-year-old son Preston (1898-1959), who joined them at the villa over Christmas – 'Virakam's brat – a most god-forsaken lout'[238] – and the relationship did not last, with Desti leaving Crowley Paris-bound before the *Book 4* manuscript was complete.

Crowley journeyed back to Paris himself, where he and Desti reunited and travelled together to London. There the liaison collapsed again, with she 'hastily marrying a Turkish adventurer[239] who proceeded to beat her and a little later, to desert her. Her hysteria became chronic and she took to furious bouts of drinking which culminated in delirium tremens.'[240]

In London Crowley also joined Waddell once more, though exactly what if anything he told her of his trans-European occult adventures with another woman isn't recorded. The only clue we have is the lengthy and quite extraordinary autobiographical poem *Chicago May*, privately published in January 1914, wherein Crowley documented the Mary Desti episode and its aftermath and made explicit his feelings for Waddell. Bearing in mind that he'd spent some months in hotels across Europe with Desti it makes for remarkable reading, contrasting the two women, Desti

> The great sow snores
> Blowing out spittle through her blubber lips
> Champagne and lust still oozes from the pores of her fat flanks...
> Like salt pools in a marsh her skin is, soiled
> With labours and abortions, stained and red
> With her low birth and her high feeding, spoiled
> With moles and wens, and fat, fat, fat...

---

237 Ibid., p 739.

238 Ibid., p 740.

The feeling was mutual; Preston – latter to find fame as Hollywood writer and Oscar-winning director Preston Sturges – loathed Crowley, commenting that 'Reading about some of his subsequent exploits, I realise my mother and I were lucky to escape with our lives. If I had been a little older he might not have escaped with his.' (*Preston Sturges* by Preston Sturges, p 77-78).

239 Named Vely Bey; he and Desti were wedded on 12 February 1912.

240 Aleister Crowley, *The Confessions of Aleister Crowley*, p 742-743.

This guzzling sow with the loose bulging belly
And sagging teats, whom fate has made my mate,
This itching mass of nastiness, this jelly
That sets all loathing tingling through my spine,

set against Waddell, 'a woman, true, fair, wise, and young, / Her soul
one flame for art and song, her soul / Pure as the thrilling musick of her
tongue, / Her heart one flame – for me.'

Through twenty-three pages Crowley insults and denounces Desti and
proclaims Waddell his love, the latter best characterised in Part IV which is
worth quoting in full; though Desti had her magical uses and would be later
be deemed a Scarlet Woman by Crowley, it was evidently Leila Waddell that
he loved and favoured.

Chicago May [excerpt]

Yes: I am you, but for a moment only.
    That leaves an ache: that leaves me less than man.
That leaves me more than God, too sad, too lonely
    To do no matter what. Since love began
With the partition of the first one thing
    That was itself, there is no hope to be
But the eternal grace – the queen and king
    Of no commensurable ecstasy.
Ah God! I am not with you even now:
    The New Moon shines on a divided love –
Christ! I will get to you somehow: somehow
    I will redeem the affright these cold hours prove.
May God damn every hour that severs us!
    May God excite each hour to holy joy
That breaks the bestially monotonous
    Madness and shame of your own boy, your boy
That is no man, no beast, not even God
    In those pale hours that you and he apart
Drain the black poison of the period,
    Smite all damnation into either heart –
O Jesus! is there pity, is there none?
    Is there no peace, no passion in the sky?
Is there no fervour in the blasting sun
    To make a symphony of sympathy?

Oh, but if I were only with you – when? –
    Who knows if all our passion would suffice
Us who were forced – we, Laylah! – now and then
    To bathe our bodies in the vats of vice?
Why is our heaven so critical a point?
    Why does life tremble on so tense a string?
Why should so rare an oil as ours anoint
    The brazen brows of a usurping king?
Is it not in our right that you and I,
    No more you and I, should be some third thing, given
Not by the Gods, nor chance, nor Destiny,
    But – by what That that is beyond hell and heaven?
Lost, lost, for ever lost we are; I know
    No word to answer the eternal Why,
No spell that may subdue the eternal woe
    That "you" are somehow different from "I!"
Lost, lost! O may not death discover spells?
    Has not the spasm of dissolution charms?
Could we not trick this trickery of hells? -
    Suppose we died in one another's arms!
Let us not wait for age to dull our eyes!
    Let us take death by his black throat and die!
Let us add murder to our mysteries,
    And face the devil together, you and I!
Let us find hope in uttermost despair,
    Delight in our division, new desire
In the black fate that takes us unaware,
    In death's dark water the eternal fire!
Come, Laylah, come, my sister and my spouse,
    Bedeck yourself with nakedness, prepare
To enter the most high, most holy house,
    Careless what gods or devils may be there.
Love me! I love you, Laylah! Laylah! mine
    Though time and space and force and being discede,
Mine is the magic that has made me thine,
    Mine from sublime unconsciousness to deed.
Laylah! oh God! the love of my whole life,
    My life concentrated in a single act,
More than a mistress, wilder than a wife,
    Who ratified our diabolic pact?

God grant my life and yours be one, be one,
    One beyond possibility, no hour
But bring to ripeness in the royal sun
    Some fruit of our fecundity, some flower
Such as no spring of earth or heaven can show; –
    Laylah! my Laylah! Laylah! Laylah! mine
Irrevocably from the hour of woe
    When I broke in upon the crystal shrine!
Oh, never falter! never fail! forget
    No second of the wonders that are past,
Foresee the greater wonders may be yet -
    Nail Love, the Son of Man, to murder's mast!
Let us be something unachieved before,
    Something intolerable, something new!
Who was the fool that preened himself and swore
    There was no further destiny to do?
Why, every thought is a new spasm of sun!
    Is there a new or old in love? What odds,
Since every one of us – yea, every one! –
    Is beyond doubt the darling of the gods?
Why then, let us die young, let us die young!
    Come, Laylah, I shall get to you so soon
This absence, a mere miserere sung,
    Seems dream. O moon! O mortifying moon!
Quicken our love! O bring me to the hour,
    Minute and second when I lose, I lose
All that I am in one fellatrix flower!
    Time, O the unsubstantial! O the ooze
Of nothingness! Come bring me to the kiss,
    The comfort of thine all-availing breast!
Bring me to the intolerable bliss
    Whose recrudescence is eternal rest –
Laylah! I come to you, I come to you –
    Three thousand miles, what are they to a soul
Whose insight baffles the blind blaze of blue
    With single effort to a single goal?
Laylah! I charge you by the love, the love
    That you and I bear to each other, come
To meet me! there's a guerdon far above
    All God's in our unalterable sum

Of infinite abasement and success –
   Come, let our spirits mingle! bodies follow
According to the grace and kindliness
   Of space's master, Zeus, and time's, Apollo.
I love you, Laylah! I am with you now.
   One kiss, one kiss! O let us part no more!
One kiss, one kiss on each beloved brow!
   One kiss, one kiss where we have kissed before!
I rise, I come to you! I come to you!
   You will be maniac to meet with me.
I ride, I race over the bounding blue: –
   You will be there to meet me on the quay![241]

Part three of *Book 4* was dictated by Crowley with Waddell transcribing at Fontainebleau in early 1912, though he was not happy with the result, and it would not be published in its complete form until 1929. The role of both Desti and Waddell, together with a third student of Crowley's named Mary Butts,[242] was acknowledged in the compiling of the book. All helped in transcribing and assembling the text and discussing its ideas with Crowley as it progressed, and all are now given a co-author credit despite their likely not having actually written much if any of it themselves. An opening note by Desti stated that

---

241 Note that this is not the complete text of *Chicago May*, only Part IV, which is the section most concerning Leila Waddell. It is likely that the title *Chicago May* alludes to the fact that, although born in Quebec, Mary Desti was raised in Chicago.

242 Mary Butts, born 1890 in Poole, Dorset, was an English author with a long-standing occult interest. Her association with Crowley was brief; she met him in 1921 and stayed at his Abbey of Thelema in Sicily in 1923 (see the chapter *Love Alway Yieldeth: Love Alway Hindereth (1914-1923)* later in this book). Disillusioned with what she found there, and acquiring a heroin habit along the way, she left after twelve weeks. She was vocal in her criticism of Crowley and the Abbey, and Crowley in turn caricatured her in his 1922 novel *Diary of a Drug Fiend* (p 14) as 'a fat, bold, red-headed slut... a white maggot. She was pompous, pretentious, and stupid. She gave herself out as a great authority on literature; but all her knowledge was parrot, and her own attempts in that direction the most deplorably dreary drivel that had ever been printed.' Though Butts' writing – originally published throughout the twenties and thirties – remained obscure for years following her death in 1937, she was rediscovered and republished in the 1980s and her work and her role in the early modernist movement finally acknowledged.

Frater Perdurabo is the most honest of all the great religious teachers. Others have said, 'Believe me!' He says: 'Don't believe me!' He does not ask for followers; would despise and refuse them. He wants an independent and self-reliant body of students to follow out their own methods of research. If he can save them time and trouble by giving a few 'tips', his work will have been done to his own satisfaction.[243]

A footnote remarkable for its hyperbole and attributed to 'Soror A' could very well be by Waddell – the reader will recall that she was initiated as Soror Agatha – though the book's later editors John Symonds and Kenneth Grant speculate that this was Roddie Minor, initiated by Crowley in 1917 as Soror Ahitha;[244] 'Frater Perdurabo, on the one occasion I was able to see Him as He really is, was brighter than the Sun at noon. I fell instantly to the floor in a swoon which lasted several hours, during which I was initiated.'[245] Another footnote added in the 1997 Weiser edition has also been credited to Waddell:

It is amusing to observe that FRATER PERDURABO, when He had completed the series of discourses in Part II, supposed that he had exhausted the subject. Everyone (He thought) would say 'Oh, that is the meaning of the Wand!' 'Now I understand about the Cup!' It never occurred to him that there were people who had not done Magick. He only thought that there might be a few who were doing it badly!!!!!

Parts one and two of *Book 4* were published separately in 1912 and 1913, with the complete version published in 1929 in a revised edition titled *Magick*, sometimes also referred to as *Book 4* or *Liber ABA* or *Magick in Theory and Practice* to further confuse matters. *Magick* sets out the theoretical and practical aspects of Crowley's magical philosophy and contains many of his most-famed and most-quoted aphorisms on the subject, for example that 'Magick is the Science and Art of causing Change to occur in conformity

---

243 Aleister Crowley, *Magick*, p xxi.

244 See the chapter *Love Alway Yieldeth: Love Alway Hardeneth (1914-1923)* later in this book

245 Aleister Crowley, *Magick*, p 223.

with Will',[246] or that 'Every intentional act is a Magical Act.'[247] Crowley endeavoured to render matters as straightforward as possible when writing;

> If at any point there appeared the slightest obscurity – obscurity from the point of view of the entirely ignorant and not particularly intelligent reader; in a word, the average lower-class man in the street – I... recast my thoughts in plainer language. By this means we hoped to write a book well within the compass of the understanding of even the simplest-minded seeker after spiritual enlightenment.[248]

Despite Crowley's desire to keep things simple and his assertion in the text that 'magick is for all',[249] *Magick* does not always make for easy reading.

> I have written this book to help the Banker, the Pugilist, the Biologist, the Poet, the Navvy, the Golfer, the Wife, the Consul – and all the rest – to fulfil themselves perfectly, each in his or her own proper function,[250]

...though it is likely that most will be left scratching their heads at some of *Magick*'s more abstruse or ponderous passages. The subject matter is obscure at the best of times, and Crowley references *Equinox* articles and his other works throughout, material with which even the most learned occult student may not be familiar. At more than five hundred pages it is far from the light read Crowley intended.

246 Ibid., p 131.

247 Ibid., p 132.

248 Aleister Crowley, *The Confessions of Aleister Crowley*, p 742.

249 Aleister Crowley, *Magick*, p 130.

250 Ibid., p 130.

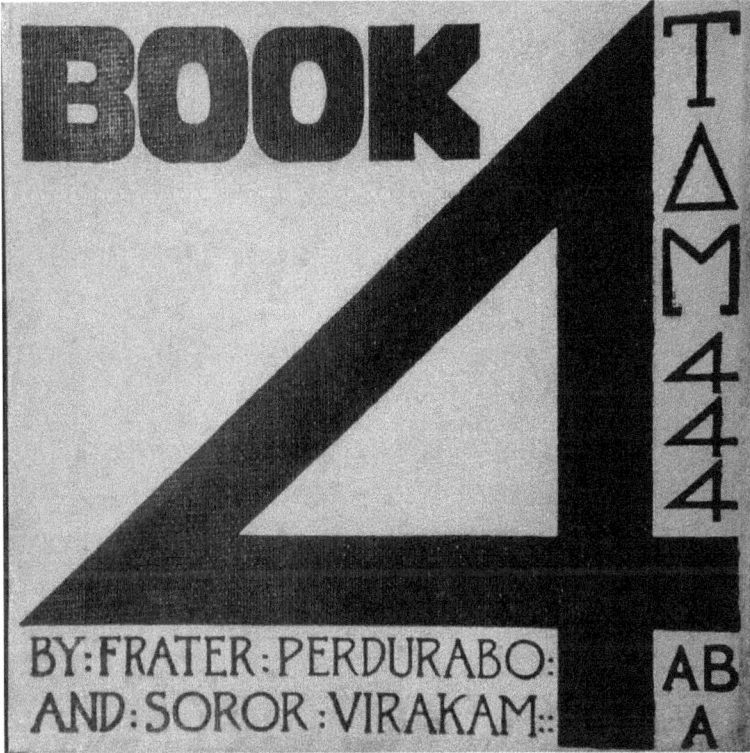

FRONT COVER OF BOOK 4 (PART I), FRATER PERDURABO AND SOROR VIKRAM, PUBLISHED BY WIELAND AND CO. LONDON, 1912. YELLOW BOARDS WITH BLACK CLOTH SPINE.

'Say: God is One.' This I obeyed: for a thousand and one times a night for one thousand nights and one did I affirm the Unity. But 'night' only means LAYLAH; and Unity and GOD are not worth even her blemishes.
Al-lah is only sixty-six; but LAYLAH counteth up to Seven and Seventy.
'Yea! the night shall cover all; the night shall cover all.'

'The Praying Mantis', Aleister Crowley
Liber CCCXXXIII: The Book of Lies, Wieland and Co.,
London, 1913, p. 83.

IT'S NICE TO BE A DEVIL WHEN YOU'RE ONE LIKE ME

(1912-1913)

By 1912 Leila Waddell was booked for further concert dates in New York. Her plan had been to secure passage across the Atlantic aboard the Titanic, on its maiden voyage from Southampton, but she was unable to buy a ticket and travelled on a different ship. When news of the Titanic's sinking upon striking an iceberg on 11 April 1912 – with the loss of more than 1,500 of its 2,224 passengers and crew – spread across the globe, Waddell's brush with death even made the newspapers in her native Australia. *The Leader of Orange*, New South Wales (25 April 1912) wrote, under the header 'How a Bathurst Girl Missed the Titanic Disaster',

> Miss Leila Waddell, the well-known violiniste, narrowly escaped being a passenger aboard the ill-fated Titanic. In the course of a letter received by her father, Mr David Waddell, of Stewart Street, Bathurst, Miss Waddell states that she had intended to proceed to America, where she had secured a six months' engagement, by the Titanic, but had just missed that vessel, and had booked her passage by the Mauretania instead.[251]

The Titanic disaster – likely the most famous ship sinking in history and an event that still resonates today – so stirred the popular imagination that even Crowley was moved to write a poem about it (not that Crowley ever needed an excuse to write a poem about something). It is one of his more conventional works, with little of the symbolism and wordplay commonly found in his poetry. It makes no mention at all of Waddell or her close escape.

The Titanic

Forth flashed the serpent streak of steel,
    Consummate crown of man's device;

---

251 *The Leader*, 25 April 1912. The same story (often with the same wording) was also reported in *The Forbes Times of New South Wales*, 27 April 1912, and in other Australian newspapers of the period.

Down crashed upon an immobile
    And brainless barrier of ice.
Courage!
The grey gods shoot a laughing lip: -
Let not faith founder with the ship!

We reel before the blows of fate;
    Our stout souls stagger at the shock.
Oh! there is Something ultimate
    Fixed faster than the living rock.
Courage!
Catastrophe beyond belief
Harden our hearts to fear and grief!

The gods upon the Titans shower
    Their high intolerable scorn;
But no god knoweth in what hour
    A new Prometheus may be born.
Courage!
Man to his doom goes driving down;
A crown of thorns is still a crown!

No power of nature shall withstand
    At last the spirit of mankind:
It is not built upon the sand;
    It is not wastrel to the wind.
Courage!
Disaster and destruction tend
To taller triumph in the end.

Waddell arrived in New York City from Liverpool on 30 March 1912, performing in the orchestra for *Two Little Brides*, a musical comedy, at the Casino Theatre and the Lyric Theatre. The show ran for sixty-three performances between 23 April and 15 June. Reviews were poor, with *The New York Times* stating that the production 'entirely lacks distinction... faith and the best intentions in the world cannot help very much.'[252] It is not known precisely when Waddell returned to London and to Crowley; likely some time in in the early summer.

---

252 *The New York Times*, 24 April 1912.

March 1912 also saw the publication of Vol 1 No VII of *The Equinox*, containing Crowley's poem *Independence*, a love song to Waddell. It was probably written some time in 1911.

Independence

Come to my arms – is it eve? is it morn?
Is Apollo awake? Is Diana reborn?
Are the streams in full song? Do the woods whisper hush
Is it the nightingale? Is it the thrush?
Is it the smile of the autumn, the blush
Of the spring? Is the world full of peace or alarms?
Come to my arms, Laylah, come to my arms!

Come to my arms, through the hurricane blow.
Thunder and summer, or winter and snow,
It is one to us, one, while our spirits are curled
in the crimson caress; we are fond, we are furled
Like lilies away from the war of the world.
Are there spells beyond ours? Are there alien charms?
Come to my arms, Laylah, come to my arms!

Come to my arms! is it life? is it death?
Is not all immortality born of your breath?
Are not heaven and hell but as handmaids of yours
Who are all that enflames, who are all that allures,
Who are all that destroys, who are all that endures?
I am yours, do I care if it heals me or harms?
Come to my arms, Laylah, come to my arms!

Crowley spent that spring between Paris and London while Waddell was in America, and wrote in his estimation 'a few first-rate lyrics, a few more or less important essays.'[253] The most significant of his literary achievements of this period was in this author's view *The Book of Lies*.

The Book of Lies, Which is Also Falsely Called BREAKS, the Wanderings or Falsifications of the One Thought of Frater Perdurabo, Which Thought is Itself Untrue, was described by Crowley as 'important as a compendium of

---

253 Aleister Crowley, *The Confessions of Aleister Crowley*, p 750.

the contents of my consciousness',[254] which is as apt a description as any. The format of the book is simple, comprising ninety-three chapters, each no longer than a page, including one consisting solely of a ? and another a !.[255] Though they run the full gamut of Crowleyana from poems to jokes to ritual workings, many are in essence love notes to Waddell. An accompanying commentary was added for the 1921 reprint and is invaluable to the reader in untangling some sometimes obscure texts. In Crowley's words, 'This book deals with many matters on all planes of the very highest importance. It is an official publication for Babes of the Abyss, but is recommended even to beginners as highly suggestive.'[256] There are numerous allusions, plays upon words, and masked occult references throughout, much of which will be lost on the general reader, and it is likely that by the time one is sufficiently knowledgeable and advanced magically – indeed a 'Babe of the Abyss' – to fully understand what Crowley is writing about, most of the contents will be irrelevant. Not that this necessarily matters; it is a book that can be enjoyed on many levels.

> Sometimes the text is serious and straightforward, sometimes its obscure oracles demand deep knowledge of the Cabbala for interpretation; others contain obscure allusions, play upon words, secrets expressed in cryptogram, double to triple meanings which must be combined in order to appreciate the full flavour; others again are subtly ironical or cynical. At first sight the book is a jumble of nonsense intended to insult the reader. It requires infinite study, sympathy, intuition and initiation. Given these, I do not hesitate to claim that in none other of my writings have I given so profound and comprehensive an exposition of my philosophy on every plane. I deal with the inmost impulses of the soul and through the whole course of consciousness down to the reactions of the most superficial states of mind.[257]

Quite how seriously we should take Crowley's lofty pronouncements on his own book is moot, but what cannot be denied is that numerous of the texts throughout *The Book of Lies* concern or mention or are inspired

---

254 Ibid., p 751.

255 For the meaning of the latter two, see Crowley's essay *The Soldier and the Hunchback, ! and ?*, *The Equinox* Vol I No I p 133.

256 Aleister Crowley, *The Equinox* Vol I No X.

257 Aleister Crowley, *The Confessions of Aleister Crowley*, p 750.

by Waddell – 'the principal character of this book, Laylah, who is the ultimate feminine symbol, to be interpreted on all planes'[258] – in particular *The Pole-Star* (28), *The Southern Cross* (29), *Waratah-Blossoms* (49), *The Drooping Sunflower* (55), *Trouble With Twins* (56), *The Duck-Billed Platypus* (57), *Margery Daw* (63), *Constancy* (64), *The Praying Mantis* (66), *Sodom-Apples* (67), *Manna* (68), *Carey Street* (74), *Plovers Eggs* (75), *Mandarin-Meals* (87), and *Starlight* (90). Of specific note is text 77, named (in capitals) *THE SUBLIME AND SUPREME SEPTENARY IN ITS MATURE MAGICAL MANIFESTATION THROUGH MATTER: AS IT IS WRITTEN: AN HE-GOAT ALSO,* the full wording of which simply reads 'Laylah' and features a photograph of Waddell. Indeed, it is possible on one level to strip *The Book of Lies* of all its occult trappings and see it as an extended love song to her.

It is worth looking at some of *The Book of Lies'* chapters in more depth. The complete text of *The Pole-Star* appears elsewhere in this book, as a preface to the chapter *Love Alway Yieldeth: Love Alway Hardeneth (1914-1923).* Crowley noted in his commentary that 'in this chapter, little hint is given of anything beyond physical love. It is called the Pole-Star, because Laylah is the one object of devotion to which the author ever turns.'[259] Likewise *The Southern Cross,* another astronomical title, 'because, on the physical plane, Laylah is an Australian.'[260] *Waratah-Blossoms* is named after 'the Waratah... a voluptuous scarlet flower, common in Australia, and this connects the chapter with [*The Pole-Star*] and [*The Southern Cross*]; but this is only an allusion, for the subject of this chapter is OUR LADY BABALON.'[261] It isn't difficult to see Crowley finding a connection in his mind between 'a voluptuous scarlet flower' native to Australia and his love Waddell.

The Drooping Sunflower sees a lovestruck Crowley missing Waddell, away in America;

my One Love was torn from me. I cannot work: I cannot think: I seek distraction here: I seek distraction there: but this is all my truth, that I who love have lost; and how may I regain? I must have money to get to America... O my darling! We should not have spent Ninety Pounds in that Three Weeks in Paris![262]

---

258 Aleister Crowley, *The Book of Lies,* p 67.

259 Ibid., p 67.

260 Ibid., p 69.

261 Ibid., p 109. Capitalisation in original.

262 Ibid., p 121.

It is the first of several mentions in *The Book of Lies* of Waddell far from him and his desire to travel to and reunite with her. He explains the 'drooping sunflower' of the text's title as 'the heart, which needs the divine light.'[263]

Trouble With Twins has Crowley proclaim Waddell holier than

OUR LADY of the STARS!... OUR LADY that rideth upon THE BEAST!... OUR LADY Isis in Her Millions-of-Names, All-Mother, Genetrix-Meretrix!... Holier than all These to me is LAYLAH, night and death; for Her do I blaspheme alike the finite and The Infinite,[264]

before closing with a breathless Crowley wondering of the titular twins 'And yet who knoweth which is Crowley, and which is FRATER PERDURABO?'[265]

The Duck-Billed Platypus was likely named due to it being an animal of Australian origin, like Waddell, and since it 'suggests the two in one, since the orinthorynchus is both bird and beast.'[266] It is one of *The Book of Lies'* more straightforward texts, called by its author 'an apology for the universe'[267] and beginning 'Dirt is matter in the wrong place. Thought is mind in the wrong place. Matter is mind so thought is dirt'.[268] Following a tantric digression Crowley concludes that 'I am glad LAYLAH is afar; no doubt clouds love',[269] perhaps an admission that although he loved her the thought was sometimes more appealing than the reality. This would also no doubt have been true of Waddell in her capacity as muse; as much as he missed her, he needed to be apart from her in order to write about and to her. As Crowley explained in his commentary, 'this doctrine is interpreted in common life by... the familiar and beautiful proverb, "Absence makes the heart grow fonder." (PS. I seem to get a subtle after-taste of bitterness.)'[270]

Margery Daw, the full text of which can be found elsewhere in this book prefacing the chapter *Laylah, My Night (1911)*, is another of *The Book of Lies'*

263 Ibid., p 121.
264 Ibid., p 122. Capitalisation in original.
265 Ibid.,
266 Ibid., p 125.
267 Ibid.
268 Ibid., p 124.
269 Ibid.
270 AIbid., p 125.

simpler texts, and again sees a smitten Crowley pining for his love. 'I love LAYLAH. I lack LAYLAH.... I am the Master of the Universe; then give me a heap of straw in a hut, and LAYLAH naked. Amen.'[271] *Constancy* continues the theme; 'Put me in LAYLAH'S arms again; the Accurst, Leaving me that, elsehow may do his worst.'[272]

The complete text of *The Praying Mantis* can also be found in this book prefacing the present chapter. It is a down-to-earth Waddell love poem, of whom 'Unity and GOD are not even worth her blemishes.'[273] *Sodom-Apples* sees the return of Crowley's Waddell-pining, as does *Manna*, wherein he asks, 'Sail I not towards LAYLAH within seven days?',[274] indicating that at one point during that spring of 1912 he joined her in America. This is tentatively confirmed by the closing lines of *Carey Street*; 'Still, the first step is not so far away: The Mauretania sails on Saturday!',[275] the Mauretania being the ship that had earlier provided Waddell's passage to New York. Crowley did admit in his commentary that although 'this is a Laylah-chapter... in it Laylah figures as the mere woman'[276] rather than as allegory, noting along the way that 'You must give up the world for love, the material for the moral idea, before that, in its turn, is surrendered to the spiritual.'[277]

Plover's Eggs, the full text of which prefaces the chapter *Marked by Charm and Refinement (1924-1932)*, finds Crowley deliberating 'If I really knew what I wanted, I could give up Laylah, or give up everything for Laylah. But "what I want" varies from hour to hour. This wavering is the root of all compromise, and so of all good sense.'[278] Giving up Laylah, or giving up everything for her, and the dichotomy between the two, had perhaps been on Crowley's mind ever since they met, and might explain the dissonance between his writing gushing love poetry to her one moment and cavorting with other women the next. His conclusion? 'I prefer to think of Laylah.'[279]

Text 77, though consisting only of one word, 'Laylah', is central to the *The Book of Lies*, as much for its title – *The Sublime and Supreme Septenary in its Mature Magical Manifestation Through Matter: As It Is Written: An He-*

---

271 Ibid., p 136. Capitalisation in original.

272 Ibid., p 138.

273 Ibid., p 142.

274 Ibid., p 144.

275 Ibid., p 158.

276 Ibid., p 159.

277 Ibid.

278 Ibid., p 160.

279 Ibid.

Goat Also – as for the fact that a photograph of Waddell is set beside it. 'As will be seen from the photogravure inserted opposite this chapter,' Crowley noted in his commentary, 'Laylah is herself not devoid of "Devil", but as she habitually remarks, on being addressed in terms implying this fact, "It's nice to be a devil when you're one like me."'[280] It is as if he were showing her off beauty to the reader, going on to confess that 'Laylah symbolises redemption to Frater P [Perdurabo].'[281]

The Book of Lies' penultimate text, *Starlight*, can be found in full form prefacing the chapter *Agatha and Perdurabo (1910)*. Crowley described it as

> a sort of final Confession of Faith. It is the unification of all symbols on all planes. The End is inexpressible.'[282] Said unification, if Crowley is to be believed, is to be found in 'the love of a good woman, and that good woman LAYLAH... In heaven all is vanity... except the love of OUR LADY BABALON... beyond heaven and earth is the love of OUR LADY NUIT... And at THE END is SHE that was LAYLAH, and BABALON, and NUIT.[283]

It is curious that Crowley switches to the past tense in this last line, as if she were Babalon and Nuit personified on one level only but was ultimately just a mere woman that he loved.

It should be noted that much of *The Book of Lies* was intended by its author to be firmly tongue in cheek, and to have multiple levels of meaning (some of them contradictory); even Crowley's comment at the beginning of the book, 'There is no joke or subtle meaning in the publisher's imprint,'[284] is untrue. *The Book of Lies* was stated within the text to have been published in 1913 but was in fact published in 1912; indeed the Vol I No VIII edition of *The Equinox* of September 1912 listed it as available for sale. In this regard, perhaps its subtitle deserves further consideration; *The Wanderings and Falsifications of the One Thought of Frater Perdurabo Which Thought Is Itself Untrue*. All thought is illusion seems to be the nub of the matter.

₭ℙ

---

280 Ibid., p 165.

281 Ibid.,

282 Ibid., p 192.

283 Ibid., p 191. Capitalisation in original.

284 Ibid., p 4.

Following the writing of *The Book of Lies* Crowley was visited by German occultist Theodor Reuss,[285] head of the Ordo Templi Orientis, an order inaugurated in 1902 by Reuss, Carl Kellner, Franz Hartmann, and Heinrich Klein. Styled after Freemasonry, initially only Freemasons were allowed entry though this restriction was soon lifted. Its first head was Kellner, who died in 1905 with the role falling to Reuss. He and Crowley had previously met in London in March 1910, and Reuss initiated Crowley into the OTO to VII° – equivalent to the 33° of Freemasonry, which Crowley already held – at that point.

During his 1912 visit Reuss accused Crowley of reproducing OTO secrets without permission in *The Book of Lies*, though it isn't clear precisely which chapter or chapters Reuss was referring to. Most Crowley writers[286] take it to have been chapter 36, *The Star Sapphire*, wherein Reuss saw reference to his Order's IX° sex magick workings. *The Star Sapphire* opens 'Let the Adept be armed with his Magick Rood (and provided with his Mythic Rose).'[287] What may seem innocuous to the casual reader was in Reuss' eyes a clear reference to sacred sex.

Crowley assured Reuss that he was entirely unfamiliar with the higher-order workings of the OTO and that any similarities were coincidental, though no doubt the thought that the OTO had sex magick rites immediately appealed to him. 'It instantly flashed upon me,' Crowley later wrote. 'The entire symbolism not only of freemasonry but of many other traditions, blazed upon my spiritual vision. From that moment the OTO assumed its proper importance in my mind. I understood that I held in my hands the key to the future progress of humanity.'[288]

The two men struck up a friendship, with Crowley elevated by Reuss to IX° in the OTO and made head of the newly inaugurated UK lodge, the

---

285 Theodor Reuss, born Albert Karl Theodor Reuss in1855 in Germany, is best-known for being head of the Ordo Templi Orientis from 1905 until his death in 1923. Formerly a singer and journalist, he was a founder member of the OTO in 1902. Resident in London since 1906, he returned to Germany at the advent of the First World War and worked for the Red Cross in Berlin before relocating to Switzerland in 1916. He was evidently much taken with Thelema, providing German translations of *The Book of the Law* and *The Gnostic Mass*. He returned to Germany in 1921, where he died two years later.

286 Except for author Robert Anton Wilson, who assumed it to have been chapter 69, *The Way to Succeed – and the Way to Suck Eggs!*, which concerns mutual oral sex in veiled magical terms and equated with the Great Work. See *Cosmic Trigger Volume I: Final Secret of The Illuminati* by Robert Anton Wilson, p 7-8.

287 Aleister Crowley, *The Book of Lies*, p 82.

288 Aleister Crowley, *The Confessions of Aleister Crowley*, p 775-776.

Mysteria Mystica Maxima. The precise date this happened is uncertain, as is the date or even month of Reuss' 1912 visit; some sources say April, some May, some June. That we don't know precisely when that year *The Book of Lies* was published only complicates matters further. Crowley's Mysteria Mystica Maxima charter may have been backdated, since it is dated 21 April 1912, and the inauguration rite itself took place on 1 June. Crowley's chosen magical name within the OTO was Baphomet, and Reuss proclaimed him – as head of the UK OTO – X° Supreme Rex and Sovereign Grand Master General of Ireland, Ionia, and all the Britons (X° being purely an administrative degree, the actual degree Crowley held for all practical purposes being IX°).

Waddell, upon her return from New York, was also initiated into the OTO, and is said to have been the first woman to attain IX⁰ in that order. Under Crowley's leadership the OTO unsurprisingly took on a Thelemic orientation, with him revising or rewriting many of their rituals and instructions – the existing ones being heavily influenced by Freemasonry – which did not sit well with some members. He later added a note to the Order's Golden Book stating that 'In all lodges of the OTO and M∴M∴M∴ in Great Britain and Ireland the Volume of the Scared Law shall be the book of Thelema, or a facsimile copy of *Liber Legis (CCXX)*, and no imitations upon any other document will be recognised by the Grand Lodge', effectively abandoning the OTO's masonic roots and making *The Book of the Law* its official text.

The OTO's higher degree secrets were now open to Crowley and Waddell. Many emphasised the ritual use of sex, something Crowley had already practised in his own occult career with both male and female partners. Such techniques included using orgasm and sexual energies to aid with mystical states, visualisation, and result, and making magical elixirs from or including the sexual secretions of both genders. Crowley also wasted no time in crafting sexual workings of his own for the OTO. Masturbatory magical methods were taught at VIII° and heterosexual ones at IX°, with Crowley adding a new degree – XI° – involving anal sex.

How much Crowley and Waddell's own sex life and private magical life was influenced by all of this is anybody's guess, but it seems highly likely that it would have been. Sadly perhaps, precisely what the two got up to in bed with each other, and Waddell's sexual tastes in particular, aren't recorded for posterity. For a clue, all that remains is Crowley's magical diary from 1914 onwards; see the chapter *Love Alway Yieldeth: Love Alway Hardeneth (1914-1923)* for further details in this regard.

Crowley referred to Waddell's own position within the Ordo Templi Orientis as THTITI (Thrice Holy Thrice Illuminated Thrice Illustrious) Soror Leila Bathurst IX° Grand Secretary General, M∴M∴M∴ (Bathurst being one of Waddell's middle names and her Australian town of origin). The title may of course have been largely an honorary one and her actual involvement minimal. *The Manifesto of the M∴M∴M∴*, published some time in 1913, pronounced on its cover and title page that it was 'Issued by Order L Bathurst Grand Secretary General. Headquarters: 33 Avenue Studios, 76 Fulham Road, London SW,' the Avenue Studios address being Crowley's then-residence. Her administrative role aside we don't know how deeply involved Waddell was with the OTO in any practical sense; Crowley doesn't specify, and Waddell didn't keep any kind of journal that we are aware of and never spoke of her magical participation in any of the interviews she gave for Australian media in the nineteen-twenties.

In amongst her OTO obligations Waddell continued to perform and to tour, including further dates with T J West's Pictures with whom she had played between 1908 and 1910. Additional appearances at Shaftesbury Hall, Bournemouth, twice daily at 3pm and 8pm from 5 September 1912 are indicated, though there would have been others of which this author has not been able to find a record. She was once more billed as 'Queen of Australian Violinists'. The Viennese Ladies' Orchestra also toured with *A Waltz Dream* during this period; a show at The Theatre Royal, Lincoln on 21 October 1912 for example was reviewed in *The Lincolnshire Echo* as 'a more delightful entertainment of its kind, as to music, would be difficult to name... excellent.'[289]

In September 1912 Waddell's composition *ΘΕΛΗΜΑ: A Tone Testament* was published in sheet music form in the Vol I No VIII edition of *The Equinox* and is the only surviving piece of music written by her that we have. It was accompanied by a poem penned by Crowley titled *Homage Preliminary* alongside a photograph of Waddell – 'sole star in my black firmament' – in profile with chin on right hand and staring wistfully away, a patterned metal disc in her left hand.

Homage Preliminary

Life that is lost in dullard
    Dream of the senses, go!
Life, by the soul fair-coloured,

---

289 *Lincolnshire Echo*, 22 October 1912.

Thy valiant trumpets blow!
Far from the world where love is lust,
And work is pain, and wealth is dust,
Rise on the wings of love, and soar
To the sun's self, the eternal shore
Where flaming streamers soar and roll,
Angels to guard its secret soul,
The Garden where my love and I
May walk to all eternity.
Who dares to force the fiery gate
May win our world inviolate.
Children whose hearts are passionate;
Maidens whose flesh is fair and fain,
And men whose souls no senses stain,
Come! These mad miles of flame of ours
Are cool as springs and fresh as flowers.

And thou, sole star in my black firmament!
    Thou, night that wraps me close, thou, moon that glimmers
Chaste, yet embraced, serenest element
    Lapping my life as the sea laps a swimmer's;
Thou. by whose strength and purity and love
I leave this land, attain to the above,

Come thou rose-red, break on my soul like dawn
    And gild my peaks, and bid their fountains flow;
For in thine absence all their life withdrawn
    Congealed my being to a sterile snow,
Snow fallen from some accursed star to ban
All the high hope and heritage of man.

Come thou, a gleaming goddess of pure pearl,
    Price of mine homage to the great glad god!
Come, saint and satyr praise alike the girl
    Who to my whole life put the period
Of all fulfilment, whose prophetic breath
Girds me with life, and garlands me with death.

Come, be thy magic in the rime and rhythm,
    Until the sea sways to the tender tune,

And the winds whisper, and the leaves wave with them,
    The leaves wherethrough we look upon the moon,
So that men hear me of the world within
Secure from sorrow, sanctified from sin.

The world of stranger deities and loves
    Than haunted Ida, or were hidden in
The Cretan bowers, the Eleusinian groves,
    A world that trembles on thy violin,
Eager to be – and then the curtain drops
Just as the music, with my heart's pulse, stops.

Nay! To this world of ours they shall not reach.
    My rimes are shadows dancing in the breeze
By moonlight; there is no delight in speech
    Such as the silence of our own heart's ease;
But even thy shadow is itself a sun
To the bleak universe of Everyone.

Then open sesame! The fairy cavern
    Of gold and gems, strange land of misty truth
As witches' eyes in a polluted tavern
    Glow with the vampire vanity of youth
Stolen from maids, so let thine own eyes shine
In this fantastic mystery of thine!

Thine eyes are love and truth and loyalty;
    Thine eyes are mystery unveiled to one.
Let them ray forth incarnate deity
    Fit to assoil the eclipse-attainted sun!
Let them point still my weather-beaten soul
Infallibly the pathway of the pole!

Ida, as well as being the highest mountain on the island of Crete and
renowned for its sacred caves (in one of which, Idaean Cave, the god Zeus
was said to have been born), was also one of Waddell's middle names. Writer
Dean Ballinger, who would appear to be more musically learned than this
author, describes Waddell's composition as a

lilting hymnal piece, bearing the influence of modernist composition in its structure – and offbeat harmonies; as such it is an interesting sonic reflection on the idiosyncratic nature of Thelema as a religion tailor-made for modernity, in its emphasis on religious syncretism and psychoanalytical notions of the 'self.'[290]

As noted, by 1913 Crowley was living at Avenue Studios, 76 Fulham Road, London, an address often incorrectly given by Crowley writers (and by the man himself) as 33 Avenue Studios; this was a Crowleyan joke, 33 being a number of magical and masonic import. He actually lived at 2 Avenue Studios, there being only fifteen properties in the building in total. Now a decidedly upmarket part of the city, Fulham was then largely a working-class neighbourhood. Peyote-fuelled parties were still popular among London's Bohemia and Crowley's associates at this time included self-proclaimed 'Queen of Bohemia' Nina Hamnett (1890-1956) and socialite Gwendoline Otter, who had first joined Crowley's circle in 1910. At a party at Otter's 1 Ralston Street, Chelsea home – precise date unknown – Crowley met Leila Waddell's friend Katherine Mansfield, still resident in London and starting to make a name for herself with the city's literati. Waddell was also present. Mansfield didn't take to Crowley at all, finding him as 'a pretentious and very dirty fellow'.[291] He gave her peyote, she adamant the drug had no effect despite her subsequent trip. As author James Laver described it,

> Katherine lay on the sofa and lit a cigarette. She threw the match on the floor and it lay crookedly on the carpet. This caused her such acute distress that Gwen [Otter] put it straight. 'That's much better,' said KM. 'Pity that stuff had no effect.' Then she began to talk, about a princess who lived at the edge of the sea and when she wanted to bathe she just called to the waves... It was as wonderful in its creation of atmosphere, thought Gwen, as one of her short stories. Gwen got rid of her guests and returned to find KM standing rather unsteadily in the middle of the room. 'Where are the others?' she said. 'Have they gone up on deck? It's lucky it is such a smooth night. Pity that stuff had no effect.' Gwen lent her a nightgown and helped her into it. 'But we can't do up all those

290 Dean Ballinger, *Looking for Laylah*, *Fortean Times* #249 (March 2023), p 35.
291 Quoted in *Do What Thou Wilt: A Life of Aleister Crowley* by Lawrence Sutin, p 230 (and elsewhere).

buttons,' she said. 'Oh yes we can,' said Katherine, 'if we talk to them very gently.'[292]

℘ℭ

On 2 February 1913 Crowley undertook another public ritual before a paying audience in an attempt at generating funds and publicity for the Ordo Templi Orientis / Mysteria Mystica Maxima. The structure of the rite was centred around the Crowley-written Mass of the Phoenix, the text of which had appeared in *The Book of Lies*. Author Elliott O'Donnell, in his 1931 book *Rooms of Mystery*, recounts attending the event at Avenue Studios during which Waddell played harp accompanied by two other unidentified female harpists;

> Arranged in a semicircle round the room there were rows of chairs for the audience, and between the chairs and the wall at the back of them there were placed, at regular intervals, busts, which we were informed were those of Pan, Lucifer, and other mystical beings of questionable reputation. A kind of altar occupied the empty space in the centre of the room, and behind it, set against the wall, in front of which were no busts and no chairs, stood three tall, wooden structures... When everyone was seated Mr Aleister Crowley, arranged in quasi-sacerdotal vestments, read extracts from a book which he told us was the Book of Death. After this we listened for a time to some rather doleful music. When that ceased, from the first (counting from left to right) of the wooden boxes arranged against the wall emerged a lady, clad in a filmy green robe and carrying a harp. She played on her harp for some minutes in front of the altar, and then tripped noiselessly back to her box, whilst another damsel, clad in the same sort of filmy garment though of some other hue, and carrying a harp, emerged from the second box. She, too, for a few minutes played on her harp in front of the altar, and then retired to her box, whilst yet another... damsel entertained us for some minutes in the same manner as her predecessors and then retired, and upon her retirement there followed a brief interval, during which the lights went lower and lower. Then, when the room was almost ominously dark, Mr Aleister Crowley strode out from behind a curtain, and advancing in approved theatrical fashion to the altar, invoked certain gods of

---

292 James Laver, *Museum Piece: The Education of an Iconographer*, p 118.

a none too respectable order. Having done this, he raised his voice to a shrill scream, exclaiming: 'Now I will cut my chest.'

Almost simultaneously with this announcement, something bright flashed through the air and a short, sharp, crinkly sound was heard, a sound which was followed immediately by horrified murmurs from most of the ladies present, and by a whisper from one of my friends, consisting if I heard right, of some vague allusion to isinglass, parchment, and potato chips.

After a dramatic pause, sufficient to allow the ladies to recover from their fright, Mr Crowley said, 'I will now dip a burning wafter in my blood.'

He passed something, I could not see what, through the flame of a candle, and then held it close to his bare chest, thereby eliciting more cries of horror from the ladies. Then after another dramatic pause, he informed us that he was going to pay his respects to the busts around the room... he paid his respects very briefly... and, after making a few passes in the air with a dagger, or... after making a few vicious jabs in the air with a bread knife; no matter whether dagger or bread knife, jabs or passes, the effect was sufficiently alarming to call forth a chorus of 'Ohs' – he announced that the ceremonies were for the time being at an end.

Later on, we understood, rites of an even more enthralling nature were performed in private.[293]

All in all O'Donnell was not impressed, finding it 'meat only for the most elementary type of thrill-hunter, the very rawest tryo in magic and occultism.'[294]

℘℃

Leila Waddell embarked on another concert tour in the spring of 1913, this time with the Ragged Ragtime Girls, a violin and dance septet purportedly under Crowley's management and of which she was the focus. Crowley had a run of a thousand promotional postcards printed featuring a photograph of the troupe and wrote an advertising blurb:

293 Elliott O'Donnell, *Rooms of Mystery*, p 157.
294 Ibid., p 157.

Seven beautiful and graceful maidens who dance and play the violin simultaneously. The strange exotic beauty of their leader Miss Leila Bathurst as she weaves her dances in the labyrinth of her attendant nymphs thrills every sense alike of the rococo and the bizarre... The weirdly fascinating appearance of the leader, Miss Leila Bathurst, first stupefied the house and then roused it to a frenzy. As exotic and bizarre as her beauty is, it is yet of that royal kind which goes straight to every heart. Her paces suggest the tiger and the snake, and her violin contains in itself all the music alike of nature and of art. The house could not wait or the all of the curtain to rise to its feet in surging enthusiasm, and the last bars were drowned in the roars of applause that greeted the march past the stalls. Women shrieked, and strange men wept. Babes at the press fainted with emotion, the very unborn emulated the execution of John the Baptist recorded in the first chapter of the Gospel according to St Mark.[295]

Crowley's assessment of the Ragged Ragtime Girls and events surrounding them is set out in *The Confessions of Aleister Crowley* and makes for curious reading;

I was... very busy helping Laylah in her career. The problem was not easy. I soon discovered that it was not in her to undergo the dreary remorseless drudgery demanded by ambition to the classical concert platform.[296]

This is an extraordinary statement; Waddell had been performing as a professional musician for more than a decade by 1913, including internationally for almost five years, and was frequently away from Crowley fulfilling concert commitments throughout their relationship. Perhaps this was more the source of his frustration; that she wasn't at his side at all times and hadn't devoted herself to him and to magick, being instead a busy independent woman with her own career. Crowley continued,

The truth of the matter was that her art was a secondary consideration with her. Secretly, she herself was probably unconscious of it. She was obsessed by the fear of poverty, the

---

295 As quoted in *Perdurabo: The Life of Aleister Crowley* by Richard Kaczynski, p 261.
296 Aleister Crowley, *The Confessions of Aleister Crowley*, p 753.

Oedipus-complex wish for a "secure future", snobbish ambition to improve her social standing. As soon as she passed the age of thirty and came into contact with the atmosphere of America, the spiritual and even the romantic sides of her character wasted away. She rushed desperately from one prospect of prosperity to another, only to find herself despised and duped by the men she was trying to deceive. At last she dropped to the depth of despair and in her drowning struggles lost her last link with life and love. She became a traitor and a thief; and bolted with her spoils to hide herself, like Fafnir, from the very eye of heaven.

I failed to divine the essential hopelessness of helping her. I idealised her; I robed her in the royal vestures of romance. The power and passion of her playing inspired me.[297] Her beauty, physical and moral, bewitched me. I failed to realize to what extent these qualities depend upon circumstances; but it was clear by the beginning of 1912 that she could never get much higher than leading the Ladies' Band [sic.] in *The Waltz Dream* [sic.] as she had been doing. The best hope was to find something equally within her powers which would yet give her the opportunity to make an individual impression. I therefore suggested that she should combine fiddling with dancing. My idea was, of course, to find a new art form. But of this she was not capable. She failed to understand my idea.

I acquiesced. I turned my thoughts to making a popular success for her. We collected six assistant fiddlers, strung together a jumble of jingles and set them to a riot of motion; dressed the septet in coloured rags, called them the Ragged Ragtime Girls and took London by storm. It was a sickening business.[298]

The sense of inconvenience and imposition with which Crowley approached the simple matter of assisting his fiancé in furthering her career is telling, as is his contention that comprehending the concept of people onstage dancing and playing simultaneously was beyond her. We don't know for certain how much the success of the Ragged Ragtime Girls was Crowley's work and how much Waddell's, or even whose idea the troupe was. Though Crowley characteristically claimed credit for it, if an interview

---

297 This despite the fact that earlier in the same book he described her as an 'ill-trained... fifth-rate fiddler', though in Crowley's eyes his influence and guidance had improved her ability in the intervening period.

298 Aleister Crowley, *The Confessions of Aleister Crowley*, p 753-754.

article in *The Australian Woman's Mirror* from December 1924 is to be believed it was Waddell and not him that came up with the idea for the Ragged Ragtime Girls and put them together.

> Miss Waddell says that while fulfilling this engagement [in New York] the rhythm of American rag-time got into her system. She learnt to dance to her own violin, then went back to London and engaged six girls, all musicians from the schools of Sevcik and Arbos. These she taught to dance to their fiddles also. They appeared at the Colosseum – the first Rag Band in London – and caused a sensation. The turn was so successful that before long the girls had to appear in four theatres nightly. 'At that time I was earning a bigger salary than the Prime Minister,' said Miss Waddell. "'It was a most inexpensive turn, too, as we were all dressed in rags. I took the girls all over Germany, Austria and Russia. We were two years on tour. In another two years, with the big bookings we had, I would have made enough to be independent for life, but the war intervened.'[299]

PROMOTIONAL POSTCARD FOR THE RAGGED RAG-TIME GIRLS, CIRCA 1913.

---

299 Interview with Leila Waddell, *Fiddled Round the World: Australian Musician's Interesting Life*, *The Australian Woman's Mirror*, 9 December 1924.

That the Ragged Ragtime Girls were regulars on the London stage that spring is true enough; they debuted at the Tivoli Theatre on The Strand on 3 March 1913, performing nightly until 8 March. They were billed as 'An Absolute Novelty: the Ragged Rag-Time Girls: Seven Pretty Girls who Play the Violin and Dance at the Same Time'. The following six weeks saw them booked at the Tivoli on and off in between shows at other venues, including Oxford Music Hall, Westminster from 10 to 15 March and 17 to 22 March at Shoreditch Empire (twice-nightly at 6.20pm and 9pm), at the London Opera House, at Chelsea Palace between 3 April and 8 April with dates at Euston Theatre Of Varieties, Euston Road from 14 to 19 April, East Ham Syndicate Halls, and the Tottenham Palace also sometime in April. A write-up from the 1 March edition of London's *The Era* gives us an idea of the nature of their performances:

> We may eventually tire of rag-time, but it will be long ere the sun of its popularity sets whilst it is presented in such a piquant fashion by the Rag-time Sisters [*sic.*], a bevy of charming girls exquisitely gowned. From the moment of their entry there is not a dull moment, and they accomplish the difficult task of introducing real novelty into their act. The ragtime lullaby, sung by one the company daintily poised upon the grand piano, is dainty in the extreme. But their show does not merely consist of singing, for one of the company essays successfully the difficult feat of doing a Russian dance to rag-time music. Another feature is a cowboy and Indian maiden dance, performed to ear-haunting refrain. The lady at the piano has an exceptionally good voice, and is such a finished artiste that we regret that the programme did not give us her name. She surely reached the limit in eccentric syncopation in her rendering of *Goodbye Summer*, in rag-time. Altogether a splendid act that should go far.[300]

Crowley's friend (and OTO member) George Cowie (1861-1948) wrote that

> I went with a friend to see [the] performance on Friday and was delighted with it – the only artistic thing in (to me) rather a dismal programme. It struck me what a very effective thing she and these

300 *The Era*, 1 March 1913. Since this article predates the Ragged Ragtime Girls' public debut on 3 March, its author may have witnessed a preview show or rehearsal, or have been working from a press release.

girls might make out of a Witches Sabbath dance and an Act that would probably fetch her double the money.[301]

Not all the reviews were as kind; *Variety* noted dismissively of the septet on 21 March that

the turn is badly dressed and as far as playing ragtime they fail miserably. However, they do play ragtime melodies. It must be granted that each is a good instrumentalist. The act is sure to get away in England if only for the idea of the number of girls playing the fiddles at once.[302]

The Ragged Ragtime Girls were not without controversy. 'English Variety Artists Are Bitter at the Prominence of American Performers' proclaimed a headline in the 9 March edition of *The New York Times*, its author or source clearly not realising that Waddell was Australian and the rest of the troupe were English.

English variety artists are up in arms against 'the Americanisation of English vaudeville theatres.' The London programmes this week present striking evidence of their reasons for complaint, outside of the very successful revue at the Hippodrome, entitled *Hallo, Ragtime*, which is almost exclusively American. The present Tivoli bill is practically American, the stars being Henry Williams and Nat D Ayer, the Ragged Ragtime Girls, Jeanette Dupre, and Harvey Dunlevy, whilst Tallman, the billiardist, tops the bill at the Oxford music hall. Variety agents say that they have armies of American performers under contract to come to England this Summer. W H Clemart, President of the Variety Artists' Federation, said to *The New York Times* correspondent with bitterness: 'The public for some reason has gone crazy over ragtime and other American notions. The managers are now ready to engage anybody who looks like an American and has a strong accent, regardless of the fact that the performer is probably neither amusing nor talented. Whilst many first-rate English artists are starving, these people are able to command any price they ask. English performers may be somewhat to blame because of their notoriously stereotyped

---

301 As quoted in *Perdurabo: The Life of Aleister Crowley* by Richard Kaczynski, p 261.
302 *Variety*, 21 March 1913.

methods, nevertheless nothing is being done to encourage native talent. If the movement continues, English artists will be starved into extinction.'[303]

Crowley's poem *Lines To a Young Lady Violinist on Her Playing in a Green Dress Designed by the Author* appeared in the March 1913 edition of the A∴A∴ journal *The Equinox*, Vol 1 No IX. Though not explicitly stated to be about Waddell, it is likely that it was. Crowley seemed proud of the fact, as mentioned on *The Equinox*'s contents page, that the poem was 'rejected by *The English Review*.'[304]

Lines To a Young Lady Violinist on Her Playing in a Green Dress Designed By the Author

Her dress clings like a snake of emerald
And gold and ruby to her swaying shape;
In its constraint she sways, entranced, enthralled,
Her teeth set lest her rapture should escape
The parted lips – Oh mouth of pomegranate!
Is not Persephone with child of Fate?

What sunlit snows of rose and ivory
Her breasts are, starting from the green, great moons
Filling the blue night with white ecstasy
Of rippling rhythms, of tumultuous tunes.
Artemis tears the gauzes from her gorge,
And violates Hephaestus at his forge.

Then the mad lightnings of her magic bow!
They rave and roar upon the stricken wood,
Swift shrieks of death, solemnities too slow
For birth. Infernal lust of dragon-hued
Devils, sublimest song of Angel choirs,
Echo, and do not utter, her desires!

I am Danae in the shower of gold
This Zeus flings forth, exhausted and possessed,

303 *The New York Times*, 9 March 1913.
304 *The Equinox*,Vol I No IX, p xxi.

Each atom of my being raped and rolled
Beneath her car of music into rest
Deeper than death, more desperate than life,
The agony of primaeval slime at strife.

I am the ecstasy of infamy.
Tossed like a meteor when the Gods play ball,
Racked like Ixion, like Pasiphae
Torn by the leaping life, with myrrh and gall
My throat made bitter, I am crucified
Like Christ with my dead selves on either side.

She stabs me to the heart with every thrust
Of her wild bow, the pitiless hail of sound;
Her smile is murder – the red lips of lust
And the white teeth of death! Her eyes profound
As hell, and frenzied with hell's love and hate,
Gleam grey as God, glare steadier than fate.

She gloats upon my torture as I writhe.
Her head falls back, her eyes turn back, she shakes
And trembles. A sharp spasm takes the lithe
Limbs, and her body with her spirit aches.
The sweat breaks out on her; there bursts a flood
Of shrieks; she bubbles at the mouth with blood.

As Satan fell from heaven, so she crashes
Upon my corpse; one long ensanguine groan
Ends her; the soul has burnt itself to ashes;
The spirit is incorporate with its own,
The abiding spirit of life, love, and light
And liberty, fixed in the infinite.

There is the silence, there the night. Therein
Nor space nor time nor being may intrude;
There is no force to move, no fate to spin,
Nor God nor Satan in the solitude.
O Pagan and O Panic Pentecost!
Lost! Lost eternally! – for ever lost.

A tour followed the Ragged Ragtime Girls' London shows, with appearances at the Sunderland Empire twice-nightly between 5 and 10 May, twice-nightly at the Grand Theatre, Derby between 12 and 17 May, at South Shields Empire Palace on 26 and 27 May and from 2 to 7 June, at the Argyle Theatre, Birkenhead from 16 to 21 June, at the Tivoli Theatre, Hull twice-nightly between 23 and 28 June, before returning to London to play Chiswick Empire twice-nightly from 30 June to 5 July.[305] A report even appeared in *The Sydney Morning Herald* dated 14 June 1913 under the header 'Music And Drama – Leila Waddell':

> Ex-Sydney music people who continue to remain well placed in the lucrative variety theatre world are Miss Violet Mount, Miss Emily Marks (now Mrs Presburg), and Miss Leila Waddell. Miss Waddell, seizing upon the London craze of the moment, has organised and leads a company of seven lady violinists who, as the Ragtime Gipsy Girls,[306] appear in picturesque costume and play with great effect a succession of popular ragtime airs, with variations by way of dances, groupings, etc. This also has caught on, and the Sydney violinist is assured of touring engagements with her little company throughout England and the Continent of Russia.[307]

Crowley accompanied the Ragged Ragtime Girls on the Russian dates; whether in a managerial capacity or just as a guest or chaperone or hanger-on is open to speculation. They departed London on 7 July 1913 and stayed for six weeks until late August, performing at a Moscow open-air venue named the Aquarium. As Crowley wrote,

> They were badly in need of protection. Leila Waddell was the only one with a head on her shoulders. Of the other six, three were dipsomaniacs, four nymphomaniacs, two hysterically prudish, and all ineradicably convinced that outside England everyone was

---

305 *The Chiswick Times* (4 July 1913) described them as 'Another fine item in the week's programme... In picturesque costume these attractive young ladies play on violins, first a selection of old-time melodies, and then up-to-date ragtimes. Their parade around the auditorium is most effective.'

306 The Ragged Ragtime Girls, though that was the troupe's name, were on occasion referred to under different monikers in contemporary media, and were often billed as the Ragged Ragtime Gipsy Girls by promoters.

307 *Music And Drama – Leila Waddell*, from *The Sydney Morning Herald*, 14 June 1913.

a robber, ravisher and assassin. They all carried revolvers, which they did not know how to use; though prepared to do so on the first person who spoke to them.

At the Russian frontier, we plunged from civilization and order, headlong into confusion and anarchy. No one on the train could speak a word even of German. We were thrown out at Warsaw into a desolation which could hardly have been exceeded had we dropped on the moon. At last we found a loafer who spoke a little German, but no man knew or cared about the trains to Moscow. We ultimately drove to another station. A train was due to leave, but they would not find us accommodation. We drove once more across the incoherent city and this time found room in a train which hoped to go to Moscow at the average rate of some ten miles an hour. The compartment contained shelves covered with loose dirty straw on which the passengers indiscriminately drank, gambled, quarrelled and made love. There was no discipline, no order, no convenience. At first I blamed myself, my ignorance of the language and so on, for the muddle in Warsaw; but the British consul told me that he had himself been held up there by railway mismanagement on one occasion for forty-eight hours. When we reached Moscow there was no one at the station who could take charge of our party. We found an hotel for ourselves, and rooms for the girls, more by good luck than design. About one in the morning they sent for Leila to rescue them. She found them standing on rickety tables, screaming with fear. The had been attacked by bed-bugs. Luckily I had warned Leila that in Russia the bug is as inseparable from the bed as the snail from his shell.[308]

Waddell's Russian days weren't just spent performing; she also 'studied dancing with Kousinetzoff, of the Imperial ballet.'[309] Crowley meanwhile took the time in Moscow to have a brief affair;

In a café, I met a young Hungarian girl named Anny Ringler; tall, tense, lean as a starving leopardess, with wild insatiable eyes and a long straight thin mouth, a scarlet scar which seemed to ache with the anguish of hunger for some satisfaction beyond earth's power to supply. We came together with irresistible magnetism. We

308 Aleister Crowley, *The Confessions of Aleister Crowley*, p 778.
309 *The Bathurst Times*, 13 December 1924.

could not converse in human language. I had forgotten nearly all
my Russian; and her German was confined to a few broken cries.
But we had not need of speech. The love between us was ineffably
intense. It still inflames my inmost spirit. She had passed beyond
the region where pleasure had meaning for her. She could only feel
through pain, and my own means of making her happy was to
inflict physical cruelties as she directed. This kind of relation was
altogether new to me; and it was perhaps because of this, intensified
as it was by the environment of the self-torturing soul of Russia,
that I became inspired to create for the next six weeks.[310]

Said flurry of creativity led to him composing poems including *Hymn
to Pan*,[311] *The City of God*, *The Fun of the Fair*, and *Morphia*, the prose pieces
The Lost Continent and *The Heart of Holy Russia*, a verse play named *The
Ship*, and the Gnostic Mass, a group ritual for the Ordo Templi Orientis.
Essentially similar in structure and intent to the Roman Catholic or Eastern
Orthodox mass, the Gnostic Mass was designed and choreographed to
communicate the core principles of Thelema in ritual. It may be a little too
ceremonial for some tastes, involving reverence of the Stele of Revealing[312]
and *The Book of the Law* (the latter being kissed at one point) and with east
being exalted as the direction of Boleskine House, the whole bringing to
Thelema a lot of the trappings many participants may perhaps have turned
from organised religion to avoid.

During a break from wild sadomasochistic sex with another woman,
Crowley wrote a second birthday poem for Waddell on 10 August 1913.
Again he has a wrong age for her, proclaiming her twenty-eight when she

---

310 Aleister Crowley, *The Confessions of Aleister Crowley*, p 778-779.

311 Likely the most famed of Crowley's poems, and arguably the best, *Hymn to Pan*
was published in Vol II No I of *The Equinox* in March 1919 and later included in the
1929 edition of *Magick*, and was one of several texts read out at Crowley's funeral.
Crowley was evidently very pleased with it himself, describing it as 'the most powerful
enchantment ever written' (*The Confessions of Aleister Crowley*, p 926).

312 A painted wooden stele dating to 680-670 BCE and located in Cairo Museum.
It depicts the priest Ankh-ef-en-Khonsu presenting an offering to the god Ra-Re-
Harakhty. Above them stretches Nut the sky goddess. There are also blocks of text on
the front and reverse. As to its relevance to Thelema, in March 1904, prior to Crowley
receiving *The Book of the Law*, his wife Rose Kelly informed him that Horus had a
message for him. Taking her to Cairo Museum and asking her to identify Horus, she
pointed to the Stele of Revealing. Crowley was impressed as its catalogue number
was 666 and it depicted what proved to be the three primary deities of Thelema, Nuit,
Hadit, and Ra-Hoor-Khuit.

was in fact thirty-three. Waddell, as previously mentioned, had been lying about her age since arriving in England, and not just to Crowley, making herself out to be five years younger than she was.

To Laylah Eight-and-Twenty

Lamp of living loveliness,
Maid miraculously male,
Rapture of thine own excess
Blushing through the velvet veil
Where the olive cheeks aglow
Shadow-soften into snow,
Breasts like Bacchanals afloat
Under the proudly phallic throat!
Be thou to my pilgrimage
Light, and laughter sweet and sage,
Till the darkling day expire
Of my life in thy caress,
Thou my frenzy and my fire,
Lamp of living loveliness!

Thou the ruler of the rod
That beneath thy clasp extends
To the galaxies of God
From the gulph where ocean ends,
Cave of dragon, ruby rose,
Heart of hell, garden-close,
Hyacinth petal sweet to smell,
Split-hoof of the glad gazelle,
Be thou mine as I am thine,
As the vine's ensigns entwine
At the sacring of the sun,
Thou the even and I the odd
Being and becoming one
On the abacus of God!

Thou the sacred snake that rears
Death, a jewelled crest across
The enchantment of the years,
All my love that is my loss.

Life and death, two and one,
Hate and love, moon and sun,
Light and darkness, never swerve
From the norm, note the nerve,
Name the name, exceed the excess
Of thy lamp of loveliness,
Living snake of lazy love,
Ithyphallic that uprears
Its Palladium above
The enchantment of the years!

Waddell, Crowley, and the Ragged Ragtime Girls departed from Moscow back to London in late August 1913. Further concert dates followed, twice-nightly at the Alhambra Theatre, Glasgow between 1 and 6 September[313] before moving on to shows at Leeds Hippodrome twice-nightly from 8 to 13 September. They are known to have played the Theatre Royal, Edinburgh twice-nightly from 15 to 20 September, Hulme Hippodrome twice-nightly from 22 September to 27 September, Sheffield Hippodrome twice-nightly from 29 September to 4 October, Liverpool Hippodrome twice-nightly from 6 to at least 8 October, Birmingham Hippodrome twice-nightly between 13 and 18 October, Preston Hippodrome on at least 3 to to 7 November, Queen's Park Hippodrome, Manchester twice-nightly from 10 to 15 November, and the Empire Theatre, Sunderland, twice nightly from 17 to 22 November, whereupon the record starts to get sketchy.

There were dates at West Hartlepool Empire (where they were billed as 'The Seven Ragged Rag-Time Gipsy Girls. Dancing Fiddlers: An Absolute Novelty. Unique! Attractive! Jolly!') between 29 November and 4 December, in Paris at Luna Park on at least 12 December, twice-nightly at the Pavilion Theatre, Liverpool between 12 and 17 January 1914, the Argyle Theatre, Birkenhead from 16 to 21 February, the Grand Hotel, Hanley, Staffordshire from 20 to 25 April, and the Pavilion, Newcastle, twice-nightly from 27 April to 2 May. There were very likely other concerts beyond those listed here, the precise details of which have been lost to history, and possibly some without Waddell leading the troupe. Other European dates beyond Paris are also suggested. It is of note that from late 1913 into 1914 they were

---

313 In anticipation of their arrival, *The Scottish Referee* wrote on 29 August that 'A novelty turn will be that presented by the Seven Ragged Ragtime Gipsy Girls. We are well acquainted with ragtime vocalists nowadays, but in the promised instance we shall have the novelty of hearing syncopated melodies played by a troupe of violinists who the while will trip the light fantastic to the lively strains of the chosen selections.'

listed as an act on the roster of Ellis Entertainments of Whitcomb Street, London, presumably a booking agency, who billed them as 'The Ragged Rag-Time Girls (Seven Dancing Fiddlers), Arouse tremendous enthusiasm wherever they go – The unanimous verdict of Press and Public'.

§§§

September 1913 also saw the publication of Vol I No X of *The Equinox*, the final issue until 1919. Crowley pronounced that five years' silence would follow after the five years of speech that constituted Vol I, but in truth the journal was expensive to produce, costing more money than it made, and funds were low. 'It is of course common knowledge,' Crowley wrote in the editorial to that last-for-now edition, 'that the A∴A∴ and *The Equinox* and all the rest of it are a stupid joke of Aleister Crowley's. He merely wished to see if anyone were fool enough to take him seriously. Several have done so, and he does not regret the few thousand pounds it has cost him.'[314]

In 1912 Crowley had assigned Vittoria Cremers, a Theosophist who joined his circle in 1910, to manage the OTO and Mysteria Mystic Maxima property and finances. He writes that Waddell first met Cremers in New York in 1912, where

> Laylah found her in a miserable room on 176th Street or thereabouts. Pitifully poor, she had not been able to buy *Liber 777* and had therefore worked week after week copying in the Astor Library. She impressed Laylah as an earnest seeker and a practical business woman. She professed the utmost devotion to me and proposed to come to England and put the work of the Order on a sound basis. I thought the idea was excellent, paid her passage to England and established her as a manageress.[315]

In October 1913 he dismissed her from the position, accusing her of embezzling funds, later writing in *The Confessions of Aleister Crowley* that 'I... found that Cremers was intriguing against me; and that, in particular, she had corrupted the heart of Leila Waddell.'[316] Frustratingly Crowley does not elaborate on this latter point at all and it is difficult to say precisely what he meant. He and Waddell were still on good terms following these events,

---

314 *The Equinox*, Vol I No X, p 8.

315 Aleister Crowley, *The Confessions of Aleister Crowley*, p 754.

316 Ibid., p 777.

and with no other accounts to draw upon we don't know what form this alleged corruption took, or its effect. The truth of Crowley's claims against Cremers with regard to M∴M∴M∴ funds are also hard to ascertain; they may have been baseless.

> I left a book of signed cheques in her charge; I allowed her access to my private papers. I gave no sign that I saw how she was corrupting the loyalty of Laylah and making mischief all round. Presently, at the end of 1913, she got influenza. I went to visit her unexpectedly; there, on the table by her bed, was a memorandum showing unmistakably that she had embezzled large sums of money by fraudulent manipulation of the aforesaid cheques. I failed to conceal from her that I had seen and understood, but I continued to act towards her with unvarying kindness and continued to trust her absolutely. It was too much for her! She had hated me from the first... and vowed to ruin me... and now, when she had robbed me and betrayed me at every turn, I had not turned a hair. The consciousness that her hate was impotent was too much for her to endure. She developed an attack of meningitis and was violently insane for six weeks, at the end of which time she melted away to hide her shame in Wales, where she supposed sensibly enough that she would find sympathetic society in thieves and traitors after her own heart. I understand in fact that she is still there.[317]

Cremers herself certainly carried no love for Crowley either and claimed in later years to have magically 'destroyed' him.[318] 'It was sex that rotted him. It was sex, sex, sex, sex, all the way with Crowley. He was a sex maniac.'[319]

Would Leila Waddell have become an occultist – much less an IX° member of one of the world's most prominent orders – had she not known Crowley? Looking at her life prior to her meeting him in the spring of 1910 it doesn't seem very likely, to this author at least. Her time until then had been almost entirely occupied with violin and with the arts. There is no indication in what we know of her history that she had any interest in matters esoteric. She is said to have been the first woman to obtain IX° in the Ordo Templi Orientis, and the first to participate as High Priestess in

---

317 Ibid., p 756.

318 See *The Magical Dilemma of Victor Neuberg* by Jean Overton Fuller, p 43-51.

319 *Quoted in The Magical Dilemma of Victor Neuberg* by Jean Overton Fuller, p 57.

the Gnostic Mass. Waddell's other magical achievements are less known, simply because she kept no record that we are aware of, and Crowley seldom mentioned them. She did participate in a number of sex magick workings of his (see the next chapter) but then so did myriad other people; she was not unique in that respect. She also took part in public performances of the Rites of Artemis and Eleusis and the Mass of the Phoenix. Though her occult involvement otherwise is strongly indicated, scant details have been left to us.

Love is all virtue, since the pleasure of love is but love, and the pain
of love is but love.
Love taketh no heed of that which is not and of that which is.
Absence exalteth love, and presence exalteth love.
Love moveth ever from height to height of ecstasy and faileth never.
The wings of love droop not with time,
nor slacken for life or for death.
Love destroyeth self, uniting self with that which is not-self, so that
Love breedeth All and None in One.
Is it not so?... No?...
Then thou art not lost in love; speak not of love.
Love Alway Yieldeth: Love Alway Hardeneth.
..........May be: I write it but to write Her name.

'The Pole-Star', Aleister Crowley
Liber CCCXXXIII: The Book of Lies, Wieland and Co.,
London, 1913, p. 38.

LOVE ALWAY YIELDETH:
LOVE ALWAY HARDENETH
(1914-1923)

I n December 1913 Crowley travelled to Paris without Waddell, who was still engaged with the Ragged Ragtime Girls on tour. There, he and Victor Neuberg undertook what was later named the Paris Working, begun at midnight on New Year's Eve and entailing six intense weeks of ritual sex, sometimes incorporating scourging and peyote and on occasion joined by a journalist named Walter Duranty.[320] Duranty's girlfriend (and future wife), Jane Chéron, was an occasional lover of Crowley's and owner of the Paris apartment where the Working took place.

It all came to an end on 12 February 1914, following which Crowley was sufficiently inspired to compose *Liber Agapé*, a treatise on sex magick written in veiled and somewhat archaic language. A clearer outline of Crowley's perspective on the subject was set out in a letter from Crowley to John Symonds in 1946:

> The close connection of sexual energy with the higher nervous centres makes the sexual act definitely magical. It is therefore a sacrament which can and should be used in the Great Work. The act being creative, ecstatic and active, its vice consists in treating it as sentimental, emotional, passive.[321]

To express it in more mystical terms, from *The Equinox* Vol III No I; 'When you have proved that God is merely a name for the sex instinct, it appears to me not far to the perception that the sex instinct is God.'[322]

---

320 Walter Duranty, born 1884, was a highly regarded Anglo-American journalist who worked as foreign correspondent for The New York Times. He later covered Russia in the early years of the Bolshevik revolution, for which he would be awarded a Pulitzer prize in 1932. This was not without controversy, amid criticism of his defense of widespread abuses and denial of famine in the country at the time, and there were calls for the award to be revoked. He died in 1957.

321 Aleister Crowley, 1946 letter to John Symonds, quoted in *Aleister Crowley: The Beast in Berlin* by Tobias Churton, p 230.

322 Aleister Crowley, *The Equinox*. Vol III No I, p 281.

Back in London Crowley's sex magick adventures continued, all documented in a journal he titled *Rex de Arte Regia* (*The King on the Royal Art*), including 'highly orgiastic'[323] sex on 3 September 1914 with a 'very weak feminine, easily excitable and very keen' married woman named Marie Maddingley, and prostitute Christine Byrne, aka Peggy Marchmont ('a sturdy bitch of 26 or so') on 6 September, with whom Crowley copulated 'with rare and brief intervals from 11am to 10pm, and the ceremony was thrice performed.' Waddell's violin-playing is said to have soundtracked at least some of Crowley's workings in an unspecified capacity.[324] Whether she also participated sexually is suggested though not stated; Crowley noted that she 'assisted in the work' with 'Violet Duval, chorus girl' on 14 October. An earlier police report from a Superintendent Quinn may yield a further clue as to how she fitted in:

In April 1914 information was received by Police that Crowley was committing certain acts of indecency in the presence of females,[325] in a room occupied by him at 2 The Avenue Studios, 76 Fulham Road, where he was visited by a woman named Waddell. Police enquiries revealed that during the time he had resided at the above address he had been holding a certain kind of service at which incense had been burnt, and various instruments played, during which time a number of both sexes were present. Although he had been seen to commit an act of indecency in his studio on one occasion, no offence on which proceedings could be taken was committed.[326]

Though sex had long formed a part of Crowley's occult practice, sexual rather than ceremonial magick had by now taken over as his favoured technique.

The simplest, most rational, and most direct method [of magick] had been known to me since the summer of 1911; but for some

323 Unless otherwise noted all quotations in this paragraph are from Aleister Crowley's *The Magical Record of The Beast 666*, p 3-4.

324 A point made in the article *Looking for Laylah* by Dean Ballinger, *Fortean Times* #429 (March 2023) p 36, though the now-deceased Ballinger doesn't provide a source.

325 It is perhaps telling of the times that police were called to a private residence to investigate purported sexual misconduct; one would hope that what consenting adults do behind closed doors is their business only.

326 Quoted in *Aleister Crowley: The Beast Demystified* by Roger Hutchinson, p 148.

reason, I had never practised it systematically or recorded my results methodically. I believe this to have been due to an instinctive reluctance in respect of the nature of the method. It was not until January 1st, 1914 that I made it my principal engine.[327]

As evidenced in his notebooks for the period, every working was defined by a fixed objective. The most common result willed for was money, which is perhaps unsurprising given the precarious financial position he was in, along with literary success, 'sex force and attraction', improved relations with others (usually a specified person), magical energy, and wisdom, amongst other goals.

Throughout Crowley's records are details of the 'elixir', the co-mingled male and female sexual fluids which he regarded as an essential component of the working, 'the most powerful, the most radiant thing that existeth in the whole universe,'[328] and which was said when consumed to bestow tremendous energy and vigour. The idea in itself should perhaps not be surprising; Christians believe that the Eucharist can transform bread and wine into flesh and blood, and Crowley felt that a kind of sexual alchemy likewise bestowed arcane properties upon bodily fluids.

Crowley liked to think that his results-based workings were successful, but if such were the case he wouldn't have continued to live in such dire financial straits, having long used up the inheritance received from his deceased father and with book sales generating only a modest revenue. As he wrote several years later,

For example, one performs an operation 'to have $20,000'. A few days later a prospect of obtaining that exact sum suddenly arises, then fades slowly away. Exactly what to do in such a case is a problem of which I have not yet found the perfect answer. Fortunately, it rarely happens that this trouble supervenes. In five out of six times the desired event comes naturally to pass without further disturbance. But I confess that I should like to make that sixth time safe, and believe that in another few months I shall have done so.[329]

---

327 Aleister Crowley, *The Confessions of Aleister Crowley*, p 758.

328 Aleister Crowley, *Liber Agapé*, online edition. <http://www.rahoorkhuit.net/library/libers/pdf/lib_0100.pdf>

329 Aleister Crowley, *The Revival of Magick*, p 36-37.

The advent of war in August 1914 changed everything, rapidly spinning out into a global conflict that would last four long years and result in the deaths of millions, but Waddell and Crowley were largely unaffected, initially at least. Crowley offered his support in the war effort immediately though this was rejected, his age (thirty-nine) or poor health or infamy rendering him unsuitable for service. 'I was more than ever convinced that I was needed by my country, which is England, and to hell with everybody. In my excitement, I had the hallucination that England needed men. I found, on the contrary, that the guiding stars of England needed "business as usual".'[330]

On 24 October 1914 Crowley travelled to New York City without Waddell on the passenger liner RMS Lusitania.[331] The day before departing he wrote to friend George Cowie; 'I hope you will write to Mother [Mother of Heaven, i.e. Waddell], and keep her happy. Luckily she is booked for next week and of course that may lead to better things.'[332] In an earlier letter to Cowie dated 17 October he wrote 'There is some hope... of mother [Waddell] getting on again, and if she can get a long tour of S America it will be splendid.'[333] Both letters suggest that performances with the Ragged Ragtime Girls had effectively come to an end (the last Ragged Ragtime Girls show this author has been able to put a date to was in May 1914) and that Waddell was looking for other work. As the reader will see, this would within a few months lead her in Crowley's footsteps to America.

Upon arrival in New York on 31 October Crowley checked in to the Hotel Wolcott at 4 West 31st Street, and with time began freelancing as a writer for *Vanity Fair*. He resumed his adventures in sex magick, sometimes solo, sometimes with prostitutes, and sometimes with the men of a local Turkish bathhouse. Amongst other partners, Elsie Edwards was described as an 'obese Irish prostitute of maternal Taurus type'[334] who cost Crowley $3 on 14 November and who he didn't much-fancy; 'the unattractiveness of the assistant made the operation difficult. But it was necessary to begin somewhere and so far New York has shown me none of its sex side.' Florence Galy on 21 November was '28-30. Keen on the whole. Lowest

330 Aleister Crowley, *The Confessions of Aleister Crowley,* p 813.

331 Which would be torpedoed by a German navy U-boat on 7 May 1915 while off the coast of Kinsale, Ireland. It sank within eighteen minutes; of its 1,266 passengers and 696 crew, only 761 survived.

332 Quoted in *Aleister Crowley in America* by Tobias Churton, p 188.

333 Ibid.

334 All quotations here are from Aleister Crowley's *The Magical Record of The Beast 666,* p 5-15.

type of prostitute. Dark mulatto, very negroid in type.' Grace Harris on 23 November was 'mediocre orgiastically'. Lea Dewey on 15 December, a 'Dutch prostitute', was 'big and tall but not fat; the muscular wolf type. Very dark hair on head; pubic hair fairer. Beautiful Yoni...[335] The operation was most orgiastic, but I formulated the God well and called aloud after his name... I think the Elixir was formed well enough.' Margaret Pitcher, on 16 January 1915, was

> a young pretty-stupid wide-mouthed flat-faced slim-bodied harlotry. Fair hair. Fine fat juicy Yoni.... The ceremony was not good, as the girl was even more concentrated than I on the object of the Operation. But the Elixir was copious, well-formed, and of very pleasing quality. It was a fairly orgiastic rite, considering all.

Despite these results Crowley found that American women weren't as much to his liking as their European counterparts, writing on 5 January that

> there is no danger of being carried away. I am left in an extraordinary state of exasperation even with the IX^0 itself! Women in America seem purely animal. They 'come like water and like wind they go'. Not one of these Operations in this country has had the flavour that one gets all the time in Europe.

 He also had no fondness for the city in which he found himself; '"Call no man happy until he is dead" or at least until he has left New York!'
 In an event Crowley dated to 'early in 1915'[336] he encountered a man named George Sylvester Viereck (1884-1962) in New York, a German-American poet and author who he says he swiftly realised was an agent for German intelligence. The two had actually met previously in London in 1911. Viereck was editor of a magazine named *The Fatherland*, a US-based German propaganda journal with a readership of around 100,000, and was keen to maintain American neutrality in the war. He offered Crowley the opportunity to write for *The Fatherland*, which was accepted. Crowley later claimed that he saw through Viereck straight away, and took the role so that he could write ironic and satirical material undermining the German war effort. Crowley's dating of this meeting however was clearly wrong; his first

---

335 From Hinduism, a Sanskrit term denoting the female genitalia.
336 Aleister Crowley, *The Confessions of Aleister Crowley*, p 817.

Fatherland article was published in the 13 January 1915 issue, so it more likely occurred some time in the final month or so of 1914.[337]

಄ ಌ

Leila Waddell left Liverpool on 13 February 1915, also via the Lusitania which had earlier served as Crowley's transatlantic passage, reaching New York on 20 February where she joined him. Copious sex aside he'd not been having a good time of things alone in the city if *The Confessions of Aleister Crowley* is to be believed, though doesn't seem particularly excited to have seen her. 'My paralysis extended to every relation of life. I had never known what it was to lack human love; and now, not only did I fail to find a single friend, but when Laylah came from England to join me, I recognised instantly that she was a stranger.'[338]

Crowley's sex magick workings continued; solo, with prostitutes and acquaintances, and with Waddell. At 6.35am on 21 February – the morning after Waddell's arrival in New York and with 'weather fine and frosty' – sex with her was described as 'as good as an early morning operation ever is. The Elixir was not very plentiful... Quality concentrated and good in all respects. I had, however, had a very tiring day[339] and so had the THTITI Soror.'[340] On 19 March with Waddell 'the Operation was undertaken in Unison by both parties. It was excellent in all respects and the Elixir of first-rate quality and vintage.' The objective on that occasion was 'All of McFall's savings'; McFall was likely an 'officer' Waddell had met on the ship from Liverpool to New York and who apparently wished to marry her. As to result, Crowley noted that 'This promises well so far (3 May), the prospects being first-rate', but this was not further elaborated upon; presumably it came to nothing. On 4 May with Waddell 'the Operation was excellent in all respects; in particular the Elixir was well formed, strong and aromatic as well as sweet.' On 28 June the objective was 'Success in Art', with no further details given.

---

337 Crowley biographer Richard Kaczynski dates it to 1 January 1915; see *Perdurabo: The Life of Aleister Crowley*, p 283. Though not impossible even this seems to be stretching things, allowing for less than two weeks between Crowley meeting Viereck and his first *Fatherland* article being commissioned, written, and making it into print.

338 Aleister Crowley, *The Confessions of Aleister Crowley*, p 875.

339 Presumably the day prior.

340 All quotations in this paragraph are from Crowley's *The Magical Record of The Beast 666*, p 19-23.

That there were intervals of a month or more between these 'operations' is curious; either the passion was no longer there between the two, or Waddell was out of town on concert engagements (Crowley was also often away from New York during his US years, as the reader will see). Unfortunately an itinerary of Waddell's bookings in America is not available to us, though there is no reason to assume that she was not performing as and where she could and as often as she could; an interview article from *The Australian Woman's Mirror* in December 1924 – which we shall return to – tells us that 'the war necessitated her making her headquarters in America. There she played everything from concertos with symphony orchestras to rag-time. She toured from coast to coast playing first violin and viol d'amore in *The Beggar's Opera*, and also appearing in vaudeville.'[341]

In July 1915 the article *Vampire Women: Eight Portraits From Life* appeared in *Vanity Fair* magazine, featuring eight drawings of women by different artists and with a 'Hokku' [*sic*.] beneath each written by 'Kwaw Li Ya, the Chinese poet', a literary pseudonym of Crowley's. One such vampire woman was named Leila, clearly modelled on Waddell, and featured a delightful line-drawing of her set above his words:

Merrily masking
Blood-lust, Leila lures me,
Glad to the graveyard!

According to the accompanying blurb,

Everybody seems to be talking, or writing, about vampires and vampire women. The Romans started the fad, of course. No fluttering bat in Rome but suggested some fascinating lady to the best selling poets and romances of the time. More lately, Kipling and Byrne-Jones have helped the bat-lady myth along. Bram Stoker has now done his share, and so has the Baroness Von Raube. Everybody seems to have one on his calling list. Reader, have you, perhaps, a little vampire in your home?[342]

Waddell is said to have connected with an Irish revolutionary group or groups while in New York, under the assumed identity L Bathurst, though

341 Interview article with Leila Waddell, *Fiddled Round the World: Australian Musician's Interesting Life*, *The Australian Woman's Mirror*, 9 December 1924.
342 *Vampire Women: Eight Pen Portraits From Life*, *Vanity Fair*, July 1915.

details regarding this are frustratingly scarce. There was tremendous political unrest in Ireland at the time, with the nation still under English rule; to many Irish nationals the advent of a global war was an opportunity to wrest freedom and independence. Waddell, being of Irish descent via her paternal grandparents, regarded herself as a patriot and was sympathetic. Unfortunately, specifics of Waddell's participation – if any – in Irish revolutionary activities in New York at this time are lost to us.

This may all be a garbled retelling or misinterpretation of what we do know: that at dawn on the morning of 3 July 1915 Crowley, Waddell, and a collective of eight of what are described as Irish-American 'revolutionaries' journeyed via thirty-foot launch from the pier at New York's West 50th Street down the Hudson towards the Statue of Liberty. Amongst said 'revolutionaries' were J Dorr, a journalist and editor, and Patrick Gilroy, described in the press as 'an Irish agitator'.[343] The remainder went unidentified in the numerous media reports detailing that morning's events.

The launch stopped offshore from Bedloe's Island, beneath the Statue of Liberty. At precisely 4.32am (the timing having been chosen for its astrological significance) Crowley, claiming to speak on behalf of the Secret Revolutionary Committee of Public Safety of the Provisional Government of the Irish Republic – an organisation he most probably invented for the occasion – embarked upon a speech in support of Irish independence:

> I have not asked any great human audience to listen to these words; I had rather address them to the unconquerable ocean that surrounds the world, and to the free four winds of heaven. Facing the sunrise, I lift up my hands and my soul herewith to this giant figure of Liberty, the ethical counterpart of the Light, Life, and Love which are our spiritual heritage. In this symbolical and most awful act of religion I invoke the one true God of whom the sun himself is but a shadow that he may strengthen me in heart and hand to uphold that freedom for the land of my sires, which I am come hither to proclaim. In this dark moment, before the father orb of our system kindles with his kiss the sea, I swear the great oath of the Revolution. I tear with my hands this token of slavery, this safe conduct from the enslaver of my people, and I renounce forever all allegiance to every alien tyrant. I swear to fight to the last drop of my blood to liberate the men and women of Ireland,

---

343 *Independence of Ireland Proclaimed From New York, The Los Angeles Times,* 13 July 1915. The same article appears in the *New York Times* on the same date, and in *The Kansas City Star* on 14 July 1915.

and I call upon the free people of this country, on whose hospitable shores I stand an exile, to give me countenance and assistance to my task of breaking those bonds which they broke for themselves 138 years ago. I unfurl the Irish flag. I proclaim the Irish Republic. Erin go Bragh. God save Ireland.[344]

The Declaration pronounced that morning stated:

1. That we put our trust and confidence in the Judge of the whole world, appealing to him to witness the rightness of our intent.

2. That, declaring England the enemy of civilisation, justice, equality and freedom, and therefore of the human race, we do hereby establish the Republic of The Men and Women of the Irish People, free and independent by right human and divine, having full power to levy war, conclude peace, contract alliance, establish commerce, and to do all other thing which independent States may of right do.

3. That we do hereby dissolve all political connection between that republic and the usurper, absolving of the allegiance to England (a) all free people of good will that are of Irish blood, (b) all free people of good will born in Ireland, (c) all free people of good will who may hereafter desire to partake of the benefits of the Irish Republic, and effectually acquire these rights by the forms provided.

4. That we do hereby declare war upon England until such time as our demands being granted, our rights recognised, and our power firmly established in our own country from which we are now exiled, we may see fit to restore to her the blessings of peace, and to extend to her the privileges of friendship.

And for the support of this declaration, with a firm and hearty reliance upon the protection of God, we mutually pledge to each other our lives, our fortunes, and our sacred honour.

---

344 Quoted in *Independence of Ireland Proclaimed From New York*, *The Los Angeles Times*, 13 July 1915. The exact same article appears in *The New York Times* on the same date, and in *The Kansas City Star* on 14 July 1915.

Long live the Irish Republic![345]

Crowley then tore up an envelope purporting to contain his passport and tossed the pieces into the waters of the Hudson below as an Irish flag was raised. Waddell soundtracked proceedings on violin, specifically *The Wearing of the Green*. Their business finished, those assembled retired to Jack's diner on Sixth Avenue and 46th Street for breakfast.

It had originally been Crowley's intention to make his speech on the steps at the base of the Statue of Liberty, and some accounts of these events this author has read have him doing precisely that, but the launch was prohibited from mooring by guards stationed there and – anticlimactically perhaps – Crowley's words were delivered from the prow of the boat. Other versions have Crowley and his companions clearly drunk for the duration.

It should be said that despite his occasional claims to the contrary Crowley was neither Irish or of Irish ancestry. The Declaration was signed 'by order and on behalf of the committee [by] Aleister Crowley, 418 [and] attested [by] L Bathurst, 11',[346] a Waddell pseudonym.

Crowley downplayed this whole event in his *Confessions of Aleister Crowley*, effectively passing it off as an elaborate practical joke and claiming that they were indeed heavily intoxicated at the time:

> It was really a minor part of my programme to wreck the German propaganda on the proof of reductio ad absurdum... Everybody assumed that the irritating balderdash I wrote for *The Fatherland* must be the stark treason that the Germans were stupid enough to think it was... I did not feel that I was advancing in the confidence of the Germans... I thought I would do something more public. I wrote a long parody on the Declaration of Independence and applied it to Ireland. I invited a young lady violinist who has some Irish blood in her... Adding to our number about four[347] other debauched persons on the verge of delirium tremens, we went out in a motor boat before dawn on the third of July to the rejected statue of Commerce for the Suez Canal, which Americans fondly suppose to be Liberty Enlightening the World. There I read my Declaration of Independence. I threw an old envelope into the bay,

345 As quoted in the article *The Irish Republic: Declaration of Independence and War in New York*, Continental Times, 11 August 1915 (and widely syndicated elsewhere).

346 As quoted in the article *The Irish Republic: Declaration of Independence and War in New York*, Continental Times, 11 August 1915 (and elsewhere).

347 Eight according to the press reports.

pretending that it was my British passport. We hoisted the Irish flag. The violinist played *The Wearing of the Green*. The crews of the interned German ships cheered us all the way up the Hudson, probably because they estimated the degree of our intoxication with scientific precision. Finally, we went to Jack's for breakfast, and home to sleep it off.[348]

Quite who to believe in the whole business, and what to make of it more than a century on, are curious issues to consider. This author frequently finds Crowley's *Confessions* unreliable, though Crowley did express disbelief therein that the incident got taken so seriously by the media, especially in England. 'Over in England there was consternation. I cannot think what had happened to their sense of humour. To pretend to take it seriously was natural enough in New York, where everybody is afraid of the Irish, not knowing what they may do next. But London was having bombs dropped on it.'[349]

℘℧

Despite Waddell and Crowley being together in New York he still had numerous relations with other partners, ranging from casual liaisons – frequently with prostitutes – to longer relationships. Soon after the Statue of Liberty stunt he was involved with a married New York poet and journalist named Jeanne Foster (1879-1970), magical name Soror Hilarion, a moniker she chose herself inspired by her Theosophical interests. Precisely what Waddell was doing during this period is unrecorded; it is possible that she was on tour or otherwise engaged with concert bookings. Foster however was clearly aware of Waddell and her place in Crowley's life; he noted in his diary on 21 September 1915 that 'H [Foster] was avoiding me though kindness for LW.'[350]

Crowley met Foster on 10 June 1915, 'ideally beautiful beyond my dearest dream and her speech was starry with spirituality',[351] though the two did not get together until 8 July. In Foster, he 'saw my ideal incarnate, and even during that first dinner we gave ourselves to each other by that

348 Aleister Crowley, *The Confessions of Aleister Crowley*, p 825.

349 Aleister Crowley, *The Confessions of Aleister Crowley*, p 825.

350 Aleister Crowley, diary, 21 September 1915.

351 Aleister Crowley, *The Confessions of Aleister Crowley*, p 876.

language of limbs whose eloquence escapes the curiosity of fellow guests.'[352]
A Theosophist with an interest in the esoteric, she was thirty-five though
like Waddell lied about her age to him, claiming to be five years younger
than she was (a not uncommon practice for women at that time). Her
marriage – to a man twenty-five years her senior – was childless and sexless
and loveless, and Crowley was not her first affair.

Crowley and Foster were much taken with each other from the outset,
he being inspired to gushing love poetry, collected (though unpublished)
under the title *The Golden Rose*. He would also later regard her as a Scarlet
Woman though quite what she did to warrant it is unclear, to this author at
least. She was far less keen on sex than he, somewhat bashful about it and
more of a romantic, enjoying the intimacy and the passion but less so the
act itself. If Crowley's diary is anything to go by she took some coaxing to
partake in his magical operations, or to bring herself to view sex in such a
fashion. Asked by him to choose an objective for a working, she replied 'the
Regeneration of Humanity', or simply 'You'. When writing up his account
of the latter episode – which took place on 12 August 1915 – Crowley noted
'This type of operation is unnecessary and frivolous in my opinion... When
she says "You" she means "Everything."'[353] He did however concede that it
'was a very great success. The elixir obtained with difficulty despite elaborate
schooling during the day was of A1 quality.'[354]

Foster's qualifying as a Scarlet Woman centred on Crowley's desire to
father a magical child with her, such being predicted by *The Book of the
Law*: 'one cometh after him, whence I say not, who shall discover the Key of
it All.'[355] She proved unable to conceive despite a working with that intent
on the 1915 autumn equinox; it is possible that she was incapable. When
Charles Stansfield Jones (1886-1950), also known as Frater Achad and a
rising star in the Vancouver lodge of the Ordo Templi Orientis, attained
the degree of Magister Templi precisely nine months later Crowley deemed
him the 'magical child' the two had created, and set about grooming Jones
as his 'son' and potential successor before they fell out in 1926, with Jones
converting to Catholicism in 1928 and later founding his own Thelemic
current centred on the goddess Maat, whose Aeon would, he alleged,
supersede the Aeon of Horus.

---

352 Ibid., p 876.

353 Ibid.

354 Quoted in *Aleister Crowley in America* by Tobias Churton, p 322.

355 *The Book of the Law*, III. 47

Crowley, Foster, and her husband Matlack Foster – who was seemingly unaware of the affair – left New York on 6 October 1915, by rail to California, with Crowley taking detours to Detroit, Chicago, Vancouver, Seattle, and Oregon along the way. In Vancouver he elevated himself in OTO degree from Magister Templi to Magus, assuming the title To Mega Therion (The Great Beast) and deeming himself Logos of the Aeon. Only seven others in world history were considered to have held such a grade – Lao Tzu, Thoth, Krishna, Gautama, Moses, Jesus, and Mohammed – putting Crowley in august company.

> The word of a Magus is always a falsehood. For it is a creative word; there would be no object in uttering it if it merely stated an existing fact in nature. The task of a Magus is to make his word, the expression of his will, come true. It is the most formidable labour that the mind can conceive.[356]

He continued west to San Francisco, Los Angeles, and San Diego. LA didn't impress him, 'the cinema crowd of cocaine-crazed, sexual lunatics, and the swarming maggots of near-occultists.'[357] By December he was back in New York.

Crowley was besotted with Foster, though she sometimes played hard to get:

> I am enjoying freely the most beautiful and voluptuous woman I have ever known. In addition, she delights me immeasurably in every way, and inspires me constantly to write poetry. She is one with me, moreover, in Spirit. And I am losing sleep wondering (a) whether she loves me (b) whether she enjoys sexual intercourse and (c) whether she has ever had another lover. If she were a simple whore I should be perfectly happy. I need medical care.[358]

He even proposed, she already being married and he engaged notwithstanding, and she accepted though this would amount to nothing. He was also still seeing Waddell, noting in his diary on 21 December 1915 'Leila's attempt to seduce me yesterday,'[359] of which Foster was aware.

---

356 Aleister Crowley, *The Confessions of Aleister Crowley*, p 879.

357 Ibid., p 846.

358 Aleister Crowley diary, 19 September 1915.

359 Ibid., 21 December 1915.

Crowley appears to have spurned Waddell's advances on this occasion which is perhaps surprising; it doesn't seem in his character to turn down an opportunity for sex.

By the end of January 1916 the affair was over, Crowley conducting a ritual banishing of Foster and replacing her that April with Alice Coomaraswamy (1885-1958), an English musician, also married though her husband appears to have been in agreement. Crowley's magical diary noted their first sexual encounter commencing 'on 15 April all the evening and continued on 16th ditto. This Operation is the most magnificent in all ways since I can remember. The Orgasm was such as to have completely drowned the memory of the Object.'[360] By June things with Coomaraswamy had also petered out, and he moved on. Foster however evidently had a lasting effect on him; on 31 May 1920 he wrote in his diary 'I have not been in love since 1915, when Jane [*sic.*] Foster inspired *The Golden Rose*. Did she really "break my heart"?'[361]

In the summer of 1916 Waddell returned to Australia to attend the funeral of her brother Wallace on 2 August. The precise cause of Wallace's death is unrecorded, only that he died at his parents' home at 64 Stewart Street, Bathurst at eight on the morning of 1 August, and 'had been ailing for a considerable time, and his death was not unexpected.'[362] He was twenty-six. That Leila Waddell got there so quickly before his death indicates that she'd been aware for a while that it was going to happen. The service, which took place at All Saints Cathedral with interment at the Church of England Cemetery, Bathurst, was reportedly well-attended, including by sisters Leila, Thelma, and Beaupre, and brothers Selwyn, Wellesley, and Beaufort, who by then held the military rank of lieutenant.

Crowley, at the time of the funeral, was staying in a cottage on the shore of Lake Pasquaney (now named Newfound Lake) near Bristol, New Hampshire, writing and undertaking what he termed a 'magical retirement,' much of it spent under the influence of peyote. He was also using ether, cocaine, opium, and possibly heroin during this period. The property belonged to astrologer and writer Evangeline Adams (1759-1932), a New York friend of Crowley's for whom he was freelancing.

---

360 Aleister Crowley, *The Magical Record of The Beast 666*, p 35.

361 Ibid., p 137.

362 *The National Advocate*, 2 August 1916. The same article notes that Wallace 'was a native of Bathurst, and for many years followed the occupation of wool-classing, in which capacity, and also in that of a private citizen, he enjoyed a large measure of esteem and popularity,' alongside mention that his siblings include 'Miss Leila Waddell, the well-known violinist.'

He remarked on 6 August in his diary that he

woke after dreaming twice that MOH [Mother of Heaven; i.e. Waddell] was dead. A close horrible night; lightning and low booming thunder. MOH is the only thing I have of value; I am not happy. She hasn't written all the week; and I know she hasn't been well. I suppose it's only a mixture of the thunder, the extreme mental fatigue and eye-strain, and possibly my new Corned Beef Croquettes. I cannot have been asleep long; an hour at most; thought it had been all night; could hardly believe combined evidence of clocks and murk.[363]

It is notable that Crowley described Waddell as 'the only thing I have of value' here, bearing in mind that he'd spent half of the previous year enamoured with Jeanne Foster and had only recently ended his affair with Alice Coomaraswamy. Leila Waddell was evidently the one woman he couldn't let go of.

Precisely how long Waddell stayed in Australia before returning to America is unclear, though return she did later that same year. It being a time of war and with German U-boats torpedoing shipping lanes, sea travel was a treacherous business, though no doubt passage from Australia to America was safer than it was from Europe. Crowley meanwhile maintained his journal, with sporadic gaps. A sex working with Waddell had been detailed on 25 February 1916 – i.e. in between the Jeanne Foster and Alice Coomaraswamy affairs – noted as being 'very good considering long restraint'[364] and with the objective of 'power over LXXVI' (unidentified, though very possibly Foster). Result was 'failure, I suppose', with Crowley also noting that 'Laylah hated LXXVI'. A further working with Waddell on 1 March at 9.50am was only vaguely described, merely with an objective of 'Thanks be unto the Lord!', along with one on 10 June, two weeks prior to Crowley's departure for Lake Pasquaney and noted as 'Operation: fair. Elixir: admirable.' Workings were documented to the end of the year with a variety of different partners as Crowley travelled throughout America, ranging from Philadelphia to Washington to Boston to Los Angeles to San Francisco and other points between. Operations on 7 and 17-18 November 1916 were recorded with the objective 'help for Soror LW [Leila Waddell]'

---

363 Aleister Crowley, diary, 6 August 1916.

364 All quotes in this paragraph are from Aleister Crowley's *The Magical Record of The Beast 666*, p 33-45.

and 'Help for LW' respectively, though why help was needed was not elaborated upon. Both occasions involved anal sex, the first with Anna Grey, 'P [prostitute]. Big fat negress, very passionate,' the second an unspecified partner. A result of 'immediate success' was recorded on 7 November but in what capacity or what this boded for Waddell was again not stated.

Crowley's notebook for December 1916 (located in the Yorke Collection at the Warburg Institute in London) features on its inside front cover a list handwritten in pencil of women with whom he had slept. Though this list does not appear to be strictly chronological, Waddell features twenty-first out of fifty-two. This likely does not include the numerous prostitutes with whom he also had sex. Crowley's infidelities throughout the Waddell relationship were myriad, though as previously noted fidelity was a concept in which he did not believe. One is left wondering what his reaction would have been had Waddell had as many other lovers during their relationship, and if he would have accepted it.

In New Orleans in 1917 Crowley wrote his first novel *Moonchild*, working title *The Butterfly Net*, which was not published until 1929. 'In this novel I have given an elaborate description of modern magical theories and practices. Most of the characters are real people whom I have known and many of the incidents taken from experience.'[365] Simon Iff, a recurring character in occult detective stories of Crowley's, leads a group of white magicians in a struggle against a black magic lodge. The main villain of the piece was based on Crowley's former Golden Dawn initiator Samuel Liddell MacGregor Mathers. Other Crowley friends and acquaintances appear under pseudonyms, including Allan Bennett (as Mahatera Phang), Isadora Duncan[366] (as Lavinia King), Everard Feilding (as Anthony Bowling), Mary Desti (as Lisa la Giuffria), and Crowley himself (as Cyril Grey). The narrative centres around la Giuffria and a plan to impregnate her with an otherworldly being, the eponymous moonchild. Waddell features under the name Sister Cybele,[367] a member of Iff and Grey's occult order, though unfortunately there isn't much in the book's slim plot for her to do:

> The face of this woman was of extreme beauty, in a certain esoteric fancy. Like her whole body, it was sturdy and vigorous, but there

365 Aleister Crowley, *The Confessions of Aleister Crowley*, p 852.

366 About whom Crowley was less than flattering; 'I used to know her pretty well myself. She was, even in those days, vulgar, stupid, heartless, and mercenary; she was a sponger, the worst type of courtesan; and she was an intolerable poseuse." Aleister Crowley, *Moonchild*, p 25.

367 Cybele being the name of the Anatolian mother goddess.

was infinite delicacy, surprising in so strong a model. Her eyes were clear and fearless and true; but one could see that they must have served her ill indeed often enough, for they were evidently capable of understanding falsity and evil. The nose was straight and broad, full of energy; and the mouth passionate and firm. The lips were somewhat thick, but they were mobile; and the whole expression of the face redeemed any defect of any feature. For while its general physical aspect was severe, even savage – she might have been a Tartar beauty, the bride of a Genghis Khan, or a South Sea Island Queen, tossing her lovers into the crater of Mauna Loa after killing them in the excess and fantasy of her passion – yet the soul within shone out and turned the swords to ploughshares. There was pride, indeed, but only of that kind which is (as it were) the buckler on the arms of nobility; the woman was incapable of meanness, of treachery, or even of unkindness.[368]

ℴ℞

Though Waddell and Crowley are often reported to have parted ways in 1916 this looks not to have been the case; a poem to her appeared in the December 1917 issue of *The International*, a monthly sister-journal to *The Fatherland* devoted to the arts and since July 1917 edited – and also largely written under multiple pseudonyms – by Crowley (freelance writing aside, editorship of *The International* was the first and only paid job ever held by him. He earned $20 a week).

Titled *A Septennial* in celebration of the seventh anniversary of Waddell and Crowley's meeting, the poem may have been composed earlier in the year, bearing in mind that they met around March of 1910. Precisely what to make of this poem and where it fits in to their relationship such as it was then is difficult to say; Waddell was clearly still an object of affection for Crowley, but if his magical diary is any indication they weren't having sex any more (not that he wasn't having a great deal of sex, with many and varied partners). Regardless of the numerous women that had come and gone throughout their relationship – some of whom Crowley would deem Scarlet Women and significant to his magical work – he still loved Waddell if the evidence of A Septennial is to be believed.

---

368 Aleister Crowley, *Moonchild*, p 76-77.

A Septennial

I.
Seven times has Saturn swung his scythe;
    Seven sheaves stand in the field of Time,
And every sheaf's as bright and blithe
    As the sharp shifts of our sublime
Father the sun. I leap so lithe
            My love today,
            My love, I may
Not tell the tithe.

II.
"But these were seven stormy years!"
    "Lean years were these, as Pharaoh's kine!"
All shapes of Life that mortal fears
    Passed shrieking. We distilled to wine
The vintage of blood and tears.
            We tore away
            The cloak of grey –
The sun uprears!

III.
We know today what once we guessed,
    Our love no dream of idle youth;
A world-egg, with the stars for nest,
    Is this arch-testament of truth.
Laylah, beloved, to my breast!
            Our period
            Is fixed in God –
Eternal rest!

Seven was a significant number for Crowley, especially with regard
to Waddell; he considered 77 her number, that by which her name could
be rendered, 'the subtle and supreme septenary in its mature magical
manifestation through matter.'[369] Despite references to Waddell as 'my love'
and 'beloved', and to 'our love no dream of idle youth', it will immediately
be noted that the tone of *A Septennial* is muted compared to Crowley's

369 Aleister Crowley, *The Book of Lies*, p 164.

previous works in homage to her. The reference to 'our period... fixed in God – Eternal rest!' suggests that their love was effectively at an end; only the line 'to my breast!' gives hope of future passion.

To further complicate matters in the Crowley/Waddell relationship and whether they even still had one and if so in what capacity, on 1 October 1917 – two months prior to *A Septennial*'s publication – Crowley met Roddie Minor (1884-1979), who he swiftly proclaimed his next Scarlet Woman, Soror Ahitha, nickname Eve. A chemist by profession and separated from her husband, Crowley noted her as

> a near artist of German extraction. She was physically a magnificent animal, with a man's brain well stocked with general knowledge and a special comprehension of chemistry and pharmacy... She was more frantically feminine than any avowed woman could possibly be. She was ruthlessly irrational.[370]

The two were soon cohabiting at 64a West 9th Street in Greenwich Village, New York, with Minor acting as seer in an extended sequence of drugs- and booze-fuelled sex magick workings, many involving astral contact with a discarnate being named Amalantrah, until they parted ways in the summer of 1918.

In 1918 another woman Crowley would deem Scarlet came and went, the Russian Marie Röhling[371] (1891-1969), also known as Marie Lavroff, magical name Soror Olun. Crowley cited her as being inspirational in the creation of *Liber CXI*, also known as *Liber Aleph*, 'an extended and elaborate commentary on *The Book of the Law*, in the form of a letter from the Master Therion to his magical son.[372] This Book contains some of the deepest secrets of initiation, with a clear solution to many cosmic and ethical problems.'[373] *Liber Aleph* was written between January and March 1918. Röhling met Crowley in mid-March 1918 and her time with him was brief, overlapping with that of Roddie Minor; some group sex workings between the three (and with others) are indicated. Quite what qualified her as a Scarlet Woman is unclear to this author; if merely being inspirational was enough, Leila Waddell should also have counted as a Scarlet Woman.

---

370 Aleister Crowley, *The Confessions of Aleister Crowley*, p 857.

371 Born Maria Eliasberg or Elsburg in Odessa, her surname was sometimes also spelled Roehling.

372 Charles Stansfield Jones, as the reader may recall from earlier in this chapter.

373 Aleister Crowley, source unknown.

Even Crowley himself seemed uncertain, later describing her as 'a doubtful case... Marie... who gave nothing, anyhow, and soon abandoned the unequal contest,'[374] though in In *Liber Aleph* itself he wrote

> My Son, I am enflamed with Love... For but now, when I cried out upon the Name Olun, which is the secret Name of my Lady that hath come to me – most strangely! – then I was rapt away altogether subtly yet fiercely into a Trance that hath transformed me with Attainment, yet without Trace in Mind... My Lady Olun hath brought unto me upon this last Day of the Winter of the thirteenth Year of the Aeon, even as I wrote these Words unto thee, is a Mystery of Mysteries beyond all these. Oh my son, thou knowest well the Perils and the Profit of our Path; continue thou therein. Olun! MAPIE! BABALON! Adsum.[375]

ॐ

As noted much of the journal *The International* was written by Crowley under numerous pseudonyms. Articles credited to 'Hautboy' or 'Haut Boy' however were most likely written by Waddell. Hautboy/Haut Boy pieces appeared in the November and December 1917 and January and February 1918 editions and were reports of musical events around New York. *The Hippodrome Horror: A Nightmare Drama*, a sketch credited to Waddell and featuring Hautboy as a character, can be found in the March 1918 issue. Also credited to Waddell under her own name was the music write-up in the April 1918 edition, and the May 1918 one – the last to be edited by Crowley – featured an account of an encounter with the violinist Leopold Auer (1845-1930), who Waddell studied under, attributed to Leila Bathurst. As to how the tutelage under Auer came about, a 1924 article for *The Australian Woman's Mirror* tells us that

> [Waddell] wanted to become a pupil of Auer but before the maestro would discuss the matter of tuition one had to pay 25 dollars for getting the great man to listen. For her trial piece Miss Waddell chose Schumann's *Abendlied*, because she felt she could play it even in her sleep. Auer accompanied her; but they did not get far.

---

374 Aleister Crowley, *The Magical Record of The Beast 666*, p 145.

375 Aleister Crowley, *Liber Aleph*, online edition. <https://sacred-texts.com/oto/aleph_index.htm>

'You are out of tune', he complained. They made four attempts and then the Australian girl, nervous and overwrought, said, 'If you say I'm out of tune, I must be, but I cannot understand it; my violin is in perfect tune and I've played the *Abendlied* thousands of times.' 'Ha, ha!' laughed the great man, 'it is that you are playing in two sharps and I am playing in the original key of five flats.' The incident made them friends and Auer accepted her for a pupil. 'What are your fees?' she enquired. 'Twenty-five roubles!' 'Oh, that is fine,' said Miss Waddell, who had just come from Russia. 'Oh, I mean dollars.' 'That is a tragedy,' complained the girl, who had mentally seen herself having limitless lessons from the great man.[376]

That Crowley featured so many Waddell-written pieces in *The International* strongly suggests the two were very much still in contact and on good terms.

The November 1917 edition of *The International* also featured the Crowley story *The Hearth*, published under the pseudonym Mark Wells. A handwritten note by Gerald Yorke on Crowley's original manuscript for this story (located in the Yorke Collection at the Warburg Institute in London) states that it was dedicated to Waddell – though the text as published in *The International* carries no mention of her – who Yorke incorrectly describes as Crowley's 'second wife'. *The Hearth* was intended by Crowley for an unpublished collection, *Golden Twigs*, a title styled after James Fraser's *The Golden Bough*. He mentions in *The Confessions of Aleister Crowley*[377] that also scheduled for this collection was a story named *The Stone of Cybele*, Cybele being the name of the character based on Waddell in his novel *Moonchild*.

The last public mention of Crowley and Waddell together that we find is from an unspecified date in 1918, as related in a sensationalistic article by journalist William Seabrook[378] whom both met in New York that year, having been introduced to him by mutual friend Frank Harris. The article was not published until 29 April 1923 in *The Indianapolis Star Sun*, under the remarkable title *Astounding Secrets of the Devil Worshippers' Mystic*

---

376 Interview with Leila Waddell in the article *Fiddled Round the World: Australian Musician's Interesting Life*, *The Australian Woman's Mirror*, 9 December 1924.

377 Aleister Crowley, *The Confessions of Aleister Crowley*, p 889.

378 William Buehler Seabrook (1864-1946) was a journalist and newspaper editor. He and Crowley were good friends for a while, with Crowley sleeping with his wife Kate with his consent and staying with the Seabrooks at their property at Decatur near Atlanta, Georgia in September and October 1919.

Love Cult: Revealing the Intimate Details of Aleister Crowley's Unholy Rites, His Power Over Women Whom He Branded and Enslaved, His Poetry and Mysticisms, His Startling Adventures Around the Globe as the Beast of the Apocalypse.

Seabrook described Waddell as being

> under the influence of this strange cult... Leila Waddell, the beautiful violinist and noted concert artist, who was Crowley's 'high priestess' when he was at the height of his fame in England, openly holding elaborate 'mystical rites', attended by many notables, in the big town house he occupied at the time.[379]

The article recounts a meeting with Crowley in New York in 1918 at which he spoke of Waddell:

> From a little iron-bound trunk which contained pictures and clippings about himself and the doings of his cult, saved from old magazines and newspapers, he produced a portrait of Leila Waddell, the beautiful violinist. From the details of the picture and from the text underneath, I judged that Miss Waddell had been a 'priestess' of the 'OTO' cult while it was at its zenith in England – at the time when Isadora Duncan, the dancer, Augustus John, the painter, and Aimée Gourand[380] were attracted to the ceremonial rites in Crowley's London house – attracted, no doubt, by their artistic beauty without knowing anything of the hidden mysteries behind them.
>
> Miss Waddell, in the photo-engraving, was shown clad in a mystical robe, bare-footed, seated upon a throne, wearing upon her head and chest the insignia of the 'OTO'.[381] The picture was from *The Sketch*, one of London's leading magazines dealing with society and art...

---

379 *Indianapolis Star Sun*, 29 April 1923.

380 Aimée Gourand (1864-1941), also known as Aimée Crocker, was a famed American Bohemian and mystic. Wealthy from an early age due to an inheritance, she was best-known for her lavish lifestyle and parties, her travels and lovers and numerous husbands. Her affair with Crowley lasted the best part of a decade on and off, and he proposed to her without success on more than one occasion.

381 Seabrook clearly has the timeline garbled here; the *Sketch* article was from 1910, three years before Crowley and Waddell became involved with the OTO. He is getting confused between the OTO and A∴A∴.

Other photographs of Miss Waddell, I discovered afterward, appeared in several volumes of Crowley's mystical books – always in the garb and role of a 'priestess' of the cult.

A week later – true to his promise – [Crowley] took me to meet Miss Waddell, who had just arrived in America[382] – in fact, to have tea with her. It was in a hotel just off Fifth Avenue, in her own apartment. She proved to be a lovely, cultured woman, a charming hostess and a brilliant musician, for I later heard her play exquisitely.

We talked of many things, but I didn't quite dare bring up directly in my conversation with her such a subject as magic. It seemed utterly impossible that two such cultured, well-bred, thoroughly modern and cosmopolitan English persons [sic.], as she and Crowley were at that moment, could have anything in common with the strange beings of whom I had glimpses – and more than glimpses – during my acquaintance with Crowley and his books.[383]

80 CR

It is not known precisely when Crowley and Waddell parted ways, or whether there was a single event or cause which precipitated their separation. It is stated in some sources to have been largely due to his numerous affairs throughout the relationship, and she is said to have been 'genuinely distressed when she found herself replaced',[384] but this is speculation; in truth we don't know. If finding 'herself replaced' was indeed the instigating event perhaps the cohabitation with Roddie Minor in 1917 was key, though bearing in mind the *Septennial* poem and Waddell's contributions to *The International*, clearly she and Crowley remained friendly until at least mid-1918.

Whether there was any bitterness on Waddell's part regarding the separation is also not recorded, but there was on Crowley's if the evidence of *The Confessions of Aleister Crowley* – written in the nineteen-twenties – is anything to go by. Despite the depth and duration of their love she is scarce-mentioned therein, and in most entries which do concern her he is critical, to the extent that the reader is left wondering why he kept her in his life for

---

382 Though from where she had travelled, or for what purpose – likely one or another concert tour or booking – is not recorded.

383 *Indianapolis Star Sun*, 29 April 1923.

384 James Laver, *Museum Piece: The Education of an Iconographer*, p 117.

as long as he did, and why he wrote the likes of the love-struck *Book of Lies* or the soppy and smitten birthday poems for her, if he truly felt the way he claimed to have done after the event. He is sniping about her ability on violin, her intelligence, her Australian accent and diction, her career ambitions. Of her ancestry he says that she 'had some Irish blood in her, behind the more evident stigmata of the ornithorhynchus[385] and the wombat.'[386]

It is worth noting that of all the women throughout Crowley's life Waddell lasted the longest, her time with him spanning seven or possibly eight years from 1910 to 1917 or 1918. She outlasted both his most famous Scarlet Women, the two of whom coincidentally bookended his relationship with her; Rose Kelly (six years between 1903 and 1909) and Leah Hirsig (five years from 1919 to 1924).

Waddell remained in New York, residing at 97 Elliott Avenue, Yonkers, and continued to give public performances. Friends to her in this period included the writers Theodore Dreiser[387] and Rebecca West.[388] Frank Harris was also a friend at this time, and it was later said that 'one of Leila Waddell's chief treasures is a signed first copy of Frank Harris' work on Shakespeare. She knows the famous littérateur well, and visited his Wednesday musical afternoons in America regularly.'[389]

---

385 Ornithorhynchus anatinus; the Latin name for the platypus.

386 Aleister Crowley, *The Confessions of Aleister Crowley*, p 825.

387 Theodore Dreiser (1871-1945) was an American author, poet, and short story writer best known for his novels *An American Tragedy, Sister Carrie, The Genius, The Financier,* and *Jennie Gerhardt.*

Dreiser had also met Crowley in New York in 1915 – possibly with Waddell present – and was introduced to peyote by him. Before taking the drug for the first time Dreiser asked Crowley whether there was a doctor in the neighbourhood to which Crowley replied that there was 'a first-class undertaker on the corner of 33rd Street and Sixth Avenue.' Dreiser was silent a moment, then responded 'I don't like that kind of joke, Crowley.'

388 Rebecca West (1892-1983) was an English novelist, journalist, and travel writer. She wrote in a variety of genres, and her journalism was widely published in England and the US. Today she is probably best-remembered for her non-fiction books *A Train of Powder* (based on her coverage of the post-World War Two Nuremberg trials), *The Meaning of Treason,* and *Black Lamb and Grey Falcon,* and her novels *The Return of the Soldier, The Fountain Overflows, The Birds Fall Down,* and *This Real Night.* Resident in England, she travelled extensively to America in the 1920s and beyond and is said to have had a number of relationships, including with Charlie Chaplin and H G Wells.

389 *A Woman of Talent, Truth (Brisbane).* 23 November 1924

Waddell stayed in America for the remainder of the war and into the early nineteen-twenties. Though past writers have largely been silent regarding this period of her life, an interview article in *The Australian Woman's Mirror* from 1924 sheds light on what she was doing:

> The war necessitated her making her headquarters in America. There she played everything from concertos with symphony orchestras to rag-time. She toured from coast to coast playing first violin and viol d'amore in *The Beggar's Opera*, and also appearing in vaudeville. But it was as cook and hostess that Leila Waddell had her most trying moment. She was acting hostess for the New American Club when Kreisler[390] was the honoured guest, and she suffered agonies of mind as to how the luncheon was going to turn out. However, Daisy Kennedy[391] told her all Kreisler's favourite dishes, and she cooked the luncheon herself. The fact that she and the famous violinist became friends proved that the cooking was a success. Miss Waddell says that Kreisler is as great a personality as he is a violinist – a most simple, kindly man, and ever ready to help any young musician along. He told her that every time he felt rusty he went to Boston for a few days to get polished up by Winternitz, who was a colleague of his and a great violinist before he lost his nerve in a railway accident and took to teaching. He advised Miss Waddell to try and study with Winternitz, and this she means to do as soon as she sees a clear year before her.[392]

Precise concert dates for Waddell for much of this period however are difficult to pin down. She is known to have appeared at Proctor's Fifth Avenue Theatre on 19 February 1918 for example, though details aren't given, and other performances in New York and beyond are clear.

Waddell's brother Wellesley died on 25 June 1919 aged twenty-five, a victim of the then on-going global flu pandemic. Also known as the Great Influenza Epidemic or Spanish Flu, it killed anywhere between seventeen and fifty million people globally – a more precise figure is not known – making

---

390 Friedrich 'Fritz' Kreisler (1875-1962} was born in Vienna though spent much of his life in America. He was widely regarded as one of the finest violinists of his era.

391 Daisy Kennedy was an Australian violinist born in 1893. She performed extensively throughout Europe and America. The grandmother of famed English violinist Nigel Kennedy, she died in 1981.

392 Interview article with Leila Waddell, *Fiddled Round the World: Australian Musician's Interesting Life*, *The Australian Woman's Mirror*, 9 December 1924.

it one of the deadliest ever disease pandemics, taking more lives than the First World War that immediately preceded it. At the time Wellesley and sister Beaupre were staying with a Reverend and Mrs H H Pritchard at the Rectory in Grenfell, Australia. Beaupre became sick and Wellesley nursed her, falling ill himself to pneumonic influenza. Her health improved but his didn't, and he died twenty-four hours later, being buried the same day at Grenfell Cemetery. It had been his parents' wish to have the body returned to Bathurst to be interred next to his brother Wallace who had died in 1916, but as was the custom during the pandemic he was buried on the day of his death. Like his sisters Leila and Beaupre, Wellesley was also musically gifted, making regular concert appearances and possessed of 'a fine tenor voice... The deceased young man was for many years a valued member of All Saints Cathedral choir. On many occasions he sang at local functions, and possessed a winning personality... He was an excellent and highly appreciated chorister.'[393] It is possible that Leila Waddell travelled to Australia for her brother's funeral; notices of his death in the Sydney newspapers mentioned her 'returning from a musical tour abroad.'[394] Whether she did or not, she was definitely in America in August 1919, as note is made in the 8 August edition of *The Kansas City Star* of her then staying with her sister Emmeline and husband Dr Edward Curran in that city.

Waddell likely returned to England in late summer or autumn 1919; *The Sydney Morning Herald* of 1 October speaks of 'Miss Leila Waddell, the Australian violinist now in London.'[395] By 20 October she was in California, where *The Riverside Daily Press* wrote that 'Mrs H W Hammond and Miss Olga Hammond entertained informally at tea in honour of their house guests, [including] Miss Leila Waddell of Bathurst, New South Wales, Australia and more recently of New York City.'[396] Though it is probable that Waddell was in California for concert bookings, we don't know for certain. She was also 'the guest of Mr and Mrs Ernest Belcher[397] at their home on Orange Drive. Miss Waddell will remain here until the arrival of her brother, Beaufort, an Australian war hero. The two will then leave for New York.'[398]

393 *The Grenfell Record and Lachlan District Advertiser*, 1 July 1919.

394 Ibid.

395 *The Sydney Morning Herald*, 1 October 1919.

396 *The Riverside Daily Press*, 20 October 1919.

397 An English choreographer and ballet dancer who worked in vaudeville, largely in London, before founding the Celeste School of Dancing in Los Angeles in 1916, providing dancers to Hollywood. His students included Fred Astaire and Cyd Charisse.

398 *The Los Angeles Herald*, 15 November 1919.

Waddell further made the Australian newspapers in October 1919 with the announcement that 'Miss Leila Waddell, the Australian violinist now doing excellent work in America, will return to Sydney in November. She has been absent from Australia for 19 years,[399] and prior to the war played in all the big cities of Europe.'[400] Quite what the purpose of her Australian return was is not specified, nor how long she stayed; perhaps it was simply to spend time with her grieving family. The record is silent and we next find her back in America in 1921, where she performed at St John's Church, Yonkers, New York on 7 December. An article in *The Yonkers Statesman and News*, 5 December, stated under the header 'Australian Violinist at St John's Choir Concert' that

St John's Church choir certainly needs no introduction to the people of Yonkers. This fine choir of 40 trained singers will give their annual concert of secular music in St John's Parish House, Getty Square, Wednesday evening, Dec 7 at 8:15 o'clock... Leila Waddell, Australian violinist, has been secured as the soloist. Miss Waddell has played at all the big cities of Europe, as well as this country, with success. She is a pupil of Emile Sauret, a great French teacher.[401]

For her part in this show Waddell performed *Berceuse* by Benjamin Godard, *Serenade* by Gabriel Pierne, Camille Saint-Saëns' *Le Cygne*, and *Poem Hongrolme* by Lederer.

Waddell most likely made other concert appearances in America in the early nineteen-twenties though this author has been unable to locate many specific details. She appeared at the Tarrytown, New York YMCA on the afternoon of 30 December 1921 and at West Side YMCA on 318 West Street, New York in March 1922. On 24 March 1922 she performed with the New York Symphony Orchestra at Aeolian Hall on 28 West 43rd Street, and at the Men's Club of Grace Church on 18 April 1922 where she was 'very pleasing in a number of selections and encores.'[402] She featured again at Aeolian Hall on 3 May 1923, at

the first of the much-anticipated interracial concerts of folk song and folk dances, given in costume by the New Music Week

---

399 Actually eleven, having departed Australia in 1908.

400 *The Daily Telegraph* (Sydney), 1 October 1919 (and elsewhere).

401 *The Yonkers Statesman and News*, 5 December 1921.

402 *Long Island Daily Press*, 19 April 1922.

Interracial Committee, of which Felix M Warburg is honorary chairman... The boxes of Aeolian Hall were occupied by the consuls general of the nearly forty different nationalities represented. They were gay with the flags of each nation of each consul general, and adjoining each consul general's box was another for his nation's patronesses, draped with American flags, these patronesses being American citizens. The sentiment was interesting; it was well carried out and it gave the well-known auditorium a gala and most unusual appearance.[403]

In October 1923 Waddell's article *Two Anzacs Meet in London*, detailing her friendship with Katherine Mansfield, was published in the journal *Shadowland: Expressing the Arts*.

...she speaks tenderly of the fragile beauty of Katherine Mansfield, her charm of manner, her deep, rather tragic insight of life. The two artists met in London when they were both on the upward struggle, and being New Zealanders, [*sic.*][404] a firm bond of friendship was woven between them.

'We were great friends,' Waddell said of Mansfield. 'Few people knew her as I did, and how the great grief of her life, the death of her beloved brother at the war,[405] changed so completely the whole of her outlook, and eventually was responsible for her own passing over. She never ceased to mourn him, and her one thought afterwards was, how soon she could join him beyond the grave. This state of mind contributed to her death, because she made no fight to live when her health broke down. The book world has lost a brilliant member. She was regarded as quite exceptionally gifted. I was privileged to write her life sketch.'[406]

Despite this, she never felt that she got to know the real Mansfield:

403 *The Morning Telegraph*, New York, 4 May 1923.

404 Even back then, the myth that Waddell was from New Zealand can sometimes be found.

405 Mansfield's brother Leslie Beauchamp was killed in October 1915 on the Ypres Salient in Belgium while on a grenade training exercise.

406 Leila Waddell, quoted in the article *A Bathurst Girl's Tour Abroad*, *Bathurst Times*, 12 June 1924.

She really was remarkable. She knew such fine things about the lowliest of people – London bus-men, charwomen and so on. How she found these things out I never could tell. To meet her was to me always an excitement, and I was for ever wondering if I would eventually pierce the chilly wall and get to the real Katherine.[407]

It is often stated that Waddell had something of a second career as a writer in this period, contributing stories and articles to journals in America and in London, though Waddell herself downplayed the extent of her literary involvement:

Curiously, it was through this article [on Katherine Mansfield] that I achieved what is really an undeserved reputation for being a newspaper woman. I think I possess a flair for writing, and I wrote of my friend with the sure pen of love and understanding, but I had never contemplated abandoning my fiddle for a typewriter. Nevertheless, a New Yorker of enterprise settled the matter for me by offering me a fee of 500 dollars for 4000 words for a special story. The data was supplied by a prominent New York society woman, who had undergone the famous gland treatment, and with the happiest results. It seemed such plain sailing; such easy money, and I thought, I shall like this. But there's a 'but' in everything, isn't there. My commissioner said: 'But, you must sign your name to the article.' Not for 20,000 dollars,' was my reply. So my writing career was merely potential. They called it good advertisement, cutting two ways. I called it something else, and so we differed, for an artist doesn't own herself after all, and I owed so much to my name and established reputation.[408]

In November 1923 Waddell helped dispose of her uncle's violin collection, with note being made in *The Northern Star of Lismore*, New South Wales, that

'My uncle's most prized treasure,' Waddell herself remarked in a 1924 newspaper interview, 'was the world-famous Betts Strad. which he bought for £1,900 years ago from Hart and Sons. It was

407 Leila Waddell, quoted in *Fiddled Round the World: Australian Musician's Interesting Life*, *The Australian Woman's Mirror*, 9 December 1924.

408 Leila Waddell, quoted in the article *A Bathurst Girl's Tour Abroad*, *Bathurst Times*, 12 June 1924.

included in the collection which I sold to Rudolph Wurlitzer in New York for 275,000 dollars, and the Betts was almost at once acquired by Mr Roberts, president of the Philharmonic Orchestra at Hartford (Conn) for £55,000. The famous 'Le Duc' Guarnerius was secured for £75,000. It is believed to be the most wonderful example in existence for largeness and sweetness of tone. There were a lot more, and I have myself a very fine Amati, the date of which is '1630 something' (I forget the exact year), but it is supposed by the date and form to be by the great Nicole Amati, the most famous of the Brescian family. New York is full of crooks, and I was much relieved when these valuable art treasures ceased to be in my possession.[409]

Waddell was set to return to Australia in 1924, though some memories of her time in America would forever remain.

With all my wanderings, and all my achievements the happiest musical moments have been those during which, I, with others, played to factory hands in luncheon hours, in cities of USA. America is really a musical country. That is explained partly by the fact that the population is polyglot, and those who have migrated, and belong to the Latin and Slav countries, will sing whatever happens. The YMCA engineered these mid-day recitals. They were unique. We played in barns and sheds and in gardens. Sometimes we would just play a simple aria, and the men would join in and sing. Again it would be almost concerto, with violin, organ and the voices of the massed men; magnificent and thrilling. I loved it so. They had no way of saying 'Thank you,' except now and again a handful of flowers; not the hothouse variety, but the common kind, some that had grown by the hedge and roadside, more often than not. These musicians were great lessons in the value and beauty of human intercourse. I have played to the mighty and the rich and the poor and the humble. I like to think that my Amati and I till now have shared a secret. We'll let the world into that secret now. Playing for those simple souls is the greatest and truest happiness, and the best service that I have known in my career.[410]

409 Leila Waddell, quoted in the *Sydney Morning Herald*, 31 May 1924.
410 Leila Waddell, quoted in the article *A Bathurst Girl's Tour Abroad, Bathurst Times*, 12 June 1924.

ℵℷ

And as for Aleister Crowley? He spent the remainder of World War One in America, coming under criticism for his *Fatherland* articles at the war's end. He maintained that he'd written them as a means of infiltrating and undermining the American pro-German movement as a spy and for the benefit of British intelligence, and his stunt before the Statue of Liberty in July 1915 where he proclaimed support for an Irish republic was framed as part of his propaganda campaign. 'I am an essentially moderate man,' he wrote in *The Fatherland*'s 11 August 1915 issue. 'I refuse to take sides in any controversy. I observe dispassionately, sit in judgment. My own Fatherland is the Sun, and while I am travelling on this planet I never forget it... I am not pro-German. I am pro-human.'[411]

In 1918 Crowley – then resident at 1 University Place, Washington Square, New York – met Leah Hirsig,[412] a Manhattan music teacher destined to be his next Scarlet Woman, initiating her in January 1919. She took the magical name Alostrael, meaning 'the womb / grail of God'. Crowley was much taken with Hirsig's genitalia, later referring to her vagina as the distinctly unromantic-sounding 'Hirsig vacuum pump'.[413] She embraced Thelema with great enthusiasm. 'I dedicate myself wholly to the Great Work,' she wrote in her 1921 diary. 'I will work for wickedness, I will kill my heart, I will be shameless before all men, I will freely prostitute my body to all creatures.'[414] She also inspired new poetry from Crowley, including the pornographic *Leah*

---

411 Aleister Crowley, *A Great Irish Poet's Indorsement* [sic.] *of The Fatherland*, published in *The Fatherland*, 11 August 1915.

412 Leila Waddell and Rose Kelly aside, Leah Hirsig is undoubtedly the most famed woman in Crowley's story. Born in 1883 and long-interested in the occult when she met him, the two would be together for five years, and have a daughter, Anne Léa, born in January 1920, who lived less than ten months, dying in a Palermo hospital while Crowley and Hirsig were resident at the Abbey of Thelema in Cefalù. Following her denouncement of Crowley and abandonment of Thelema she returned to America in December 1929, converted to Catholicism, and resumed her teaching career, before relocating to Switzerland in the nineteen-seventies where she died in 1975 aged ninety-one.

413 Aleister Crowley, *The Magical Record of The Beast 666*, p 252.

414 Leah Hirsig, magical diary, 1921. Hirsig clearly knew *The Book of the Law* well; her words echo the III.44 passage describing the Scarlet Woman: 'But let her raise herself in pride! Let her follow me in my way! Let her work the work of wickedness! Let her kill her heart! Let her be loud and adulterous! Let her be covered with jewels, and rich garments, and let her be shameless before all men!'

Sublime, precisely 666 words in length and with its famed lines 'Stab your demoniac / Smile to my brain! / Soak me in cognac / Cunt and cocaine.'[415]

Crowley returned to England on 21 December 1919, amid controversy from the British media for his seeming support of Germany during the war.[416] The poverty in which he was then living meant he lacked the funds to sue the publications accusing him of treachery. He later recalled being

> amazed... when my patriotism was doubted... I am perfectly aware that I am irrational. The traditions of England are intertwined inextricably with a million abuses and deformities which I am only too eager to destroy. But all Englishmen keep their brains in watertight compartments... I am quite prepared to die for England in that brutal, unthinking way. *Rule, Britannia* gets me going as if I were the most ordinary music-hall audience. This sentiment is not interfered with by my detestation of the moral and religious humbug which one is expected to produce at moments of national crisis.[417]

He moved on to Paris with Hirsig in January 1920, though not before he'd acquired a heroin habit in London after a doctor prescribed the drug for his asthma and bronchitis. Crowley evidently thought addiction a weakness of character, and that anybody who had mastered their True Will should easily be able to exhibit control over drugs. As *The Book of the Law* states,

> I am the Snake that giveth Knowledge & Delight and bright glory, and stir the hearts of men with drunkenness. To worship me take

---

415 Crowley was so fond of these lines that he later painted them on the wall of his room at the Abbey of Thelema in Cefalù.

416 The journal *The John Bull* took particular exception, writing in its 10 January 1920 issue that 'we have heard that the traitorous degenerate, Aleister Crowley, is anxious to sneak back to the land he has sought to defile. Crowley is no stranger to the columns of John Bull. As long ago as November 1910, we pilloried this man for his bestial posturings and his disgusting blasphemies. He was then, forsooth, the inventor of a new religion, with its pseudo-teaching supposed to be derived from the medieval alchemists, and its licentious cult in which dark rooms, impressionable women and poems recited to throbbing music played their appointed part... Now we ask, in all seriousness, can such a dirty renegade be permitted to return to the country he has spurned and insulted? We await reassurance from the Home Office or the Foreign Office that steps are being taken to arrest the renegade or prevent his infamous feet from ever again polluting our shores.'

417 Aleister Crowley, *The Confessions of Aleister Crowley*, p 90.

wine and strange drugs whereof I will tell my prophet, & be drunk thereof! They shall not harm ye at all. It is a lie, this folly against self. The exposure of innocence is a lie. Be strong, o man! lust, enjoy all things of sense and rapture: fear not that any God shall deny thee for this.[418]

Crowley's own addictions embarrassed him.

From France Crowley and Hirsig relocated to Italy, founding the Abbey of Thelema in Cefalù, Sicily on 2 April 1920. The place was remote, Cefalù a small coastal village with the nearest sizeable town, Palermo, being forty miles east. It was intended as

an archetype of a new society. The main ethical principle is that each human being has his own definite object in life. He has every right to fulfil this purpose, and none to do anything else. It is the business of the community to help each of its members to achieve this aim; in consequence all rules should be made, and all questions of policy decided, by the application of this principle to the circumstance. We have thus made a clean sweep of all the rough and ready codes of convention which have characterised past civilisations.[419]

The term 'Abbey' gives the impression of a greater scale and grandeur than it had, the building itself being little more than a six-room farmhouse. Crowley lived there for three years with Hirsig and a number of his students and was content for a while; 'I care nothing for public opinion. I care nothing for fame or success. I am perfectly happy in my retirement. The full leisure to work, the freedom from all interruption, the absence of temptations to distractions. Cefalù realises my idea of heaven.'[420] He loved Hirsig too; 'I love Alostrael; she is all my comfort, my support, my soul's desire, my life's reward, my dream's fulfilment.'[421] In a more carnal not to mention brutal light he later wrote of her

I have made my Scarlet Woman, perfect beyond all praise, from a dull ugly school-teacher, ignorant, tired, old and common. Only

---

418 *The Book of the Law* II 22.

419 Aleister Crowley, *The Confessions of Aleister Crowley*, p 934.

420 Ibid., p 834-835.

421 Aleister Crowley, *The Magical Record of the Beast 666*, p 210.

three years and three months – behold a perfect Proctophile,[422] a Priestess of Passion, prehensile to the Phallus of Pan... her faith, her courage, her candour unmatched in the world... No deed but we dared it and did it! No sorrow but we suffered it. No filth and no venom but we made it our meat and drink.[423]

The Abbey of Thelema would probably be deemed a commune these days, its occupants wearing ritual garb[424] and performing the Gnostic Mass and other Thelemic rites including four-times-daily sun salutations. Animals and children roamed freely throughout the building, which soon became unsanitary, cleaning and housework seemingly not being any of the residents' True Will. Drugs and sex were plentiful.

In the Abbey of Thelema at Cefalù sex is studied scientifically without shame or subterfuge. Passions are physiologically assayed; all acts are allowed, if they injure not others; approved, if they injure not self. This liberty, far from fomenting lust, destroys sex-obsession.[425]

Addictions to heroin and cocaine[426] notwithstanding, Crowley considered himself a virtual ubermensch by this point, writing in his diary on 18 June 1920 that

I am drunk with the pride-absinthe that I am great, the greatest man of my century, its best poet, its mightiest mage, its subtlest philosopher... I am aflame with the brandy of the thought that I am the sublimest mystic in all history, that I am the Word of an

---

422 Likely in appreciation of Hirsig's eagerness to partake in Crowley's anal sex-based magical workings.

423 Aleister Crowley, diary, March 1922, quoted in *City of the Beast: the London of Aleister Crowley* by Phil Baker, p 110.

424 Which was only a requirement for non-A∴A∴ initiates; initiates could wear what they wished. That said, Crowley was also often robed when at Cefalù.

425 Aleister Crowley, quoted in *A Magick Life: The Biography of Aleister Crowley* by Martin Booth, p 366.

426 Though not physiologically addictive like heroin, cocaine is certainly psychologically addictive, and Crowley made excuses with himself to use more of it. 'What is stronger, my will or the drug? I must prove myself the master. How do I do this? By taking cocaine!' Aleister Crowley, quoted in *A Magick Life: A Biography of Aleister Crowley* by Martin Booth, p 370.

Aeon, that I am the Beast, the Man Six Hundred Sixty and Six, the self-crowned God whom men shall worship and blaspheme for centuries that are yet wound on Time's spool.[427]

On 26 July 1920 at Cefalù Hirsig challenged him to eat her excrement to prove that he had indeed transcended the base mundane and could perceive all things as being of equal and exalted worth; he did.

My mouth burned; my throat choked; my belly retched, my blood fled whither who knows, and my skin sweated. She stood above me, hideous in contempt; she fixed snake's eyes on mine, and with most patient discipline as with most eager passion, as with sublime delight, was face to face with me, epiphany of my duty's archetype... My teeth grew rotten, my tongue ulcered; raw was my throat, spasm-torn my belly... So with my body shuddering, retching, fainting, and convulsed; with my mind tempest, my heart crater, my will earthquake, I obeyed Her lash... I passed ordeal, I took oath; I am indeed High Priest.[428]

By 23 May 1921 Crowley deemed himself to have attained the magical rank of Ipsissimus, the highest A∴A∴ or OTO grade possible and one held by nobody else;

the Ipsissimus is wholly free of all limitations soever, existing in the nature of all things without discriminations of quality between them... The Ipsissimus is pre-eminently the Master of all modes of existence; that is, his being is entirely free from internal or external necessity... [he] has no relation as such with any Being: He has no will in any direction, and no consciousness of any kind involving duality, for in him all is accomplished.[429]

This placed him, on a spiritual level, above comparative dabblers such as Jesus, Buddha, and Thoth. 'I am by initiation and insight an Ipsissimus; I'll face the phantasm of myself and tell it so to its teeth. I will invoke Insanity

---

427 Aleister Crowley, *The Magical Record of The Beast 666*, p 177-178.

428 Ibid., p 235.

429 Aleister Crowley, *Magick*, p 329-330.

itself; but having thought the Truth, I will not flinch from fixing it in word and deed, whatever come of it... As a god goes, I go.'[430]

On a break from the Abbey in May 1922 Crowley and Hirsig returned to London, where publisher William Collins commissioned him for two books, a novel and an autobiography. Crowley wrote the former in a rented Chelsea flat between 4 June and 1 July, dictating to Hirsig who transcribed the book longhand. They averaged 5,000 words daily, an impressive feat for any writer, let alone an addicted one. Both Crowley and Hirsig were heroin-dependent, and the novel was in large part autobiographical. Its narrator Peter Pendragon, addicted to heroin and cocaine, meets Basil King Lamus, a magus (and thinly veiled Crowley analogue) who invites him to his Thelemic abbey named Telyphus, promising that magical practice and the exercise of True Will can cure his addictions. Crowley liked to believe as much, as if considering the very concept of dependency something he'd transcended; 'I have tried the hashish-life, the opium-life, the alcohol-life, the ether-life; the heroin-life; none of them has held me for a moment, or interfered with any of the other lives. I seem to enjoy anything that comes along, but to bid it cheerfully farewell.'[431] In reality of course this simply wasn't true, and a heroin habit would dog him on and off for the rest of his life. Cocaine was also still a problem:

Why is it that one takes Cocaine (but no other drug) gluttonously, dose upon dose, neither feeling the need for it, nor hoping to get any good from it? I have found that every time 3 doses, intelligently taken, secure all one wants. Yet, if the stuff is at hand, it is almost impossible not to go on. One resists successfully (perhaps) for a few nights, then slides into a 'go as you please' race without rime or reason. One even goes on while actually cursing oneself for one's folly... Why take thirty doses (or is it sixty? I haven't a ghost of a guess) to get into a state neither pleasant nor in any other way desirable, but fraught with uneasiness, remorse, self-contempt, alarm, discomfort & irritation at the ever-present thought of 'Hell! now I have to endure the reaction' while well aware that with 3 one can get all one wants without one single drawback?[432]

430 Aleister Crowley diary, April 1921, quoted in *Do What Thou Wilt: A Life of Aleister Crowley* by Lawrence Sutin, p 290.

431 Aleister Crowley, *The Magical Record of The Beast 666*, p 204.

432 Aleister Crowley, *Magical Diaries of Aleister Crowley*, Tunisia 1923, p 162-163.

Diary of a Drug Fiend came out in November 1922, Crowley's first book not self-published, and though it sold respectably 'drug addict' was swiftly added to his rap sheet in the popular press. In their review *The Sunday Express* declared it 'A Book For Burning', and ran a sensationalised exposé of Crowley's life and work, going into exaggerated detail about the degenerate nature of life at Cefalù, replete with tales of orgies and animal sacrifice. The article also mentioned Leila Waddell, stating incorrectly that she and Crowley were married following his divorce from Rose Kelly. Crowley's books were described as 'either incomprehensible or disgusting – generally both. His language is the language of the pervert, and his ideas are negligible.'[433] Amid media furore William Collins scrapped plans to publish the autobiography, but allowed Crowley to keep the £120 advance they'd paid.

Crowley and Hirsig returned to Cefalù, where newcomers continued to arrive. One, Raoul Loveday,[434] died from a liver infection on 16 February 1923 after drinking from a polluted stream in the woods near the Abbey[435] and his wife Betty May[436] went to the press. The media in Europe once again

---

433 *The Sunday Express*, 26 November 1922. The source of the claims about Cefalù was an unhappy Mary Butts, disgruntled with Crowley's portrayal of her in *Diary of a Drug Fiend* as 'a fat, bold, red-headed slut... a white maggot... pompous, pretentious, and stupid. She gave herself out as a great authority on literature; but all her knowledge was parrot, and her own attempts in that direction the most deplorably dreary drivel that had ever been printed.' (Aleister Crowley, *Diary of a Drug Fiend*, p 14).

434 Born Frederick Charles Loveday in Rangoon in 1900, an Oxford undergraduate long fascinated with ancient Egypt and the occult. He was an ardent Thelemite much-taken with Abbey life though his wife was far less keen. Crowley was fond of him, seeing in him much magical potential, and was said to have been greatly upset by his death. Loveday's burial rites were conducted at Cefalù according to an A∴A∴ funerary ritual devised by Crowley, which was the first time it was ever performed. The body was later exhumed by Loveday's parents and transferred to England.

435 Another story, spread by Betty May and which may have had its foundation in a real event, has it that Loveday died following the drinking of the blood of a sacrificed cat during a ritual at Cefalù.

436 Betty May seems to have been quite a colourful character in her own right. Born c.1892, she, according to her own account, grew up in a Limehouse brothel, working as an artist's model before moving to Paris and joining a robber gang named the Apaches in which she was known as Tiger Woman. A heavy drinker fond of cocaine, she first met Crowley at the Café Royal in 1914 and didn't much like him. Raoul was her third husband by the age of thirty. They married in 1922, within weeks of meeting each other, and their relocation to the Abbey of Thelema was at his instigation. She later wrote an autobiography, *Tiger Woman: My Story*. She died some time after 1955.

turned against Crowley, with UK journal *The John Bull* (which as the reader may recall had never liked him) denouncing him under the headlines 'The King of Depravity',[437] 'A Wizard of Wickedness', 'A Man We'd Like to Hang', and 'The Wickedest Man in the World'. Crowley was evicted from Cefalù on 23 April 1923 by the Italian government, then led by the fascist Benito Mussolini.[438]

Crowley and Hirsig moved on, this time to Tunis. He continued to write, beginning work on his 'autohagiography' *The Confessions of Aleister Crowley*, which would not be finished until 1929. In October 1923 Theodor Reuss, head of the Ordo Templi Orientis, died, and Crowley announced himself as successor; 'I have proclaimed myself OHO [Outer Head of the Order] Frater Superior of the Order of Oriental Templars',[439] he had earlier written in his diary. This was not without controversy; Reuss was said to have favoured Charles Stansfield Jones for the role, while Crowley maintained that Reuss had designated the position to him shortly before his death. Either way Crowley would remain head of the Order until his own death in 1947.

In Tunis Crowley made a concerted effort at quitting heroin, undergoing heavy withdrawal symptoms. He succeeded but lasted two days before he was using again. The drug was clearly still a source of pleasure for him and perhaps he simply didn't want to give it up; in his 1924 diary he described it as 'like thirteen masturbations, a menstruation orgie, a five-man buggery competition, sixteen rapes of assorted quadrupeds... and a pot

437 In its 10 March 1923 issue: 'It is over twelve years since *John Bull* first exposed the corrupting infamies of that arch-traitor, debauchee and drug-fiend, Aleister Crowley, whose unspeakable malpractices are said to have driven his former wife and at least one other of his victims mad, while they have already ruined the lives of numerous cultured and refined women and young men... Many highly intelligent women – and even men – have been convinced that the Master Therion (as Crowley calls himself) is a Saint, to discover too late a devil possessed of indubitable occult power. It is these powers which, used as they are, make Crowley one of the most dangerous men alive...'

438 Which caused much celebration at *The John Bull*. Under the header 'The Man We'd Like to Hang' in their 16 May 1923 issue: 'The infamous Aleister Crowley, who has been expelled from Italy, proposes to return to this country. He is not wanted here. We do not want a man of his record on British soil. Apart from anything else, he is a beast whose disloyalty is only exceeded by his impudence... It is at least a tribute to public decency that this man should be bundled unceremoniously out of his Abbey at Cefalù, where he practised his horrible rites and perverted his victims. But clearly what is required is concerted international police action. Otherwise Crowley will simply transfer his malevolent activities elsewhere, and continue to find fresh followers.'

439 Aleister Crowley, diary, 27 November 1921.

of marmalade thrown in.'⁴⁴⁰ He was also still using cocaine and ether. This period saw Crowley at his poorest and most despondent, his time divided between Tunisia and France;

> I seem to have no strength or energy left. I take no real interest in anything for more than a few minutes at a time. I have no real hope, that is the root of the matter... I have but a few minutes a day when I feel really fit. I resent dressing and undressing. I sleep late after going to bed early; I sleep long, yet wake weary. It is a dreadful effort to rise, even by 1 pm... I long for death – simply to be away from the body which weighs me down instead of being my chariot.⁴⁴¹

So much for being a godly Ipsissimus. 'Have I ever done anything of value, or am I a mere trifler, existing by a series of shifts of one kind or another? A wastrel, a coward, a man of straw.'⁴⁴²

Crowley and Hirsig became increasingly remote from each other and by September 1924 he had replaced her, the role of Scarlet Woman now being taken by American devotee Dorothy Olsen (1892-1930), magical name Soror Astrid. In Tunis he wrote *To Man* that same year, in which he proclaimed himself a prophet entrusted with spreading the word of a New Aeon across the globe.

> I took upon myself, in my turn, the sin of the whole world, that the Prophecies might be fulfilled, so that Mankind may take the Next Step from the Magical Formula of Osiris to that of Horus. And mine hour being upon me, I proclaim my Law. The word of the law is θέλημα [Thelema].⁴⁴³

In March 1925 Olsen miscarried and was nursed by the ever-dependable Leah Hirsig of all people, who for a while acted as Crowley's secretary despite no longer being his lover or Scarlet Woman. Crowley and Olsen relocated to Paris, and though Hirsig began to distance herself from

---

440 Aleister Crowley, March 1924 diary, quoted in *City of the Beast: The London of Aleister Crowley* by Phil Baker, p 226.

441 Aleister Crowley, diary, 13 January 1924.

442 Aleister Crowley, letter to Norman Mudd, quoted in *Aleister Crowley: A Biography* by Tobias Churton, p 276.

443 Aleister Crowley, *To Man*.

Crowley, renouncing any belief in him – 'The question remains "Who are you?"... You are no more a Magus than you are a cunt. You seem to disregard all Holy Books, etc in your sexual stupidity.'[444] – she continued for some years as a dedicated and practising Thelemite.

By 1926 Crowley and Olsen were no more; she found solace in alcoholism and was dead by 1930. He still attracted new followers seeking occult tuition or wanting to learn about Thelema though his health remained poor, with a lingering heroin addiction. In November 1928 in Paris he met the woman destined to be his second wife, the half-Nicaraguan and half-French Maria Teresa de Miramar (1894-1955), also known as Maria Teresa Sanchez or Maria Teresa Ferrari. 'She is marvellous beyond words, but excites me too much, so that I cannot prolong... She has absolutely the right ideas of Magick and knows some Voudoo...[445] We did proper ritual consecrations, and arranged for the next Work.'[446] They were married on 16 August 1929[447] but it was over in less than a year, Crowley moving to Berlin and deciding on the German Hanni Jaeger (1911-1932?) – who at nineteen was thirty-five years his junior – instead; 'Met and won Hanni Jaeger. Dismissed wife, without notice.'[448] Like many of Crowley's women de Miramar was prone to alcoholism, and ended up in Colney Hatch asylum suffering from depression, paranoia, and delusions, including – her doctors noted with incredulity at first – claims that she was Scarlet Woman to the infamous Wickedest Man in the World. She remained there, still legally married to but abandoned by him, until her death in 1955.[449]

---

444 Leah Hirsig, unsent letter to Aleister Crowley, 28 October 1924, reproduced in *Three Chapters in My Life* by Leah Hirsig, p 116.

445 It is possible Crowley had little knowledge of African diaspora traditions, and didn't recognise what he was seeing. His descriptions of her practices seem a fair way from Vodou as we currently understand it.

446 Aleister Crowley, diary, 14 November 1928.

447 Some authors contend that the marriage was one of convenience to allow de Miramar entry into England since she lacked a residence permit, though since Crowley noted a sex magick working with her in his diary on their first night together as a married couple for 'success to our campaign and happiness in marriage' this likely wasn't the case.

448 Aleister Crowley, diary, date unknown, quoted in *A Magick Life: A Biography of Aleister Crowley* by Martin Booth, p 439.

449 For more information regarding her life and her brief association with Crowley, see the article *Aleister Crowley, Marie de Miramar and the True Wanga* by Christopher Josiffe.

Crowley's magnum opus *Book 4* – much of which had been written in 1911 and 1912 while he was still with Leila Waddell – was finally published in April 1929 under the title *Magick*, and may be his greatest single contribution to western occult literature.[450] It didn't sell well in his lifetime. Hanni Jaeger's stint with him was brief, and she too was soon history and under psychiatric care before later committing suicide. By September 1931 he was living in Berlin with Bertha Busch (1895-?), also known as Bill or Billie, another woman prone to excessive boozing. He declared sex with her 'the best fuck within recorded memory of living man,'[451] but the relationship was volatile and violent on both sides and not prolonged. He was soon back in London, taking yet another heavy-drinking Scarlet Woman, Pearl Brooksmith (1899-1967), in July 1933. He commemorated her alcohol habit and sexual appetite[452] in an imagined epitaph written soon after they met; 'Here lies a Pearl of a woman / Who lived in open sin. / One end collected semen, / The other guzzled gin.' She resigned herself to his magical requests and requirements with the words 'all great saviours have been bastards.'[453] Brooksmith lasted until 1937 and also ended up in an asylum, suffering hallucinations of devils. It was perhaps less the case that Crowley drove his women to their fates and more that he attracted or was attracted to those already vulnerable to addiction and instability and madness.

Financial difficulties persisted, and Crowley was rendered destitute following a failed legal action against Nina Hamnett, an author and friend and former A∴A∴ member who he claimed had libelled him in her 1932 memoir *Laughing Torso*, which featured allegations of black magick and nefarious goings on at Cefalù; 'Crowley had a temple in Cefalù in Sicily. He was supposed to practice Black Magic there, and one day a baby was said to have disappeared mysteriously.[454] There was also a goat there.[455] This all

---

450 Though it isn't this author's favourite Crowley book; that would be *The Book of Lies*.

451 Aleister Crowley, diary, 6 September 1931.

452 Brooksmith was also noted as having come out with the wonderful seductive line 'I feel the flame of fornication creeping up my body.'

453 Quoted in *Do What Thou Wilt: A Life of Aleister Crowley* by Lawrence Sutin, p 366.

454 Possibly a garbled retelling of the fate of Anne Léa Crowley, the daughter Crowley had with Leah Hirsig who died aged nine months on 18 October 1920 while they were resident at the Abbey.

455 Hamnett was not mistaken; there was indeed a goat at Cefalù, which Leah Hirsig once tried to have sex with. The animal could not be tempted however, and Crowley took over; in his words, 'I atoned for the young He-goat at considerable length.'

pointed to Black Magic, so people said, and the inhabitants of the village were frightened of him.[456] Crowley sued Hamnett and her publisher, losing the case in court in April 1934, with the judge Mr Justice Swift commenting that

> I have been over forty years in the administration of law in one capacity or another. I thought I knew of every conceivable form of wickedness. I thought that everything that was vicious and bad had been produced at some time or another before me. I have learnt in this case that we can always learn something more if we live long enough. I have never heard such dreadful, horrible, blasphemous, and abominable stuff as that which has been produced by a man who describes himself to you as the greatest living poet.[457]

Crowley was ordered to pay Hamnett's costs, and with debts totalling £4,695 (equivalent to approximately £430,000 today) spread between forty-eight creditors he was declared bankrupt in April 1935. His court submission in his defence in this respect stated 'I am the author of some of the noblest prose and poetry with which the English language has ever been enriched, and I cannot also have the talents of an accountant.'[458]

Now in his sixties, Crowley managed to continue living simply in London, partly on book sales, partly on a small trust fund, and partly on donations from the California lodge of the Ordo Templi Orientis, fervent Thelemites later led by famed rocket engineer Jack Parsons.[459] Another minor

---

(Quoted in *Perdurabo: The Life of Aleister Crowley* by Richard Kaczynski, p 373).

456 Nina Hamnett, *Laughing Torso*, p 174-175.

457 Quoted in *Do What Thou Wilt: A Life of Aleister Crowley* by Lawrence Sutin, p 372 (and elsewhere).

458 Quoted in *Aleister Crowley: The Biography* by Tobias Churton, p 363.

459 Born 1914 as John Whiteside Parsons, Jack Parsons was an American rocket engineer and Thelemite. He joined the California branch of the Ordo Templi Orientis, the Agape Lodge, in 1941, and was appointed by Crowley as its head in 1943. He would be expelled from work at Aerojet Engineering Corporation and the Jet Propulsion Laboratory (both of which he was a co-founder of) in 1944 for his occult associations and the OTO's poor reputation, though the significance of his work in rocket science was later acknowledged. He is probably best remembered now for his involvement in the famed Babalon Working with later Church of Scientology founder L Ron Hubbard, intended to manifest Babalon and carried out in 1946. For some this manifestation was intended as literal and physical, whereas others saw it more as the manifestation of a divine feminine archetype or Babalon current. Parsons considered the working a success, meeting occultist and actress and poet (and later

source of income at this time was through the sale of Crowley's Elixir of Life pills, a weekly supply of which cost 25 guineas and which were purported to increase energy and sexual vitality; Crowley neglected to mention to his meagre customers that the primary ingredient of the pills was his own semen. In his book *Little Essays Toward Truth* published in 1938 he wrote that 'the whole and sole object of all true Magical and Mystical training is to become free from every kind of limitation.'[460] He'd certainly managed that, but what had it left him with? His health was precarious, he was living in poverty, and heroin remained the one 'limitation' he never quite managed to transcend; though he'd quit once more by this point it would not last. During the years of the Second World War he offered his services as an agent for British intelligence, but this came to little. Not that there haven't been numerous sometimes fanciful stories of Crowley's magical involvement during the war, including that he worked alongside occult novelist Dennis Wheatley, James Bond author Ian Fleming and others for the intelligence services, and that he engaged in rituals designed to repel the Luftwaffe and the threat of German invasion.

At the close of 1941 Crowley's last sex partner came and went, Alice Speller, a secretary some fifteen or so years his junior. Now aged sixty-six, his erections were failing him, and on 23 December 1941 he recorded in his diary 'Alice here: frigged her',[461] his final sex act magical or otherwise. Though he still had a number of friends and acquaintances in this period he had alienated many of the more significant people who had come and gone throughout his life, writing in his diary in June 1942 'Mental state v. bad; no clearness, no power to concentrate... I feel the need of a loyal friend as never before. Not one in England who really cared a nickel.'[462] His drug use prevailed; on 7 March 1943 he wrote an untitled poem which it has to be said is a long way from the finest of his literary works: 'I sit and smoke / Until I choke, / Take heroin / To breathe again, / And then cocaine / To clear my brain. / To top with hashish / Much too rash is; / So let me clear / My mind with beer, / And call upon the loftiest genii / With Anhalonium Lewinii!'

Crowley produced his last significant books, *Magick Without Tears*

---

wife) Marjorie Cameron shortly afterwards. He deemed her a Scarlet Woman, and the two attempted without result to manifest a magical child. Parsons died in 1952 in an accidental explosion at his home laboratory.

460 Aleister Crowley, *Little Essays Toward Truth*, online edition. <https://sacred-texts.com/oto/aleph_index.htm>

461 Aleister Crowley, diary, 23 December 1941.

462 Aleister Crowley diary, June 1942, quoted in *City of the Beast: The London of Aleister Crowley* by Phil Baker, p 239.

(originally titled *Aleister Explains Everything*, and not published in his lifetime) and *The Book of Thoth*, published in 1944; the latter was written to accompany a set of tarot cards designed by Crowley and illustrated by Lady Frieda Harris,[463] an OTO member and artist of some ability. Originally intended to be a six-month project, it ended up taking five years from 1938 to 1943. Now often called the Thoth deck, these beautifully painted cards are commonly used by tarot practitioners today.

On 1 February 1945 Crowley moved to Hastings, residing in a boarding house named Netherwood. He took on a new student, Kenneth Grant,[464] who he hoped might be his magical successor. Grant acted as his secretary for a while and Crowley, still destitute, paid him in magical tuition. He would soon dismiss Grant as 'a Bore with no interest in the world in general.'[465] He appointed Karl Germer[466] to be his successor as head of the OTO, with Grady

---

463 Frieda Harris (1887-1952) is best-remembered these days for her association with Crowley, and for the striking and instantly recognisable images that make up the Thoth deck. She actually met Crowley and began work on the cards before being initiated by him into the OTO, being elevated to IV°due to her existing esoteric knowledge and past association with Freemasonry. She and Crowley remained good friends after the project was complete, and she visited him regularly at his Netherwood lodgings. Though *The Book of Thoth* was published in 1944, a complete run of the deck as cards wasn't printed until after both its creators had died.

464 Kenneth Grant, born 1924, was an English occultist and writer. He was tutored by Crowley in the nineteen-forties and initiated into the Ordo Templi Orientis. Grant also befriended the then-little-known occultist Austin Osman Spare, and was instrumental in bringing his works to a wider audience following Spare's death. In 1955 Grant founded his own New Isis Lodge, which later became the Typhonian Ordo Templi Orientis, Thelemic in essence but introducing numerous new elements, in particular from Hindu tantra and ufology and the works of H P Lovecraft (as an aside, it is sometimes claimed that Lovecraft and Crowley met, and were influenced by each other, neither of which are true). In the nineteen-sixties and seventies Grant co-edited many of Crowley's books for republication, and played a vital role in the revival of interest in Crowley. He also wrote numerous works of occultism, fiction, and poetry of his own throughout his life. He died in 2011, aged 86.

465 Quoted in *Aleister Crowley in England* by Tobias Churton, p 294.

466 Karl Germer was born in 1885 in Elberfeld, Germany. He served in military intelligence in the First World War, for which he was twice awarded the Iron Cross. He stayed at the Abbey of Thelema in the early twenties, relocating to America afterwards. He was deported from America following the expiry of his visa in 1935, returning to Germany where he was held in a sequence of concentration camps for his occult beliefs and associations. Released in 1941, he returned to America. He assumed leadership of the OTO following Crowley's death in 1947, a position he held until his own death in 1962.

McMurtry[467] – a friend and US military officer stationed in England – to assume the role upon Germer's death. He also selected author John Symonds (1914-2006) as his literary executor. Symonds, despite taking a negative view of Crowley in his 1951 biography *The Great Beast: The Life of Aleister Crowley*, would later – along with Kenneth Grant – be instrumental in republishing Crowley's books. Crowley also met the up-and-coming Gerald Gardner,[468] and (it is said) drafted rituals for his nascent witchcraft movement known as Wicca. However unlikely, the truth of whether Crowley wrote Gardner's rituals is difficult to ascertain – both were prone to self-aggrandisement and tall tales – though Gardner's work was certainly borrowed from and influenced by Crowley regardless of who wrote it.

The years and drugs had not been kind to Crowley. As author James Laver, meeting him for the first time in more than thirty years, described him in March 1947,

> he seemed to have shrunk both in height and girth and he wore a little straggly beard... His face was the colour of mud. His clothes, a tweed coat, a double-breasted waistcoat and voluminous plus-fours of different material seemed to hang loosely about him... He took up the syringe, dissolved a little scarlet pellet in the glass chamber, rolled back his sleeve and gave himself a *piqure*. The heroin injection seemed to give him new life. The muddy look in his face vanished, and the wonderful brown eyes glowed. From time to time he turned them upon me, and I began to understand the hypnotic fascination that he must have once possessed.[469]

---

467 Grady McMurtry was born in 1918. He came to the work of Aleister Crowley initially through his friendship with Jack Parsons. An officer in the US military, he took part in the Normandy landing in 1944 and the subsequent liberation of France and Belgium, and also served in the Korean War. He was initiated by Crowley into the OTO in 1941, assuming the magical name Hymenaeus Alpha, and by 1943 had attained IX°. He did not claim his role as head of the OTO until 1969, a position he held until his death in 1985. He was succeeded by William Breeze, known as Hymenaeus Beta, was still head of the OTO at the time of writing.

468 Gerald Gardner, born 1884, was a prominent author instrumental in popularising modern paganism, witchcraft, and Wicca. He authored numerous influential books on the subject, and founded his own sect which came to be called Gardnerian Wicca and which continues to this day. His efforts in the promotion of interest in and acceptance of contemporary paganism were immeasurable, though there is no evidence for the commonplace assertion that Wicca is the direct continuation of an older, pre-Christian religion. He died in 1964, aged 79.

469 James Laver, *Museum Piece: The Education of an Iconographer*, p 227-228.

Aleister Crowley died at Netherwood on 1 December 1947, aged seventy-two. Cause of death was chronic bronchitis worsened by pleurisy and myocardial degeneration. Aside from journalists approximately a dozen people attended his funeral, which was held at Brighton crematorium and featured readings of his poem *Hymn To Pan* and selections from *The Book of the Law*, *The Ship*, and the Gnostic Mass.

There is some disagreement as to Crowley's last words. The oft-quoted 'I am perplexed' comes from Frieda Harris, who visited him shortly before he died, possibly the day before. Another – 'Sometimes I hate myself' – comes (according to Crowley biographer John Symonds) from a Mr Rowe who was present with Crowley's nurse, though again precisely when is unclear. There is a good chance that neither was Crowley's final pronouncement. A third account has him dying alone in his room; according to Thelemite and author Gerald Suster (1951-2001), 'Crowley used to pace up and down his living-room. One day the Beast was pacing and Mr W H [otherwise unidentified] was on the floor below, polishing furniture. Suddenly there was a crash. Mr W H went upstairs and entered Crowley's rooms to find him dead on the floor.'[470] A fourth account still – and perhaps the one most likely to be true – has Crowley dying peacefully and silently in bed as thunder rumbled beyond the window.

Since his death Crowley's fame and notoriety have only increased, and these days he is seen by many not only as a countercultural icon and Thelemic prophet but also as one of the most significant, if not the most significant, figures in twentieth century occultism. His works continue to be read and studied globally, and there are more practitioners of the Thelemic current now than there were in his lifetime. Regardless of one's thoughts on Crowley as a man there can be little doubt that he fully lived what he believed, that – as he would put it – he did his True Will. 'Magic is not *a* way of life,' he told author E M Butler the year before he died. 'It is *the* way of life.'[471]

470 Gerald Suster, *The Legacy of The Beast: The Life, Work, and Influence of Aleister Crowley*, p 75.
471 E M Butler, *Paper Boats: An Autobiography*, p 173. Italics in original.

ALEISTER CROWLEY, CIRCA 1925

Spring beans and strawberries are in: goodbye to the oyster!
If I really knew what I wanted, I could give up Laylah, or give up
everything for Laylah.
But 'what I want' varies from hour to hour.
This wavering is the root of all compromise,
and so of all good sense.
With this gift a man can spend his seventy years in peace.
Now is this well or ill?
Emphasise gift, then man, then spend, then seventy years, and
lastly peace, and change the intonations – each time reverse the
meaning! I would show you how; but – for the moment! –
I prefer to think of Laylah.

'Plovers' Eggs', Aleister Crowley
Liber CCCXXXIII: The Book of Lies, Wieland and Co.,
London, 1913, p. 92.

MARKED BY CHARM AND REFINEMENT
(1924-1932)

n 1924, her Crowley and occult days behind her, the then forty-three-year-old Leila Waddell returned alone to Sydney, Australia. Setting out from Vancouver onboard the Niagara on 10 April 1924, she arrived at Sydney harbour on the Sonoma, having changed ships en route, on 27 May. Her homecoming was quite the news item in the Australian press;

> 'Glad to be home,' she echoed from behind a floral model of her precious Amati, given her on arrival by some friends – 'I should just say so. Coming home is the wonderful happening in any traveller's life. Whether I'll stay put, as they say in America, is another matter. Wanderlust is a wicked little germ, and we all get it, once having crossed the line with face towards foreign lands.'[472]

It is often stated that the reason Waddell returned to Australia in 1924 was to act as nurse to her ailing father, though this was not the case; he didn't sicken and die until 1929, still five years away. She swiftly got back into things in Sydney, finding that she was still fondly remembered and highly regarded as a musician in her homeland and could make a living there. She would go on to perform with the Conservatorium Orchestra under Dr William Arundel Orchard and the Royal Philharmonic Society Orchestra under Gerald Peachell, at the Criterion and Her Majesty's Theatres with JC Williamson Limited Orchestra, and even took on some teaching at the Covenant School of the Sacred Heart (later known as the Kincoppal-Rose Bay School of the Sacred Heart), a day and boarding school sited east of Sydney in Elizabeth Bay.

It would be some months before Waddell returned to public performance, with note being made of her appearing at an entertainment in late October 1924 for a Mr and Mrs Alfred Edward of Leith Links, Elizabeth Bay, who were set to depart for England the following January. 'Songs were given by Mrs Edward and Mrs White, and Miss Leila Waddell, who has just returned from a prolonged tour of the world, gave several delightful violin solos.'[473]

---

472 Leila Waddell, quoted in the article *A Bathurst Girl's Tour Abroad*, *The Bathurst Times*, 12 June 1924.

473 *The Daily Telegraph* (Sydney), 24 October 1924.

Waddell's first return show proper took place at the Haymarket Theatre on George Street, Sydney on 1 November 1924. She played using the Amati violin given to her by her former tutor Émile Sauret, as part of the Nellie Leach-Leila Waddell Trio (with the third member of the trio being Alfred Lawrence for some shows and Beatrice Tange, also known as Trixie Tange, for others). Nellie Leach was an opera singer recently returned from stints on the London stage and in America. Lawrence was an Australian composer and pianist as was Tange. Their set is known to have included the songs *I Wouldn't Leave My Little Wooden Hut For You*, *Somebody Is Waiting for Me*, *Live Laugh and Love*, *Because*, *Wonderful One*, and *My Radio Girl* performed by Leach and Lawrence, *Hungarian Rhapsodie* and *Ziguemeweisen* performed by Waddell on violin, together with a final medley, *Memories From the Operas*. A mention in the gossip pages of the Australian journal *The Bulletin* from 13 November 1924 tells us that

> Leila Waddell and Nellie Leach, who are off with their trio to Brisbane, gave a party last week, between turns, in the lounge of the Haymarket. The two clever girls, with composer Lawrence (he's the man who gave *My Little Wooden Hut* to the world), have been putting on a bright act at the Haymarket – Nellie singing, Leila at the fiddle, and Lawrence making the piano earn its living. Their tea-drinking was a great success... Trixie Tange brought her nearly-as-young-as-herself mother, and of the forty gathered together nobody left till the last possible minute.[474]

The Trio played the Haymarket again on 5 and 10 November, before performing at the Tivoli Theatre, Brisbane[475] twice daily between 17 and 29 November, as well as a show at the Lennon's Hotel as guests of Deputy Mayoress Mrs T Wilson on 19 November where 'Miss Leila Waddell gave much pleasure with her violin solos.'[476] *The Truth* newspaper of Brisbane, speaking to Waddell for the Tivoli shows, described her as

> one of the most interesting personalities we have met for some time.. A secret of her success is adaptability, for she plays any kind of music, which is particularly useful in America, where one

---

474 *The Bulletin*, 13 November 1924.
475 *The Brisbane Courier* (15 November 1924) comments that these are the first dates Waddell ever played in Brisbane.
476 *The Brisbane Courier*, 20 November 1924.

has the opportunity of playing so many different engagements –
orchestral, clubs, concerts, and vaudeville. There being such vast
territory to cover, a well-known musician is kept busy, and very
high fees are paid... This is the violinist's first visit to Australia after
many years in Europe, and she likes our calm and the restfulness
of the people.. Miss Waddell gives out a serious warning to those
thinking of going overseas. 'You must have a good nest-egg,' she
said, 'and many introductions. Without either, the fight is heart-
breaking.'[477]

The Brisbane Courier's review gives us an idea of what these shows
were like:

The speciality trio, consisting of Miss Nellie Leach, Leila Waddell,
and Trixie Tange, opened their season before crowded audiences at
the Tivoli yesterday. The three young artists provided a delightfully
varied programme of combined and solo numbers. Miss Nellie
Leach, a Sydney singer, who has had continental training possesses
a light soprano voice of considerable charm. She was heard to
advantage in *Somewhere Somebody's Waiting For Me*, *Live, Laugh,
and Love. The Radio Girl* and *Because*. In the first three numbers
she was accompanied by Miss Waddell (violiniste) and Miss Tange
at the piano. She was most becomingly gowned as the radio girl.
Miss Tange's pianoforte solo was the finale of a Grieg concerto,
which she played with considerable strength, varied with the
delicacy of tone so necessary in the more subdued passages of a
Grieg number. Miss Waddell, a native of Bathurst, New South
Wales, who also studied abroad, gave a fine rendition of Hauser's
Hungarian Rhapsodie.[478]

Waddell returned from Brisbane on 2 December 1924. Following some
minor concert appearances around Sydney[479] she departed Australia for

---

477 *A Woman of Talent, Truth* (Brisbane) 23 November 1924

478 *The Brisbane Courier*, 18 November 1924.

479 This author doesn't feel the need to include every concert by Waddell in the
primary text; she is known to have played at a musical event hosted by Mrs T Wilson,
Deputy Mayoress of Brisbane at Lennon's Hotel on 19 November, at a musical party
hosted by a Mrs Hugh D M'Intosh at Astor, in honour of Dame Mary Hughes on 17
December 1924 at which 'Miss Waddell's violin solos were much appreciated' (Sunday
Times, Sydney, 21 December 1924), at Waverley College Garden Fete on 12 February

Vancouver on board the Aorangi with Nellie Leach in March 1925, arriving on 3 April to fulfil Canadian concert bookings. Leach's aunt is said to have accompanied them as 'chaperone'.[480] Waddell's touring commitments took her across America, including concerts in New York and Chicago, returning to Sydney by mail steamer before leaving for England and thence on to Paris, where she wrote to *The Bathurst Times* in August. *The Bathurst Times* – who state 'how proud Bathurstians were of the wonderful successes of Miss Leila Waddell, affectionately known in musical circles as "The girl whose fiddle has taken her around the world"'[481] – reproduce her letter in their 29 August 1925 edition:

> Greetings to my home town from Paris, the loveliest and most charming city in the world. I think the gardens at Versailles, and Forest at Fontainebleau are a dream of beauty now. The English country too is magnificent and such a marvellous summer. I have filled engagements in Canada, USA and England since leaving Australia recently, I sail on July 17th on the Mongolia. My book is accepted by a London publisher, and I will revise it during my stay in Australia. Please tell the kind man who believed in me as a writer. Yours sincerely, Leila Waddell.[482]

It is unfortunate that for much of the later part of Waddell's life, from her parting of ways with Crowley until her death, we are reliant almost entirely upon newspaper articles to piece together the narrative. The identity of 'the kind man who believed in me as a writer' is unknown, and information about Waddell's writing is likewise only known to us from the journalism of others. In this respect *The Sydney Morning Herald*, in the article *Violinist as Author* dated 5 September 1925, elaborates:

> Miss Leila Waddell, whose reputation in Sydney as a violinist has been enhanced by appearances abroad, returned to this city this week by the Mongolia in a new capacity – that of an author. Miss Waddell has written a novel and a volume of short stories, and these having been accepted by a London publishing house, she has

---

1925, and at an event held for the Young Australia League at the Ambassadors on 20 February 1925.

480 According to *The National Advocate*, 21 March 1925.

481 *The Bathurst Times*, 29 August 1925.

482 Ibid.

come back to Australia to give them the finishing touches before publication. In entering with this substantial success upon another attractive field of activity, she does not by any means propose to abandon music in favour of literature, since she perceives no reason why they cannot be carried on together. Miss Waddell has already had some considerable experience as a writer, in contributing short stories to the magazines within the past three years,[483] and in the work of musical criticism for two seasons in America.[484]

Sadly, it seems that neither Waddell's novel or short story collection were finalised let alone published, despite the clear indication here that both were essentially complete by 1925 save for some editing. Even if they were finished, we do not know what became of the manuscripts; they appear to be lost.

Waddell returned to Sydney on the Mongolia in the first week of September 1925, initially staying at the Australia hotel before renting a flat at Donna Roma, a block on Farrell Avenue, Darlinghurst, Sydney. It is to the benefit of later scholars that the Australian media continued to praise her and to cover her activities around Sydney and beyond, with *The Sunday Times* writing that 'altogether she's enormously interesting and a very charming personality.'[485] She continued to perform as a violinist wherever she could. Though some of her lesser bookings are now lost to history there is note of her appearance at an entertainment for a Mr Stanley Long at the Wentworth Cafe in early December 1925, at an entertainment in aid of the Woolahra branch of the District Nursing Association on 15 December, at an event hosted by the Musical Association of New South Wales on 17 May 1926, at a Red Cross Appeal for the Rosemary Cabaret on 8 June, at a 'welcome back' cabaret for Miss Marie Burke at the Ambassadors on 16 August, and at the annual conversazione of the Dalcroze Society of New South Wales held at the Royal Art Society on 27 August. An afternoon tea was held at the Australia hotel on 10 September in Waddell's honour, organised by Miss Elizabeth Plummer and hosted by Mr Stanley Long, acknowledging

---

483 Presumably *The Sydney Morning Herald* was referring here to her music-related articles for *The International a*nd her Katherine Mansfield piece; see the previous chapter *Love Alway Yieldeth: Love Alway Hardeneth (1914-1923)*.

484 *The Sydney Morning Herald*, 5 September 1925.

485 *The Sunday Times* (Sydney), 4 October 1925.

her leaving Australia once more for overseas concerts. 'Cerise flowers were arranged as this is the favourite colour of the departing guest.'[486]

Waddell embarked on 15 September 1926, arriving in London from Sydney on the Jervis Bay on 29 October. Once again her bookings were international. She was still in Europe in January 1927, and a piece in Waddell embarked on 15 September 1926, arriving in London from Sydney on the Jervis Bay on 29 October. Once again her bookings were international. She was still in Europe in January 1927, and a piece in *The Sydney Morning Herald* gave an enlightening account of her travels:

Miss Leila Waddell... spent some time in London at the theatres and saw Chekov's *The Three Sisters*, beautifully acted at the Barnes Theatre, the *Rosmersholm* of Ibsen admirably presented, and Galsworthy's *The Escape*, also very well done. Miss Waddell went from London to Paris on her way to a touring engagement, which will keep her for several weeks in the Riviera. She praises two revues she saw in Paris and is glowing in her enthusiasm over the autumn tints in e Bois. The glories of the dying year followed her all the way to Marseilles, and the wonderful cultivation by which not an inch is wasted was indescribably impressive after Australia. Monte Carlo thrilled her, but its crowds of wealthy folk from England and America threw a mantle of conventionality and sameness over every scene and she preferred Nice as 'so French and full of striking contrast.'[487]

By February Waddell was 'at present touring the Riviera',[488] and *The National Advocate* noted in March that

Miss Leila Waddell, who is known as 'the girl who fiddled her way around the world', and is a Bathurst native of whom we have reason to be proud, sends greetings to her many friends from St Raphael, a charming little place where Gounod wrote *Romeo and Juliet*. The musician's villa overlooks the sea and has a delightful garden with palms, wattle and gum trees.[489]

486 *The Grenfell Record and Lachlan District Advertiser*, 23 September 1926.
487 *The Sydney Morning Herald*, 1 January 1927.
488 *The Sun* (Sydney) 20 February 1927.
489 *The National Advocate*, 5 March 1927.

She is known to have also performed in Monte Carlo and Menton around this time.

Waddell was back in Australia on 17 December 1927, having been overseas for fifteen months. Mention was made in *The Sydney Morning Herald* of her

> returning by the Suevic to spend Christmas with her parents at Randwick. Before sailing from Liverpool, the Sydney violinist spent a few weeks in London, and on October 8 heard Miss Jelly d'Aranyi at Wigmore Hall. She describes this artist as physically of a distinct gipsy type, and her style of playing corresponds, as it was characterised by marvellous vitality, backed by a fine technique. 'On Sunday,' Miss Waddell continues, 'I went to a concert at the Royal Albert Hall by Sir Thomas Beecham's orchestra, at which one of the star attractions was Miss Florence Austral, whose great warm dramatic voice was admirably employed in *Ocean, Thou Mighty Monster*, the declamatory passages in which were effectively enhanced by the precision and spirit of the orchestral accompaniment. At this concert a great success was made by Madame Alvarez in the *Air de Lia* from Debussy's opera *L'Enfant Prodigue*, in which the passionate lamentation was emphasised by the richness of the beautiful contralto voice. I also heard Mr Tom Burke, the Lancashire-Irish tenor (who possesses a fine voice), in the two principal airs from Puccini's *La Tosca*. A new Russian basso, Zaporojetz, rolled out his stately tones in Mozart's *Qui Sdegno*, so that the concert was in every respect memorable.[490]

Media coverage of Waddell went very quiet following her return to Sydney, with only a couple of minor public appearances (at Hunter Baillie Memorial Presbyterian Church, Sydney, around 25 February 1928, and at an 'at home' for the wife of Mr Stanley Long of Coomerah, Darling Point, around 7 April 1928) until the death of her uncle James Waddell, who died at home in Double Bay, Sydney in early April 1928, precise date and cause unspecified. He was seventy-five, and stated to have been officer of the Australian Joint Stock Bank and later of the Australian Bank of Commerce.[491] At proceedings at the Supreme Court of New South Wales held in June 1928 Leila Waddell was named as sole beneficiary of her

---

490 *The Sydney Morning Herald*, 12 November 1927.

491 *The Sydney Morning Herald*, 12 April 1928.

uncle's estate in accordance with his Last Will and Testament, though the circumstances of this were not elaborated upon.

Her next public appearance was low-key, as one of several musical guests at a matinee and musicale arranged by Miss Josephine Marks of the Women's Country Club for the Deaf, Dumb and Blind Children's Building Appeal on 26 July 1928. Two days later notice appeared in *The Sydney Morning Herald* that 'Miss Leila Waddell, Pupil of Leopold Auer and Émile Sauret, will accept 6 Pupils for Violin. Address, c/o Carnegie's, George Street.'[492] A second Women's Country Club musicale took place on 11 September, 'a delightful programme'[493] that was well-attended, followed by a performance for the Arts Club of Sydney on 2 October where she was described as 'a violinist of sympathetic charm',[494] at a musicale arranged by Mrs Rosalind Treleaven on 15 October, again for the Women's Country Club on 15 November, at Feminist Club on 22 November, and once more at the Women's Country Club around 4 December. Waddell made a further showing at a Women's Country Club musicale on 12 February 1929, while 27 February saw the first radio appearance this author can find by her in the listings, merely as 'violinist'. Waddell became a weekly regular on Australian radio in the ensuing years, including on what is curiously described as 'Theosophical Station, Ltd, 2GB – Wave Length, 316 metres.'[495] It is tantalising link to Waddell's occult and mystical past, though whether she still held any interests or sympathies in that regard can only be speculated upon.

On 5 March 1929 a party was held at the Feminist Club in honour of the musicians who had performed for free the previous year, of which Waddell was one:

> Quaint name cards marked each guest's place at the Feminist Club yesterday when artists who had given their services to the club during the past year were entertained at a social afternoon. Competitions and community singing were features of the entertainment and the lady guests were presented with floral tributes.[496]

---

492 Ibid., 28 July 1928.

493 *The Sunday Times* (Sydney), 16 September 1928.

494 *The Week* (Brisbane), 12 October 1928.

495 *The Sydney Morning Herald*, 13 March 1929.

496 *Evening News* (Sydney), 6 March 1929.

As 1929 progressed Waddell's public performances continued to be minor; just a farewell hosted by Mr and Mrs Walter Treleaven at the Ambassadors for Mr and Mrs R A Cameron, departing for Europe, on 8 March, at a Feminist Club musicale on 2 April, at Mrs Garlick's musicale at Sydney Town Hall in support of the National Association for the Prevention and Cure of Consumption on 30 July, and at a Hellenic Ball held at the Greek Cathedral, Sydney as a benefit for the Royal Hospital for Women on 5 August. The reason for the lapse in the number of public performances Waddell was undertaking was soon apparent; her father David Waddell had for some time been sick and her time was taken up with nursing him. He died at a private hospital in Randwick on 14 August 1929, aged eighty.[497] Note was made in the newspaper coverage of his death that he had until recently been resident in St Aubyn, Waverley Street, Randwick. He was the only one remaining of his four brothers, the former owners of Waddell Bros wool-washing works in Rankin Street, Bathurst, and was also one of the oldest members of the Phoenix Masonic Lodge. He was survived by his widow Mary Waddell, Leila's mother (who herself died 20 April 1940). Of his once-eleven children only six remained; Emmeline, Beaupre, Thelma, Leila, Beaufort, and Selwyn. His funeral service took place on 15 August at St Michael's Church,Vaucluse, with interment at South Head Cemetery.

Leila Waddell's remaining public appearances were few; on 20 September 1929 she played the Arts Club Sydney at a farewell party for Mrs Herbert Nelson, departing Sydney for San Francisco, then at an event in support of a Reunion Club in Randwick on 9 October 1929, followed by a musicale for Mr George Irvine, discussing his experiences in wartime England, on 11 March 1930, the final public appearance by her that this author has been able to find record of. It made for a depressing damp squib of an ending to a long and illustrious musical career.

On 9 August 1930 – the day before her fiftieth birthday – a letter from Waddell was published in *The Sydney Morning Herald* with regard to a debate about her former tutor Leopold Auer and the claim that he had declined to perform a Tchaikovsky concerto in Petrograd, finding it unsatisfactory. She writes:

This statement differs radically from the account Professor Leopold Auer gave to me, when I was studying with him in New York a few years ago. We were discussing the question of nervousness in

---

497 At least, according to *The National Advocate*, 16 August 1929. *The Sydney Morning Herald* on 15 August 1929 lists him as having been seventy-nine.

public performances. 'Tchaikovsky dedicated his Violin Concerto to me,' said Professor Auer, 'and I was playing it in public for the first time. All went well until I came to the cadenza. Then, realising that I had to play it alone, I became terrified, so, giving one quick glance at the large audience, I rushed off the platform. Tchaikovsky was very angry, and the Concerto was no longer dedicated to me.'[498]

A Mr L Noskowski wrote in response on 16 August that

Miss Leila Waddell's claim regarding this Concerto is strangely different from Professor Auer's own remarks in his memoirs, published about six years ago in New York, for in these he takes the blame for neglecting the work on his own shoulders. Auer thought that the Concerto required a good deal of revision, and as he was very busy at the time, a long delay occurred. 'I deferred the matter of this revision so thoroughly,' he states, 'that after waiting two whole years, the composer, very much disappointed, withdrew the original edition. Quite frankly admitting that I was to blame, I thought him perfectly within his rights. He re-dedicated it to Adolphe Brodsky, who played it for the first time in Vienna.' Considering that Auer was already Professor of the St Petersburg Conservatorium, and conductor of the Russian Musical Society's symphonic concerts, it is rather strange that he should have been frightened to play the cadenza in public, and that he should have taken the unusual procedure of rushing off the platform. Even admitting this possibility, the statement still contradicts Auer's original version in his memoirs.[499]

It was a very minor exchange of correspondence, one that likely didn't even register with the majority of *The Sydney Morning Herald*'s readers. This author only includes it here because it marks the last public notice we have concerning Leila Waddell until her death.

Leila Waddell died aged fifty-two on 13 September 1932 while still resident in Sydney, at Malpas Court, Darling Point. She was single and unmarried. Cause of death was uterine cancer and the process was noted as being prolonged and painful. She was buried at South Head Cemetery in Sydney, beside her father, with her mother joining them in 1940. There

---

498 *The Sydney Morning Herald*, 9 August 1930.
499 Ibid., 16 August 1930.

was nothing to mark her grave or even denote her brief significance on the London and global musical and magical circuits or her years spent with the Wickedest Man in the World.

From the obituary of Leila Ida Bathurst Waddell, *Sydney Morning Herald*, 14 September 1932, p 15. Original source unknown.

That Waddell was still considered a notable figure in Sydney despite the relative quietude of her later years is demonstrated by the fact that *The Sydney Morning Herald* ran an obituary for her, which perhaps unsurprisingly makes no mention at all of her involvement in the occult or with Crowley (if indeed the obituary's author was even aware of those things; it isn't implausible to suggest that they weren't).

The death occurred yesterday of Miss Leila Ida Bathurst Waddell, the Sydney violinist, who achieved considerable fame abroad. She was the daughter of Mr David Waddell, of Bathurst and Randwick, and Mrs Waddell, of Bellevue Hill.

A pupil of Mr Henri Staell, Miss Waddell became teacher of the violin at the Presbyterian Ladies' College, Croydon, and Ascham and Kambala schools. She made her public debut at the organ recitals of the then city organist (Mr Arthur Mason), and joined, as soloist, The Brescians, a party from Europe, who appeared in peasant festival costumes in association with J T West's early cinematograph shows. Mr West introduced her to London, and she achieved success as the leader of the Gipsy Band [*sic.*] in *The Waltz Dream* [*sic.*] at Daly's Theatre. As The Ragtime Gypsy, [*sic.*] Miss Waddell won fame in vaudeville throughout England. She toured Europe with a party which she formed of six girl violinists with a talent for stately dancing, and also with trios and quartets. Miss Waddell next visited the United States, and stayed there for many years. She studied under great teachers, including Leopold Auer. She travelled across the country, appearing in all the great cities. She returned to Sydney a few years ago after a long absence. She has since been a member of J C Williamson Ltd orchestras at Her Majesty's and the Criterion, and was also engaged for the Conservatorium and Philharmonic Society's orchestras. Despite a recent serious illness, she retained her position as teacher of the violin at the Convent School of the Sacred Heart, Elizabeth Bay.

Besides possessing an excellent technique, Miss Waddell's style as a violinist was particularly marked by charm and refinement.[500]

The Sydney Mail ran a belated short piece on 21 September 1932, under the header 'The Late Leila Waddell':

On Tuesday, September 14, a vivacious and charming stage violinist and orchestral player, popular in Sydney over thirty years ago, passed away after a painful and protracted illness in the person of Leila Ida Nerissa Bathurst Waddell, of Bathurst and Randwick. Miss Waddell made her first professional appearance at the concert recitals given by the City organist (Mr Arthur Mason), and in 1906 her services in the cause of charity and her high personal character were recognised by a concert in her honour. This led to her engagement by Mr Henry Hayward with a concert party from Europe, known as The Brescians, which toured Australia and New Zealand for long seasons. In 1908 the young player left Australia

---

500 Leila Waddell obituary, *The Sydney Morning Herald*, 14 September 1932.

to try her fortune in England. Her principal experience there was as leader of the Gipsy Band [*sic.*] on the stage in *A Waltz Dream* at Daly's theatre, London. This gave her an impetus in a new direction, and in the character of the Ragged Gipsy [*sic.*] she appeared with a group of girl violinists during a period of years at the Coliseum, Palladium, and other theatres, and ultimately toured France and Germany and other countries as far as Russia.[501]

A notice in *The Sydney Morning Herald* on 13 September 1932 reads:

WADDELL – A tribute of love to the splendid,
glorious memory of my Leila.
The name of death was never terrible
To her who knew how to live.
From her friend, Hettie Elliston.[502]

Hettie Elliston lived at the same property as Waddell, though there is nothing to indicate that they were any more than friends. They were evidently very close; Elliston was named sole beneficiary in Waddell's will. Unfortunately, we don't know a great deal about her. Born Harriet Jane Allestone in England in 1887, she used a number of pseudonyms. She returned to England sometime during the years of the Second World War, and died in Waltham Cross, Hertfordshire, in 1973.

৪০৫৪

Following her death Leila Waddell might have been forgotten were it not for her association with Aleister Crowley, which has all but overshadowed her musical career. Crowley himself might also have been overlooked were it not for John Symonds, who Crowley had met in the last years of his life and appointed his literary executor. Symonds (with Kenneth Grant) co-edited and republished many of Crowley's books, and wrote the first significant biography, titled *The Great Beast: The Life of Aleister Crowley*, published in

---

501 *The Late Leila Waddell, The Sydney Mail*, 21 September 1932.
     There were other brief obituary notices in the Australian press, but the author doesn't feel the need to include them all; see also *The Dubbo Liberal And Macquarie Advocate* 17 September 1932, *The Grenfell Record and Lachlan District Advertiser* 19 September 1932, *Mudgee Guardian* and *North-Western Representative* 22 September 1932, *Gilgandra Weekly and Castlereagh* 22 September 1932.
502 *The Sydney Morning Herald*, 13 September 1932.

1951 and subsequently revised in 1973. Symonds didn't much like Crowley it has to be said, but his book succeeded in massively increasing Crowley's fame and notoriety. Indeed *The Great Beast* was for a long time many people's first introduction to Crowley and his work, and it would some years before other biographies giving a more nuanced account of him began to appear. Among the numerous releases of Crowley's books co-edited by Symonds was *The Confessions of Aleister Crowley*, a slight abridgement of the original eight volume manuscript written in the nineteen-twenties, which was first published in 1969. Leila Waddell received a number of mentions in both books, along with the inclusion of the famed topless photograph of her in the images section of *Confessions*; the two in conjunction did much to cement Waddell's place in history as one of the most famed of Crowley's numerous women, a role she still occupies to this day.

ℬℭ

There is little else of note related to Leila Waddell although two fictional appearances bear mentioning. 1978 saw the publication of the Sherlock Holmes novel *The Case of the Philosopher's Ring*, credited to Dr. John H Watson, wherein Waddell appears as a character along with Crowley.[503] The novel is described as having been 'unearthed' by author Randall Collins, though there is nothing to indicate that Collins didn't write it. As for the plot, in the summer of 1913 Holmes receives a telegram from Bertrand Russell imploring him to come to Cambridge to investigate the 'theft' of the mind of Ludwig Wittgenstein. Naturally the nefarious Aleister Crowley accompanied by 'the Scarlet Woman' Leila Waddell is behind everything, including 'the blood and guts of occult murder'[504] and with 'nothing less than the fate of civilisation'[505] being at stake. During his investigations Holmes encounters figures such as John Maynard Keynes, Lytton Strachey, Virginia Woolf, Annie Besant, and Bertrand Russell himself. Despite a photograph of her appearing on the book's back cover and within Waddell only features in one chapter and all of eight pages, and the reader is left wondering why she was even included save as a narrative device. Her character differs greatly from what we know of the real Waddell, as does her relationship with Crowley; 'I've worked for Crowley. He set me up to play on some public

503 It is difficult to say whether Crowley would have been offended or flattered; he is known to have not been a fan of the Sherlock Holmes books.
504 *The Case of the Philosopher's Ring*, Dr. John H Watson [attrib.], unearthed by Randall Collins, Crown: New York, 1978, cover blurb.
505 Ibid.

stage where he put on the Rites of Eleusis, some Greek thing. And we've done some private turns.'[506] She responds to a newspaper advert placed by Holmes, agreeing to play violin for him and to betray Crowley in exchange for money and cocaine. In her dialogue she sounds more like a Londoner than an Australian; indeed, her country of origin is not even mentioned, and it is very possible that the author was not aware of it. 'He's a very devil, isn't he?' she says of Crowley. 'You'd know it just to look at him. But then he starts coming on to you, and before you know it he's got you hooked. Even before he starts handing out the snow [cocaine], I mean.'[507] She sides with Holmes against Crowley in exchange for 'ten guineas a go and all the snow I want',[508] and Holmes hypnotises her whereupon she quotes directly from The Book of the Law and from Crowley's comment upon it (the latter of which wasn't even written until 1926;[509] clearly the author doesn't know his Crowley texts).

'The study of the Book is forbidden,' she said. 'It is wise to destroy this copy after the first reading.' She was silent again.

'In the name of the demon,' cried Holmes, 'say on!'

She spoke again. 'Whosoever disregards this does so at his own risk and peril. These are most dire.' Once more she reverted to silence.

'Shall I speak his name?' said Holmes. 'Shall I utter it loudly, for all to hear?'

'Those who discuss the contents of this Book are to be shunned by all, as centres of pestilence,' came the reply. 'The study of this Book is forbidden. It is wise to destroy this copy after first reading.'

I had no idea what this extraordinary performance might mean, and even Holmes sat silently for a few minutes. Presently Leila opened her eyes, and shook her head vigorously. She seemed very pleased with herself...

She got up suddenly and glared at him, swinging her sequinned handbag menacingly. 'You blokes are all alike, aren't you? Where's my reward? What was all that talk about ten guineas?'

'The ten guineas were for services implied but not rendered,'

---

506 Ibid., p 124.

507 Ibid., p 125.

508 Ibid., p 126.

509 On a similar note the book's characters frequently refer to Crowley as 'The Wickedest Man in the World', which he was not called until 1923.

said Holmes. 'But I think this packet will pay you for your help this evening.'

He handed across a small brown envelope.

Leila opened it and with one deft movement had it to her nose. 'Good enough, Mr. Holmes. You're an all-right bloke after all. It's been a pleasure. You know where to reach me when you want me again.'[510]

Another fictional account of Waddell appears in the 2013 screenplay to the never-made film *Aleister Crowley in the Mouth of Hell* by Carlos Atanes. The blurb says all one needs to know; 'this script is structured in the reverse order of the Major Arcana of Crowley's Tarot. The plot describes the mystical trip of Crowley through the Duat – the Egyptian underworld, the encounters with significant characters in his real life – people as Hanni Jaegger [*sic.*], Fernando Pessoa, Leila Wadell [*sic.*], Victor Neuburg, Raoul Loveday – and the confrontation with the demon Choronzon, his old adversary.'[511] That the script's author could not spell Waddell's name correctly doesn't instil one with any confidence that he has accurately captured her character.

As a fitting coda to Leila Waddell's story, in 2016 David Bottrill of the Canberra, Australia branch of the Ordo Templi Orientis set out to get her grave marked and her significance in Australian history acknowledged. In Bottrill's words,

For 84 years she has lain in an unmarked grave in a cemetery in Sydney, New South Wales in Australia. A nearby rubbish bin was the only visual marker for those looking for the plot. The burial licence for the plot has long expired which raised the possibility (albeit slight) that it could be reused. The cemetery management were completely unaware of Laylah's history when I called them. I provided Laylah's story to them. I advised them of the coverage, by Australian newspapers, throughout her life of her musical career, liaison with Crowley and death... I also alerted them to the ongoing interest in Laylah on the internet, the National Library of Australia's online holdings, in the biographical project being undertaken by Sr Osis of OTO New Zealand and in the installation of a life-size figure of Laylah (by Collective 777) installed as part

---

510 *The Case of the Philosopher's Ring*, p 128-130.

511 Quoted from the blurb to the self-published book version of the script on the Amazon website.

of Bathurst's 200th anniversary celebration. As a result Laylah, (under her legal name) will be included on a register of internees of historical significance and the indignity of the rubbish bin was promptly removed. The cemetery advised that with a monument in place the plot would be preserved. I asked for and was given permission to make arrangements for this to happen.[512]

At the time of writing this project has not been a success and Leila Waddell's burial site remains unmarked.

---

512 Laylah Memorial Fund, David Bottrill, 22 September 2016, LAShTAL (website no longer active).

BIBLIOGRAPHY

Please note that there are many books by or about Aleister Crowley
and this list does not pretend to be exhaustive, merely containing –
in the Crowley works – those drawn upon or quoted from, and –
with the biographies – those the author found most useful.

Baker, Phil, *City of the Beast: The London of Aleister Crowley*, Strange
    Attractor Press, 2022

Blyth, Üna Maria, *Muses No More: Portraits of Occult Women*, Hexen Press,
    (undated)

Booth, Martin, *A Magick Life: A Biography of Aleister Crowley*, Coronet,
    2000

Churton, Tobias, *Aleister Crowley in America*, Inner Traditions 2017

Churton, Tobias, *Aleister Crowley in England*, Inner Traditions, 2021

Churton, Tobias, *Aleister Crowley in Paris*, Inner Traditions, 2022

Churton, Tobias, *Aleister Crowley: The Biography*, Watkins Publishing, 2012

Churton, Tobias, *Aleister Crowley: The Beast in Berlin* by Tobias Churton,
    Inner Traditions, 2014

Collins, Randall, *The Case of the Philosopher's Ring* by Dr John T Watson,
    Crown Publishers Inc, 1978

Crowley, Aleister, *The Book of Lies*, Samuel Weiser Inc edition, 1981

Crowley, Aleister, *The Book of the Law*, online edition <https://
    nofaithinthehumanrace.com/legis/>

Crowley, Aleister, *Chicago May*, privately published, 1914

Crowley, Aleister, *The Confessions of Aleister Crowley*, edited by John
    Symonds and Kenneth Grant, Bantam Books edition, 1970

Crowley, Aleister, *Diary of a Drug Fiend*, Weiser edition, 1979

Crowley, Aleister, *The Equinox of the Gods*, online edition <https://ia804602.
    us.archive.org/28/items/Equinoxs/Eq-gods.pdf>

Crowley, Aleister, *Household Gods*, Pallanza (privately published), 1912

Crowley, *Aleister, Liber 0*, online edition <https://hermetic.com/crowley/
    libers/lib6>

Crowley, Aleister, *Liber Agapé*, online edition <http://www.rahoorkhuit.
    net/library/libers/pdf/lib_0100.pdf>

Crowley, Aleister, *Liber Aleph*, online edition <https://sacred-texts.com/oto/
    aleph_index.htm>

Crowley, Aleister, *Little Essays Toward Truth*, online edition <https://sacred-
    texts.com/oto/aleph_index.htm>

Crowley, Aleister, *Magical and Philosophical Commentaries on the Book of the Law*, edited by John Symonds and Kenneth Grant, 93 Publishing edition, 1974

Crowley, Aleister, *Magical Diaries of Aleister Crowley*, Tunisia 1923, edited by Stephen Skinner, Samuel Weiser Inc edition, 1996

Crowley, Aleister, *The Magical Record Record of The Beast 666*, edited by John Symonds and Kenneth Grant, Duckworth Publishing edition, 1972

Crowley, Aleister, *Magick*, edited, annotated and introduced by John Symonds and Kenneth Grant, Guild Publishing edition, 1989

Crowley, Aleister, *Magick* Without Tears, Llewellyn Publications edition, 1973

Crowley, Aleister, *Moonchild*, Samuel Weiser Inc edition (undated)

Crowley, Aleister, *The Revival of Magick*, online edition <https://www.100thmonkeypress.com/biblio/acrowley/periodicals/revival_1/revival_of_magick.pdf>

Crowley, Aleister, *The Vision and the Voice*, Samuel Weiser Inc edition, 1988

Fuller, Jean Overton, *The Magical Dilemma of Victor Neuberg*, Mandrake, 1990

Hirsig, Leah, *Three Chapters in My Life*, edited by Jon Lange, The Cefalù Press, 2022

Hutchinson, Roger, *Aleister Crowley: The Beast Demystified*, Mainstream Publishing, 1998

Jay, Mike, *Mescaline: A Global History of the First Psychedelic*, Yale University Press, 2021

Kaczynski, Richard, *Perdurabo: The Life of Aleister Crowley*, North Atlantic Books, 2010

Laver, James, *Museum Piece: The Education of an Iconographer*, Andre Deutsch, 1963

Neuberg, Victor, *The Triumph of Pan*, Equinox 1910

Spence, Richard B, *Secret Agent 666: Aleister Crowley, British Intelligence and the Occult*, Feral House, 2008

Suster, Gerald, *The Legacy of the Beast: The Life, Work, and Influence of Aleister Crowley*, Weiser. 1989

Sutin, Lawrence, *Do What Thou Wilt: A Life of Aleister Crowley*, St Martin's Griffin, 2000

ARTICLES

The author hasn't listed every available article concerning Leila
Waddell, only those found useful. There are a great many newspaper
articles from the period – particularly from Australia – that mention
her or are quoted from, too numerous to list here; see the footnotes
throughout the text for sources.

Ballinger, Dean, *Looking for Laylah*, *Fortean Times* #249, March 2023
Bottrill, David, Laylah Memorial Fund, 22 September 2016, LAShTAL
    website (no longer online)
Josiffe, Christopher, *Aleister Crowley, Marie de Miramar and the True Wanga*,
    online   edition   <https://sas-space.sas.ac.uk/5642/1/REDACTED_
    Aleister_Crowley_Marie_de_Miramar__the_True_Wanga_v_2.pdf>
Uncredited article, *A Bathurst Girl's Tour Abroad*, *The Bathurst Times*, 12
    June 1924
Uncredited article, *Fiddled Round the World: Australian Musician's
    Interesting Life*, *The Australian Woman's Mirror*, 9 December 1924
Uncredited article, *Leila Waddell*, *The Voice Of Fire Volume 1 Number 9*, 21
    June 2015

ONLINE RESOURCES

The author utilised a number of online archives in writing this book;
the following proved to be the most helpful.

100th Monkey Press for their extensive archive of Aleister Crowley texts
    and press cuttings, in which the author also found mention of Leila
    Waddell <https://www.100thmonkeypress.com>
Hermetic Library for its archive of Crowley texts < https://hermetic.com>
Trove, excellent Australian newspaper and journal archive website, which
    proved invaluable < https://trove.nla.gov.au>

www.ingramcontent.com/pod-product-compliance
Lightning Source LLC
Chambersburg PA
CBHW051208090426
42740CB00021B/3422